CHRISTMAS
Celebrations

The essential guide for festive gatherings

Pictured on front cover:
New Year's Eve Celebration
1. Raspberry Sparklers, page 166
2. Bacon Feta Turnovers, page 160
3. Tourtière Meatball Skewers, page 162
4. Smoked Salmon Spears, page 160
5. Onion Pepper Pizzettes, page 159
6. Lemon Herb Lamb Chops, page 165

First Printing October 2006

Library and Archives Canada Cataloguing in Publication

Paré, Jean, date
Christmas celebrations / Jean Paré.
(Special occasion series)
Includes index.
ISBN 1-897069-08-1
1. Christmas cookery. 2. Entertaining. 3. Christmas decorations. I. Title. II. Series.
TX739.2.C45P367 2006   641.5'686   C2006-900480-3

Published by
Company's Coming Publishing Limited
2311 – 96 Street
Edmonton, Alberta, Canada T6N 1G3
Tel: 780-450-6223   Fax: 780-450-1857
www.companyscoming.com

Company's Coming is a registered trademark owned by Company's Coming Publishing Limited

Printed in China

CHRISTMAS
Celebrations

Author	Jean Paré
President	Grant Lovig
Vice President Product Development	Derrick Sorochan
Research & Development Manager	Roxanne Higuchi
Design Director	Jaclyn Draker
Editorial Director	Eleanor Gasparik
Food Editors	Lynda Elsenheimer
	Patricia Meili-Bullock
Recipe Editors	Stephanie Amodio
	Joan McManners
Contributors	Paula Bertamini
	Debbie Dixon
	Eleanor Gasparik
	Mary Anne Korn
	Patricia Meili-Bullock
	Laurie Stempfle
	Lovoni Walker
Senior Copyeditor	Amy Hough
Copyeditors	Janet Fowler
	Laurie Penner
	Connie Townsend
Proofreader	Connie Townsend
Publishing Coordinator	Laura Hussein
Registered Dietitian	Margaret Ng
Kitchen Services Manager	Jill Corbett
Senior Tester	James Bullock
Tester	Allison Dosman
Photo Editor	Patricia Meili-Bullock
Photography	Stephe Tate Photo
Photographer's Assistant	Ron Checora
Prop Stylists	Paula Bertamini
	Snez Ferenac
Food Stylist	Ashley Billey
Prep Kitchen Coordinator	Audrey Smetaniuk
Prep Assistant	Linda Dobos

We gratefully acknowledge the following suppliers for their
generous support of our test kitchen and photo studio:
Broil King Barbecues
Corelle®
Hamilton Beach® Canada
Lagostina®
Proctor Silex® Canada
Tupperware®

Our special thanks to the following businesses
for providing props for photography:

Anchor Hocking Canada	Michaels The Arts & Crafts Store
Browne & Co.	Mikasa Home Store
Canhome Global	Out of the Fire Studio
Casa Bugatti	Pfaltzgraff Canada
Cherison Enterprises Inc.	Pier 1 Imports
Corelle®	Proctor Silex® Canada
Danesco Inc.	Pyrex®
Emile Henry	Stokes
Island Pottery Inc.	Strahl
Linens 'N Things	The Bay
	Tupperware®

Table of Contents

Festive gatherings can range from simple to elaborate, from casual to sophisticated. The results may look quite different but the same party-planning principles apply. Our guide will help you plan with confidence and entertain with success.

Be it morning, noon or night, buffets are a fun, friendly and flexible way to entertain throughout the holidays. Five thematic gatherings are presented with all the information and ideas you need to plan and host buffet-style.

Table of Contents

Foreword

The sound of carollers at the piano, the scent of gingerbread wafting from the kitchen, the look of wonder in a child's eyes—what glorious treasures Christmas brings. It's no surprise that these magical moments occur most often as family and friends gather to celebrate the season with good cheer and great food.

It seems a pity to miss any of the magic because you're in the kitchen preparing the meal. Some of the best parties I attend are those where the host has time to mingle with the guests, disappearing only occasionally into the kitchen to refresh a serving tray or pop something into the oven. Magic? Not really. All it takes is good planning, organization and make-ahead recipes that will allow you to enjoy your party as much as your guests do.

You'll find everything you need in *Christmas Celebrations,* the essential guide to hosting a holiday event. From an open house gathering or elaborate dessert buffet to an intimate lunch with friends or a new take on turkey dinner, we've created 12 wonderful, well-planned occasions to ring in the season.

Follow our suggested menus or mix and match recipes as you please (I'd add the Tartufi to every meal, they're just *so* good!). Our *Holiday Cocktail Party,* for example, offers an international theme, with menus from Mexico, India and the Far East: you could choose some of these appetizers to spice up your standard dinner for company. Our index, with helpful headings such as Appetizers, Main Dishes and Desserts, will help you quickly find your best-loved recipes.

We've included updates on traditional dishes such as Sweet And Smoky Brussels Sprouts, as well as interesting new flavour combinations like Holiday Turkey Roulade. And if your mother's sweet potato casserole or Auntie Irma's cornbread stuffing are family favourites, add them to the menu—that's how holiday memories are made!

With *A Guide to Entertaining* on page 7, *Christmas Celebrations* walks you through those important first decisions when hosting a party, from choosing the style of food service to planning the menu and creating the setting. Then, to make it even easier, we've divided the book into three sections according to serving style: buffets, sit-down meals and cocktail parties, with specific information at the beginning of each section. If you've ever wondered how many hors d'oeuvres you need per person, the best way to set up a buffet table, or where to put the dessert forks for a formal dinner, it's all here.

Whenever I host a gathering, I make lists and write down every detail, including those I know I won't forget, just because it makes me feel good to cross them off! Use the timelines for our 12 celebrations as your preparation lists. We keep you on track by itemizing tasks—beginning weeks before your event, and running right up to serving time.

Many of our delicious recipes have make-ahead elements. The Chipotle Mayonnaise for the Roasted Corn Crab Cakes, for example, can be prepared three days in advance, while the Mincemeat Bites or the Kofta hors d'oeuvres can be tucked into the freezer in November.

Christmas Celebrations is full of entertaining tips, decorating ideas and tidbits about the season...who knew that poinsettias had such a lovely legend about the origin of their crimson leaves? (See page 85 for details!) We've even tossed in a craft or two for those of you who can't let your hands stay idle as you watch television holiday specials.

With detailed directions and delicious fare, *Christmas Celebrations* will soon become your essential festive guide, whether you're an experienced host or just starting out. Let us help you entertain with confidence so you can take part in the magic of the season!

Merry Christmas!

Jean Paré

Each recipe has been analyzed using the most up-to-date version of the Canadian Nutrient File from Health Canada, which is based on the United States Department of Agriculture (USDA) Nutrient Data Base. If more than one ingredient is listed (such as "butter or hard margarine"), or a range is given (1 – 2 tsp., 5 – 10 mL), then the first ingredient or amount is used in the analysis. Where an ingredient reads "sprinkle," "optional," or "for garnish," it is not included as part of the nutrition information. Milk, unless stated otherwise, is 1% and cooking oil, unless stated otherwise, is canola.

Margaret Ng, B.Sc. (Hon), M.A.
Registered Dietitian

A Guide to Entertaining

Planning a Party

All entertaining starts with decisions that define and shape your gathering, and provide a basis for subsequent decisions, such as menu planning.

Guest List
The comfort of your guests is of primary importance. Look at the compatibility, tastes and ages of your guests. Consider the space available—it may be better to have just the right number at two parties rather than too many at one party.

Style of Entertaining
Your gathering may be influenced by a particular theme, activity or focus—such as a New Year's Eve party or a cookie exchange. This may have bearing on the time of day you host your event. An important consideration is the ambience you want to create. Casual entertaining favours a more relaxed approach, typically with food served buffet- or family-style. Formal entertaining is usually more refined and elegant, with food served in courses at a fully set table. Your choice will influence the style of service, table setting, seating arrangements, pace and decor—but either choice should be comfortable, welcoming and enjoyable for your guests.

Your Time and Budget
Extend your budget beyond food and beverages. Decorations (candles, flowers and such), additional plates, glasses or flatware and serving or cleanup help should all be considered to aid you in creating the style of party you want with the money and time you can afford.

Deciding on Serving Style

Buffet
Food is presented in bowls and on platters set out on a table or sideboard. Guests pick up plates and move past the food while serving themselves. This approach works well with any type of meal and size of gathering.

Sit-Down Meal
Family-style service This is a familiar style in most homes. Platters and bowls are passed from person to person at the table. Serving vessels are left on the table for second helpings. This is best for smaller gatherings—though the camaraderie and conversation it sparks is appealing even when there are many people gathered around the table.

Plated or restaurant-style service Typically used for a small dinner party, food is placed on each individual plate then brought to the guest, course by course. The host determines the amount of food on each plate and how it is presented. As guests have little input at the time of service, it's best to inquire about dietary preferences or restrictions beforehand.

Cocktail
Appetizers, snack-type foods, dips and crudités are the usual fare. Food can be circulated among the guests on trays or set on various tables throughout the rooms. Drinks, with alcohol or without, are often an important consideration. All food and beverages should be presented in a manner that encourages mingling.

Planning Beverages

If ever a time of year called for particular attention to beverages, it's the season of good cheer. The following tips will help ensure that your guests are looked after and that your holiday celebration goes smoothly:

Choices
Offer guests an assortment of alcohol-free drinks—punch, pop, juice, water, tea and coffee. Use the same glassware for both alcohol and alcohol-free beverages.

Fizz-Free
Punches can be pepped up with ginger ale or club soda, but if you're serving a punch containing alcohol, use a non-carbonated base, such as fruit juice. Carbonation makes the body absorb alcohol faster.

Do-It-Yourself
If possible, mix and serve drinks yourself or appoint a bartender—and always measure the alcohol when pouring drinks.

Food and Drink
If you're serving alcohol, make sure food is part of your beverage plan, whether it's appetizers with pre-dinner cocktails or dessert with late-night liqueurs.

Serving Portions for Beverages

One standard drink is equivalent to:
12 oz. (341 mL) of beer (5% alc./vol.) or
5 oz. (142 mL) of wine (12% alc./vol.) or
1 1/2 oz. (45 mL) of spirits (40% alc./vol.)

Wine and Champagne	By standard serving, a 26 oz. (750 mL) bottle will yield five glasses.
Liquor and Mix	A 26 oz. (750 mL) bottle will yield approximately 17 standard drinks. Plan on three similarly sized bottles of mix.
Punch	One gallon (4 L) will provide 20 to 25 servings.
Liqueurs	A 26 oz. (750 mL) bottle will yield approximately 25 standard 1 oz. (30 mL) drinks.
Alcohol-Free Beverages	Allow about three to five 6 oz. (170 mL) drinks per guest. Allow two to three cups of coffee or tea per guest.

Planning a Menu

Whether you're considering one of the occasions in this book or creating your own menu, keep the following in mind:

Be Realistic
The size of the guest list, the style of the party, your skills in the kitchen and the demands on your time must be factored in.

Stay in Season
You will often save money and get better quality produce if you use seasonally available fruits and vegetables.

Think Through the Menu
It's important to look at your menu from different perspectives, such as:

❋ How much time is needed to do everything? Tip: Overestimate the time required.

❋ Are there any potential preparation problems between recipes? For example: With only one oven, you can't bake two dishes at two different temperatures at the same time.

❋ Does the food suit the type of gathering and service? For example: Hors d'oeuvres that are bite-sized are more suited to a cocktail party than appetizers that need to be eaten with a knife and fork.

❋ Is there a way to make things easier? Tip: Shop for shortcuts like pre-washed lettuce and frozen hors d'oeuvres. Also plan to use a mix of make-ahead and last-minute baking and preparations.

❋ Are there guest considerations to bear in mind, such as allergies, dietary restrictions, preferences or lifestyle choices?

Table Decor

How your table looks is very important. All your decorations—tablecloth, napkins, centrepiece, place settings—are intended to accentuate the food and add to its presentation. Here are a few planning tips to keep in mind:

Choose colours that reflect the style and type of occasion and coordinate them with the colour and pattern of your dishes. Most important, to save time, money and effort, consider what you already have on hand that can be used.

Use tablecloths in unusual ways: double layers, runners and varying overhang lengths can create distinctive effects.

Fold napkins in interesting patterns or use rings or ties as an accent.

Arrange your tableware, glassware, place settings and such to suit the type of service. Keep in mind that dessert plates and cutlery, coffee and tea cups can be set out when needed rather than at the beginning of the meal.

Plan your centrepiece keeping in mind how full your tabletop will be—this will enable you to choose the right size and shape.

Serving Portions for Food

The style of gathering and its duration, the time of day, even the ages of your guests will affect the quantity of food needed. The menus in this book do the portioning for you, but the following guideline is useful if you're adding or substituting dishes.

Appetizers	Three to four items per guest if serving a meal; 10 to 12 per guest if no other courses.
Cheese	1 to 2 oz. (28 to 57 g) per guest if there are other appetizers and a meal is being served. Allow 3 to 4 oz. (85 to 113 g) if there are other appetizers and a meal is not being served.
Salad	About 1 cup (250 mL) of green leafy salad per guest.
Meat	An average of 3 to 5 oz. (85 to 140 g) of cooked meat per guest.
Pasta	About 3 oz. (85 g) of uncooked pasta per guest if it is the main course, about 1 1/2 to 2 oz. (43 to 57 g) if it is a side dish or starter.
Starch	1/2 cup (125 mL) of cooked rice or 1/2 to 1 cup (125 to 250 mL) of potatoes, depending on whether they are mashed or cubed.
Vegetables	About 1/2 cup (125 mL) per guest of each vegetable if only two vegetables are being served. If more than two vegetables are being served, allow 1/4 cup (60 mL) of each vegetable per guest.
Dessert	Approximately one-eighth of a 9-inch (22 cm) pie or one 3-inch (7.5 cm) square piece of fancy pan dessert per guest.
Squares	About three 1-inch (2.5 cm) pieces per guest.

Preparing Your Home

Keeping in mind the tone and style of your party, here are a few areas to consider when you're creating the perfect setting:

Traffic Flow and Seating
Will people be able to move easily between and within rooms? Does furniture need to be rearranged to relieve congestion or encourage mingling? Is there adequate seating?

Creating a Mood
What type of lighting, scents or music would contribute to the desired mood? Flickering candles, dimmer-adjusted lighting, seasonal potpourri and fresh flowers or greenery are worth considering. Choose music wisely so it's not too intrusive, especially if conversation is a big part of the gathering.

Decor
Are there decor touches or accessories that could enhance your setting? A little visual lift is as simple as fresh flowers, pretty straws or shiny ribbon on elegant glasses. Think of creative ways to use your favourite items.

Special Attention
Beyond the main entertaining rooms, what are the other areas guests will pass through?

Make sure there's adequate room in your entryway for the doffing and donning of coats and boots. Have somewhere for people to sit, if possible, and lay out an additional mat or two for boots. You might even want to designate a room for storing coats—make sure it is tidy and easily accessed from the entryway.

Assume that guests may need to use every bathroom you have and ensure all are company-worthy. Consider carrying the party theme into the bathroom—sprigs of holly berries and greenery in a Christmas vase are a simple yet charming touch. A couple of long-lasting votive candles will create a nice mood. Stock extra toilet paper, tissues and fresh towels, and make sure the supply is easy for guests to see.

Cleaning Up

Cleanup may be a reality of entertaining, but a little planning before the party can make it less of a chore.

* Bake on foil-lined pans or in foil containers for less mess and quicker wash up.

* Wash, dry and put away all the preparation dishes that you can.

* Empty your dishwasher, sinks and kitchen garbage receptacles before the party.

* Set up a large plastic outdoor garbage can (dressed up for Christmas in wrapping paper) in the kitchen or near the back door.

* Make room in your refrigerator for leftovers to help keep cleanup quick.

* Have two or three clean dishcloths ready in case of spills or splashes.

* Let others help.

Staying Organized

Behind every smiling, relaxed host is time spent listing, checking, doing and organizing so everyone enjoys the party. Seamless, successful gatherings don't happen by accident. Here are our top tips for staying organized from start to finish:

Make Lists
Whether you're hosting a small family gathering or a large cocktail party, the three must-have lists are:

Menu Include all the recipes and other necessities such as condiments, butter, rolls, etc.

Tasks Note *everything* that needs to be done, from shopping, cooking and cleaning to setting the table, clearing out the front closet and decorating the living room.

Timeline Knowing when things will be done gives you confidence and control. Make sure you have a detailed timeline that includes the day of your party as well as the days leading up to it.

Plan Ahead
Check supplies From groceries, glasses and garnishes to tablecloths, trivets and trash bags, menu and task lists are a great help in making sure you have what you need when you need it.

Maximize space where you can Give yourself room to work by removing any unnecessary appliances and canisters from the countertop. Clear out room in the freezer, fridge and pantry for party food storage.

Make menu decisions Select which make-ahead options you'll use from your menu and when you'll prepare them.

Prepare for serving Set your table the day before. Select, clean and place your tableware, glassware, serving vessels and utensils. Put a small note next to each serving vessel with the name of the food that it will hold.

The Three Most Important Rules of Entertaining

1. Always make time on the day of the party to relax and get ready without being rushed.

2. Delegate whatever you can and warmly accept offers of help.

3. Never apologize for something you might have forgotten or didn't get done from your to-do list. No one knows but you!

Buffets

Buffet Guide

A buffet is a casual style of service, with flexibility being one of its best features. Well-suited to a large crowd of people in a limited space, it's also a comfortable style for a small group when convenience is an important factor.

Whether you're serving brunch or supper, buffet menus can be tailored to your budget without compromising the quality or quantity of food for your party guests. In fact, buffets can be one of the least expensive ways to entertain nicely.

The secret to a great buffet is timing. Your guests will be expecting a meal, so they'll probably arrive hungry. Allow about an hour from the start of the party for guests to arrive and do a little mingling, and nibbling if you're serving appetizers. At that point your table should be ready and you can orchestrate the buffet line.

Buffet Serving Style

A traditional buffet will have all the food, beverages, dishes and cutlery set out in one location, often the dining room or kitchen, where guests may select the food they wish, then move to another area to eat. Once done with the main course, guests help themselves to dessert and after-dinner beverages.

As a variation on the traditional buffet try placing only the food and plates on the buffet table. Your guests can help themselves, then move to a seating area where tables are set with cutlery, napkins and glasses. Or seat guests at two or more tables with an appetizer or salad already at their places. The tables can be completely set, including condiments, with only the main course dishes on the buffet table where guests can help themselves. Dessert and coffee may be served by the host.

Whichever style you choose, the food on your buffet table should be arranged in a logical order. For example, sauces should be placed right after the item that they go with so your guests know to take some as well.

Planning Beverages

By their natures, both bars and buffets create traffic. To avoid congestion, have beverages on one table and food on another—if possible, significantly apart and, ideally, in separate rooms.

Depending on the ages and number of guests and the type of gathering, you might have cold (alcohol and alcohol-free) drinks in one place and hot (coffee and tea) in another. If there are lots of children, their beverages could be placed on their own separate table. Make sure to have appropriate glassware, napkins and fixings available at each station.

Planning a Menu

A bountiful buffet table laden with tempting food awakens hearty appetites. Help guests enjoy the meal even more by offering a well-organized menu.

Points to Consider
* Dishes don't have to be passed around, so you can offer more variety.

* One-pot dishes such as casseroles are a natural for buffets.

* Cut food into smaller portions so guests can take a little of everything if they wish.

* Vegetables and salads add colour and selection without blowing your budget.

* Choose one or two desserts that can be pre-cut and arranged on plates on a dessert table.

* Opt for bite-sized finger and fork food if guests are managing the meal on their laps or while standing.

* The rule of thumb is one extra portion of each dish for every six guests.

Company-Friendly
* Guests can choose what and how much they eat.

* Dietary needs and preferences, from diabetic to low-carb or vegetarian, can usually be accommodated.

* If the guest list increases at the last minute, simply add a convenience dish like a gourmet frozen pizza cut into very thin wedges or increase the quantity of a last-minute dish such as scrambled eggs.

Serving Tips

For Presentation
* Think vertical and be creative: Stand crudités or bread sticks in water glasses that take less room than sectioned platters.

* Fill the platters and bowls with enough food to serve everyone at least one helping to avoid frequently disrupting the line to replenish the dishes.

* Pre-portion messier items into small containers for easy pick up. Try putting fruit salad in small disposable wine glasses or an egg dish in single-serving ramekins.

* Pre-slice meats and other dishes in the kitchen for smoother and easier service. If carving is to be done at the table, do it yourself rather than leaving it to each individual guest.

On the Table
* Set out large plates at the start of the buffet and smaller plates beside the desserts.

* Position all serving dishes and utensils in advance. Set out pads on which to place hot vessels.

* Use chafing dishes to keep food either warm (with hot water or a flame) or cold (with ice). Slow cookers are also great for keeping food warm.

* Provide the proper utensils so all food can be served with one hand. Dishes that require two-handed serving can be placed near the beginning of the line with extra room for guests to set down their plates.

* Stack dinner-sized napkins between the plates or wrap them around the flatware to save space.

* If you wish, print the names of the dishes on small cards and place them in front of each dish.

Away from the Buffet
* Set out salt and pepper away from the buffet table where guests can access them easily without disrupting the line.

* For extra convenience, if guests are eating in different rooms, supply each area with napkins, salt and pepper to save guests an extra trip to the buffet table.

Food Safety
* To stay on the safe side, food should not sit at room temperature for more than two hours—the danger zone for bacterial growth is between 40°F (4°C) and 140°F (60°C).

Table Decor

Give careful thought to the placement of everything on the table—from the cloth to the serving vessels to the plates and napkins to the centrepiece. You want to avoid a cluttered-looking table even if there's a lot to fit on it!

First and Foremost
* Leave as much table surface as possible for the food, plates, napkins, cutlery and so forth—centrepieces and table decor elements should take second position.

* Plan the table layout in advance, using the actual serving pieces, plates and so on. As a reminder, place a little note where each food dish goes.

* Add drama and interest, and maximize use of the table surface area, by presenting dishes at different levels:
  - Use pedestal serving dishes and tiered serving platters.
  - Place sturdy boxes or upside-down pans or bowls on the table, drape them with a tablecloth or napkin, and arrange serving bowls and plates on top.

Added Touches
* A centrepiece on a buffet table can be taller, larger and showier. Arrange platters and bowls right up to the base of a narrow, tall centrepiece. If your table is against a wall, position your centrepiece against the wall also.

* Instead of a centrepiece, dress the table in pretty linens, add seasonal touches to the hanging skirt of the tablecloth or lay boughs of greenery under serving platters.

Traffic Flow and Seating

The distinctive feature of a buffet setting is that the guests come to the food rather than the reverse. When guests start moving towards the buffet, you want to maintain the convivial mood by ensuring a smooth flow of people to, through and away from the buffet line—and by making sure that all guests can sit down and enjoy their meal. Keeping these points in mind will help:

* Allow plenty of room for people to line up.

* Plan a clear exit path for guests with filled plates, one that allows them to move freely to the seating area.

* Guests should be able to move easily around the buffet table and serve themselves in a logical order.

* Depending on your space and number of guests, the buffet table can be positioned in the centre of the room, allowing traffic to flow comfortably around the table. Alternately, the table may be against a wall with the food line moving along one side only.

* A place to sit should be available for every guest, even if it's not on a traditional chair—a piano bench, sturdy toy box or fireplace hearth can work in a pinch.

* Arrange your furniture to accommodate small seating groups, with surfaces close by for setting drinks and plates.

* Create a picnic area for kids in a quiet corner of a room. Put a blanket or two on the floor to free up chairs for adults. The blankets will also catch any crumbs and spills, making cleanup easy.

* Set out lap trays, TV trays or small tables for the use of individual guests, especially the elderly.

Cleaning Up

Buffets often bring out the best in guests when it comes to cleanup. They may carry their own dirty dishes and even ask where to put them! As with the buffet line, plan a clear path to the designated location (say the kitchen table or counter, tidied of any clutter). Set up a logical sequence, making sure there's a garbage can for refuse and a place to stack dirty dishes for washing.

Tree & Tinsel Party

~

The annual trimming of the tree is always a highlight of the season. It seems to mark for many of us, especially children, the official start of Christmas. That's why we thought it an occasion worthy of a party.

At this gathering, everyone lends a creative hand—from decorating the tree to making ornaments to building their own supper sandwiches.

The party food matches the party mood: snacks to start and a do-it-yourself sandwich-making spread for supper. We've created two menus, each with a simple, low-key main course, served buffet-style. The bustle of activity at the heart of this party means not every dish needs to be made ahead. You can easily and conveniently slip away as needed to tend to the food.

Before, during or after the tree trimming, our candy cane angels Christmas craft is a terrific activity for school-aged children—but plan on having enough supplies on hand for any adults itching to make an ornament or two or three!

Of course, the most spectacular part of this occasion is the beautiful tree, so build up the final presentation. Gather everyone together to officially light up the tree, ceremoniously place an angel or star at the top and sing a few Christmas carols.

1. Christmas Bundt Cake, page 22
2. Fuss-Free Focaccia, page 20
3. Pepperoni Pizza Pinwheels, page 18
4. Christmas Sandwich Tree, page 18

Tree & Tinsel Party

Casual Sandwich Supper for 8

Two sandwich menus, one cold and one hot, offer a convenient selection of recipes for hand-held food, perfect for this bustling gathering. Set everything out casually on the dining or kitchen table, and include plates and napkins. Only a few food-related tasks—such as blending a new batch of eggnog, setting out fresh appetizers, warming items or laying out platters of food—will require your attention during the party.

Menu 1 – Cold Sandwiches
Frothy Eggnog, page 17

Sugar And Spice Nuts, page 20
Chicken Artichoke Dip, page 17
Crispy Tortilla Trees, page 19

Pepperoni Pizza Pinwheels, page 18
Christmas Sandwich Tree, page 18
Fuss-Free Focaccia, page 20

Christmas Bundt Cake, page 22

Menu 2 – Hot Sandwiches
Spiced Apple Cider, page 20
Sugar And Spice Nuts, page 20
Pine Forest Dip, page 19
Crispy Tortilla Trees, page 19

Saucy Braised Beef, page 21
Balsamic Vegetable Medley, page 22
Fuss-Free Focaccia, page 20

Christmas Bundt Cake, page 22

Timeline

Menu 1 – Cold Sandwiches

Up to One Month in Advance
Make and freeze Crispy Tortilla Trees
Bake and freeze focaccia

Up to Two Weeks in Advance
Make Sugar And Spice Nuts

Day Before
Make bundt cake
Assemble artichoke dip
Make pinwheels

Day Of
Just before guests arrive:
Set out nuts
Bake artichoke dip
Make eggnog

30 minutes before serving:
Assemble Christmas Sandwich Tree
Reheat focaccia
Reheat pinwheels

Menu 2 – Hot Sandwiches

Up to One Month in Advance
Bake and freeze focaccia
Make and freeze Crispy Tortilla Trees

Up to Two Weeks in Advance
Make Sugar And Spice Nuts

Day Before
Make sandwich fillings (Saucy Braised Beef and Balsamic Vegetable Medley)
Make bundt cake

Day Of
Up to 4 hours in advance:
Make cider
Make Pine Forest Dip

Just before guests arrive:
Arrange Crispy Tortilla Trees in dip
Set out nuts

30 minutes before serving:
Reheat sandwich fillings
Reheat focaccia

Frothy Eggnog

So easy to make! This delicious beverage has a rich, frothy texture that will remind you of traditional homemade eggnog—without the raw eggs and fuss. If you'd like, add rum to the punch bowl or to individual glasses.

Milk	4 cups	1 L
Eggnog ice cream	4 cups	1 L
Ground nutmeg, sprinkle		

Process milk and ice cream in 2 batches in blender or food processor until frothy. Pour into small punch bowl or pitcher. Sprinkle with nutmeg. Makes about 8 cups (2 L).

1 cup (250 mL): 243 Calories; 14.0 g Total Fat (4.0 g Mono, 0.5 g Poly, 8.7 g Sat); 53 mg Cholesterol; 24 g Carbohydrate; 0 g Fibre; 7 g Protein; 108 mg Sodium

Pictured at right.

Chicken Artichoke Dip

This warm, hearty dip is perfect with veggies, bread sticks or Crispy Tortilla Trees, page 19. The recipe makes plenty and leftovers are just as delicious warmed up the next day.

Cooking oil	1 tsp.	5 mL
Lean ground chicken	1 lb.	454 g
Garlic clove, minced (or 1/4 tsp., 1 mL, powder)	1	1
Chili powder	1 tsp.	5 mL
Tub of vegetable spreadable cream cheese	8 oz.	250 g
Mayonnaise	1/2 cup	125 mL
Sour cream	1/2 cup	125 mL
Can of artichoke hearts, drained and chopped	14 oz.	398 mL
Medium salsa	1/2 cup	125 mL
Grated jalapeño Monterey Jack cheese	1 cup	250 mL
Grated Parmesan cheese	1/2 cup	125 mL

Heat cooking oil in large frying pan on medium. Add ground chicken, garlic and chili powder. Scramble-fry for about 10 minutes until chicken is no longer pink. Drain. Cool.

Combine next 3 ingredients in medium bowl. Spread evenly in 2 quart (2 L) shallow baking dish.

Combine artichoke and salsa in small bowl. Spread on top of cream cheese mixture. Scatter chicken mixture over top.

Frothy Eggnog, this page

Sprinkle with Monterey Jack and Parmesan cheeses. Bake, uncovered, in 350°F (175°C) oven for about 30 minutes until heated through and edges are golden. Makes about 7 cups (1.75 L).

1/2 cup (125 mL): 393 Calories; 32.2 g Total Fat (11.2 g Mono, 4.6 g Poly, 10.1 g Sat); 53 mg Cholesterol; 6 g Carbohydrate; 1 g Fibre; 20 g Protein; 667 mg Sodium

Make Ahead: Assemble the dip in the baking dish up to 24 hours ahead of time, cover and chill until ready to bake. Bake as directed.

Entertaining Tip

Before Everyone Arrives

❋ Position the tree in the room for stability and to show its "best side."

❋ Generously space ornament storage boxes around the tree (keep treasured ornaments out of children's reach, to be handled with adult assistance).

❋ Check string lights for burnt out bulbs. (Or even put the lights on the tree in advance.)

❋ Buy or restock tree-trimming supplies (icicles, tinsel, etc.).

Christmas Sandwich Tree, below

Arrange remaining 9 ingredients in decorative pattern on top of lettuce, filling in tree shape (see photo). For smaller version of tree, use a smaller serving platter and arrange remaining 9 ingredients higher on top of each other instead of spreading them out. Serves 8.

1 serving: 304 Calories; 18.3 g Total Fat (6.7 g Mono, 1.2 g Poly, 9.1 g Sat); 78 mg Cholesterol; 6 g Carbohydrate; 2 g Fibre; 29 g Protein; 1137 mg Sodium

Pictured at left and on page 14.

Special Touch

Sandwich Board

If you want to do something extra-special for the presentation of your Christmas Sandwich Tree, make an easily constructed serving board that better fits the tree's form.

Cut a trapezoid shape from heavy cardboard or foam core board. Make the top (where the apex of the "tree" starts) 8 inches (20 cm) across and make the base (where the bottom of the "tree" ends) 20 inches (50 cm) across. The height from top to bottom should be 20 inches (50 cm). Cover the board with decorative paper, then plastic wrap or food-safe cellophane. (The photo on this page shows the Christmas Sandwich Tree presented on the custom-made sandwich board.)

Christmas Sandwich Tree

Add a whimsical touch by arranging sandwich fillings to resemble a tree. (Follow our Special Touch suggestion, this page, to make a tree-shaped serving board.) Set out butter, mayonnaise, mustard and assorted breads for guests to help themselves.

Head of green leaf lettuce, torn into sandwich-sized pieces	1	1
Black Forest ham slices	1/3 lb.	150 g
Deli smoked turkey breast slices	1/3 lb.	150 g
Deli roast beef slices	1/3 lb.	150 g
Deli salami slices	1/3 lb.	150 g
Provolone cheese slices	1/3 lb.	150 g
Cheddar cheese slices	3 1/2 oz.	100 g
Roma (plum) tomatoes, sliced	4	4
Dill pickles, sliced	4	4
Unpeeled English cucumber, thinly sliced	1	1

Arrange bed of lettuce in shape of tree on top of an extra-large serving platter, cutting board, inverted baking sheet or our custom-made sandwich board.

Pepperoni Pizza Pinwheels

An attractive spin on pepperoni pizza. These will disappear quickly.

Tube of refrigerator pizza dough	10 oz.	283 g
Pizza sauce	1/4 cup	60 mL
Deli pepperoni slices, chopped	12	12
Grated mozzarella cheese	1/4 cup	60 mL

Unroll dough into rectangle. Spread sauce on dough, leaving 1/2 inch (12 mm) edge on 1 short side.

Scatter pepperoni on top of sauce. Roll up from covered short side, jelly-roll style. Press seam against roll to seal. Cut into 8 slices. Arrange, cut-side up, about 2 inches (5 cm) apart on greased baking sheet.

Sprinkle with cheese. Bake in 350°F (175°C) oven for 20 to 25 minutes until golden. Makes 8 pinwheels.

1 pinwheel: 147 Calories; 5.3 g Total Fat (1.9 g Mono, 0.4 g Poly, 1.7 g Sat); 3 mg Cholesterol; 18 g Carbohydrate; 1 g Fibre; 6 g Protein; 378 mg Sodium

Pictured on page 14.

Make Ahead: The pinwheels may be baked up to 24 hours ahead of time and stored in an airtight container in the refrigerator. To reheat, wrap them with foil and bake in a 350°F (175°C) oven for about 10 minutes or until warm.

Pine Forest Dip With Crispy Tortilla Trees, below

Pine Forest Dip

As a festive garnish, stand a few Crispy Tortilla Trees, this page, in the dip just before serving. For a little extra zip, serve with a bowl of salsa on the side.

Tub of herb and garlic spreadable cream cheese	8 oz.	250 g
Sour cream	1/2 cup	125 mL
Ripe large avocados, mashed	2	2
Salsa	1/4 cup	60 mL
Lime juice	2 tbsp.	30 mL
Pine nuts, toasted (see Tip)	1/4 cup	60 mL
Chopped fresh chives	2 tbsp.	30 mL

Combine cream cheese and sour cream in medium bowl. Spread evenly on small serving plate.

Combine next 3 ingredients in separate medium bowl until almost smooth. Spread on top of cream cheese mixture.

Scatter with pine nuts. Sprinkle with chives. Serves 8.

1 serving: 221 Calories; 20.2 g Total Fat (9.3 g Mono, 2.6 g Poly, 6.7 g Sat); 26 mg Cholesterol; 8 g Carbohydrate; 2 g Fibre; 6 g Protein; 253 mg Sodium

Pictured above.

Tip: To toast the pine nuts, place them in an ungreased frying pan. Heat on medium for 3 to 5 minutes, stirring often, until they are golden.

Make Ahead: The dip may be made up to 4 hours ahead of time, covered with plastic wrap and stored in the refrigerator.

Crispy Tortilla Trees

Why not cut the tortillas into Christmas tree shapes? Use different flavours of flour tortillas for a festive mix of colours.

Butter (or hard margarine), softened	1 cup	250 mL
Finely chopped fresh parsley (or 1 tbsp., 15 mL, flakes)	1/4 cup	60 mL
Sesame seeds	1/4 cup	60 mL
Seasoned salt	1/2 tsp.	2 mL
Chili powder	1/2 tsp.	2 mL
Flour tortillas (9 inch, 22 cm, diameter)	10	10

Combine first 5 ingredients in medium bowl.

Spread 2 tbsp. (30 mL) butter mixture on each tortilla. Cut each tortilla into 12 wedges. Arrange in single layer on 2 greased baking sheets. Bake on separate racks in 350°F (175°C) oven for 12 to 15 minutes, switching position of baking sheets at halftime, until crisp and golden. Makes 120 tortilla wedges.

3 tortilla wedges: 33 Calories; 2.1 g Total Fat (0.7 g Mono, 0.3 g Poly, 1.1 g Sat); 4 mg Cholesterol; 3 g Carbohydrate; trace Fibre; 1 g Protein; 46 mg Sodium

Pictured above.

Make Ahead: The tortilla wedges may be stored in an airtight container at room temperature for up to 2 days, or in the freezer for up to 1 month.

Spiced Apple Cider

A traditional winter beverage, simmered to bring out the essence of fresh orange and mulled spices. Try this beverage chilled for an equally good summer treat!

Whole cloves	12	12
Small orange	1	1
Apple cider	8 cups	2 L
Ginger ale	4 cups	1 L
Cinnamon sticks (4 inches, 10 cm, each)	2	2

Press cloves, evenly spaced apart, into orange peel. Cut orange into quarters. Put into 4 to 5 quart (4 to 5 L) slow cooker.

Add remaining 3 ingredients. Cook, covered, on Low for about 4 hours or on High for about 2 hours until heated through (see Note). Makes about 12 cups (3 L).

1 cup (250 mL): 111 Calories; 0.2 g Total Fat (trace Mono, 0.1 g Poly, trace Sat); 0 mg Cholesterol; 28 g Carbohydrate; trace Fibre; trace Protein; 11 mg Sodium

Pictured on page 21.

Note: When the cider is hot, turn the slow cooker to its lowest setting to keep it warm. Keep the cover on the slow cooker to avoid evaporation.

Sugar And Spice Nuts

Your guests will enjoy nibbling on this fruited nut mix. Put some in a pretty glass bowl near the tree for munching as you decorate.

Butter (or hard margarine)	2 tbsp.	30 mL
Liquid honey	2 tbsp.	30 mL
Brown sugar, packed	2 tbsp.	30 mL
Ground cinnamon	1 tbsp.	15 mL
Ground ginger	2 tsp.	10 mL
Chili powder	2 tsp.	10 mL
Mixed salted nuts	3 cups	750 mL
Dried cranberries	1/2 cup	125 mL
Chopped dried apricot	1/2 cup	125 mL

Combine first 3 ingredients in small microwave-safe bowl. Microwave, covered, on high (100%) for 1 minute. Stir. Microwave for another 20 to 30 seconds until brown sugar is dissolved and butter mixture is bubbling.

Add cinnamon, ginger and chili powder. Stir.

Put nuts into large bowl. Pour butter mixture over top. Stir until coated. Spread evenly on greased baking sheet with sides. Bake in 300°F (150°C) oven for about 20 minutes, stirring occasionally, until toasted. Remove from oven.

Add cranberries and apricot. Stir. Let stand on baking sheet on wire rack until completely cooled. Makes about 4 1/2 cups (1.1 L).

1/4 cup (60 mL): 185 Calories; 13.8 g Total Fat (8.0 g Mono, 2.7 g Poly, 2.5 g Sat); 4 mg Cholesterol; 14 g Carbohydrate; 2 g Fibre; 4 g Protein; 179 mg Sodium

Make Ahead: Sugar And Spice Nuts may be stored in an airtight container at room temperature for up to 2 weeks.

Fuss-Free Focaccia

Fresh-baked bread fragrant with garlic, herbs and cheese is an enticing invitation to supper—and easier to make than you might think!

Frozen white bread dough, covered, thawed in refrigerator overnight	1	1
Garlic butter, melted	2 tbsp.	30 mL
Grated Parmesan cheese	1/3 cup	75 mL
Dried oregano	1 tsp.	5 mL
Dried basil	1 tsp.	5 mL

Roll out dough on lightly floured surface to 6 × 12 inch (15 × 30 cm) rectangle. Transfer to greased baking sheet.

Brush with garlic butter. Sprinkle with remaining 3 ingredients. Using fork, poke holes about 1 1/2 inches (3.8 cm) apart through dough to surface of pan to prevent dough from puffing. Bake in 350°F (175°C) oven for 20 to 25 minutes until golden and hollow sounding when tapped. Cool. Cut into 4 rectangles. Cut each in half diagonally, for a total of 8 triangles.

1 triangle: 197 Calories; 6.3 g Total Fat (2.1 g Mono, 0.6 g Poly, 3.1 g Sat); 12 mg Cholesterol; 28 g Carbohydrate; 1 g Fibre; 7 g Protein; 412 mg Sodium

Pictured on pages 15 and 21.

Variation: Use grated Asiago cheese instead of Parmesan cheese. Use 2 tsp. (10 mL) Italian seasoning instead of basil and oregano.

Make Ahead: The focaccia may be wrapped tightly with plastic wrap and stored at room temperature for up to 24 hours, or in the freezer for up to 3 months. To reheat from frozen, wrap with foil and bake in a 350°F (175°C) oven for 10 to 15 minutes or until warm.

Spiced Apple Cider, page 20   Saucy Braised Beef, below   Fuss-Free Focaccia, page 20   Balsamic Vegetable Medley, page 22

Saucy Braised Beef

This dressed-up version of beef-on-a-bun is a delicious choice for any sandwich buffet. Serve on focaccia bread or crusty rolls.

Dried oregano	1 tsp.	5 mL
Salt	1/2 tsp.	2 mL
Pepper	1/4 tsp.	1 mL
Boneless beef brisket roast	2 lbs.	900 g
Garlic cloves, minced	2	2
Large onion, sliced	1	1
Dry (or alcohol-free) red wine (or prepared beef broth)	3/4 cup	175 mL
Ketchup	1/4 cup	60 mL
Sun-dried tomato pesto	2 tbsp.	30 mL

Combine oregano, salt and pepper in small bowl. Rub mixture over entire surface of roast. Place, fat-side up, in greased 2 quart (2 L) shallow baking dish.

Spread garlic evenly on top of roast. Top with onion. Bake, uncovered, in 350°F (175°C) oven for about 1 hour until onion starts to brown. Remove from oven. Reduce heat to 300°F (150°C).

Pour wine around roast in baking dish. Bake, covered, for another 2 to 2 1/2 hours until beef is very tender and pulls apart easily. Scrape onion from roast into drippings. Transfer roast to large bowl. Shred roast with 2 forks. Cover to keep warm.

Skim any fat from surface of drippings. Transfer drippings to blender or food processor. Add ketchup and pesto. Process until smooth. Pour over beef. Toss until coated. Serves 8.

1 serving: 177 Calories; 7.7 g Total Fat (3.5 g Mono, 0.3 g Poly, 2.7 g Sat); 44 mg Cholesterol; 5 g Carbohydrate; 1 g Fibre; 18 g Protein; 290 mg Sodium

Pictured above.

Make Ahead: Shred the beef and toss it with the sauce up to 24 hours ahead of time and store it in an airtight container in the refrigerator. To reheat, transfer the meat to a 2 quart (2 L) shallow baking dish and bake it, covered, in a 350°F (175°C) oven for about 20 minutes, stirring occasionally, until heated through.

Christmas Bundt Cake

A simple spice cake glazed with orange-flavoured white chocolate becomes a holiday treat.

Box of spice cake mix (2 layer size)	1	1
Orange juice	1 1/3 cups	325 mL
Sour cream	1/3 cup	75 mL
Large eggs	3	3
WHITE CHOCOLATE GLAZE		
White chocolate chips	1 cup	250 mL
Whipping cream	3 tbsp.	50 mL
Grated orange zest	2 tsp.	10 mL

Beat first 4 ingredients on low in large bowl for about 1 minute until moistened. Beat on medium for 2 minutes. Pour into greased and floured 12 cup (3 L) bundt pan. Bake in 350°F (175°C) oven for 35 to 45 minutes until wooden pick inserted in thickest part of cake comes out clean. Let stand in pan on wire rack for 20 minutes before inverting onto serving plate. Cool completely.

White Chocolate Glaze: Heat chocolate chips and whipping cream in small heavy saucepan on lowest heat, stirring often until chocolate chips are almost melted. Do not overheat. Remove from heat. Stir until smooth.

Add orange zest. Stir. Makes about 2/3 cup (150 mL) glaze. Slowly pour over cake, allowing some glaze to run down side. Chill for at least 2 hours until glaze is set. Cuts into 12 pieces.

1 piece: 317 Calories; 13.0 g Total Fat (4.6 g Mono, 2.2 g Poly, 5.1 g Sat); 65 mg Cholesterol; 46 g Carbohydrate; trace Fibre; 5 g Protein; 313 mg Sodium

Pictured on page 14.

Make Ahead: The glazed cake may be stored in an airtight container in the refrigerator for up to 24 hours before serving.

Entertaining Tip

Table Duty

Designate a table for serving the supper buffet. Set up a separate craft area. If you have to use the same table for both food service and crafts, then plan for crafts to be finished at least 30 minutes before serving supper.

Balsamic Vegetable Medley

Versatile and very tasty. Serve the vegetables warm on focaccia bread or crusty rolls, or serve them cold as a side dish. If you have a clear path to the barbecue, the vegetables may be grilled.

Balsamic vinegar	1/3 cup	75 mL
Liquid honey	2 tbsp.	30 mL
Dried basil	2 tsp.	10 mL
Dried oregano	2 tsp.	10 mL
Garlic powder	1 tsp.	5 mL
Salt	1/2 tsp.	2 mL
Pepper	1/8 tsp.	0.5 mL
Unpeeled Asian eggplants, cut into 1/4 inch (6 mm) slices	2	2
Small red onion, cut into 8 wedges	1	1
Medium unpeeled zucchini, cut into 1/4 inch (6 mm) slices	2	2
Large red pepper, cut into 8 pieces	1	1
Large yellow pepper, cut into 8 pieces	1	1

Combine first 7 ingredients in small bowl.

Arrange eggplant and onion on greased baking sheet. Brush all sides of each with 1/2 of vinegar mixture. Reserve remaining vinegar mixture. Broil on centre rack in oven for about 20 minutes, turning once, until vegetables are softened. Transfer to large bowl. Cover to keep warm.

Arrange zucchini and red and yellow pepper on same baking sheet. Brush with remaining vinegar mixture. Broil on centre rack in oven for about 20 minutes, turning once, until vegetables are softened. Add to eggplant mixture. Toss gently. Serves 8.

1 serving: 75 Calories; 0.4 g Total Fat (trace Mono, 0.2 g Poly, 0.1 g Sat); 0 mg Cholesterol; 18 g Carbohydrate; 4 g Fibre; 2 g Protein; 155 mg Sodium

Pictured on page 21.

Make Ahead: The vegetables may be broiled ahead of time. Store the cooled vegetables in an airtight container in the refrigerator for up to 3 days. Serve them cold, or reheat them by baking in a covered baking dish in a 350°F (175°C) oven for 5 to 10 minutes until warm.

Candy Cane Angels

This will make a pair of angels—one boy and one girl. So simple, school-aged children can make both in about 10 minutes. The adults at your party may want to join in, too!

MATERIALS

1 red chenille stem
4 small cellophane-wrapped candy canes
    (2 1/2 inch, 6.4 cm, length)
2 1/2 white chenille stems
2 Styrofoam balls (1 inch, 2.5 cm, diameter)
2 silver glittered stems (4 inch, 10 cm, length)
Tightly curled white craft hair
2 small red ribbon bows

TOOLS AND SUPPLIES

Scissors, white craft glue, needle, white thread

Boy Angel

To make pants, hold the red chenille stem about 1/2 inch (12 mm) from the bottom of 1 candy cane. Wrap the stem tightly around the candy cane 4 times, wrapping upward toward the hook, to form a pant leg.

Hold another candy cane beside the first with the hooks turned slightly away from you for wings. Wrap the chenille stem tightly around both candy canes 3 times to form the waistband of the pants (see photo). Wrap the remainder of the stem downward around the second candy cane to form the other pant leg.

To make a shirt, wrap the half-stem of white chenille tightly around both candy canes, starting at the waistband of the pants and wrapping upward toward the wings. Leave about 1/2 inch (12 mm) of the chenille stem sticking out between the wings for a neck. Push a Styrofoam ball onto the neck for a head.

To make a halo, shape 1 silver glittered stem into a small circle, leaving a 1/2 inch (12 mm) end. Insert the stem end into the back of the head to hold the halo in place above the head.

To finish, cut several 1 inch (2.5 cm) lengths of craft hair and glue them to the head. Glue 1 ribbon to the top of the shirt for a bow tie. Sew a loop of thread through the back of the head for hanging.

Girl Angel

To make the body, hold two candy canes together with the hooks turned slightly away from you for wings. Starting about 1/2 inch (12 mm) from the bottom, wrap a white chenille stem tightly around both candy canes, wrapping upward toward the wings. Leave about 1/2 inch (12 mm) of the chenille stem sticking out between the wings for a neck. Push a Styrofoam ball onto the neck for a head.

To make a dress, wrap a second white chenille stem loosely around the body, starting from the base of the neck and spiralling downward, forming gradually larger loops.

To make a halo, shape 1 silver glittered stem into a small circle, leaving a 1/2 inch (12 mm) end. Insert the stem end into the back of the head to hold the halo in place above the head.

To finish, cut several 2 inch (5 cm) lengths of craft hair and glue them to the head. Glue 1 ribbon to the top of the dress. Sew a loop of thread through the back of the head for hanging.

Family Breakfast

~

For many families, the first and most exciting tradition of Christmas Day is opening the presents! The day may start shockingly early or agreeably late, depending on the ages of children in your home, but everyone—young and old—is drawn from their beds to the Christmas tree to exchange and open gifts.

Christmas morning is usually equal parts lively activity and leisurely ease, and that can affect when and how breakfast gets served. Not to mention when and how it gets cooked!

We've opted for two menus with simple, distinctive dishes, including some that can be made ahead. The best part of this gathering is both menus are served in courses. You can choose the timing, pacing and style of service that best suits your family's traditions.

If your Christmas morning is spent around the tree, serve course-by-course in the room where you're opening the gifts. Or, if you prefer, set all the dishes out at once, buffet-style, so everyone can help themselves however and whenever they wish. If it's your family's custom to gather at the table, either menu also makes a fitting banquet.

One thing's for sure: No matter how you unwrap this breakfast, it will wrap up your Christmas morning in style.

Top left: Holiday Morning Refresher, page 27
Top right: Spiced Fruit Salad, page 29
Centre: Freezer Almond Cranberry Buns, page 28

Family Breakfast

Leisurely Breakfast for 6

Whether you choose to serve each course individually, lay out the food buffet-style for people to help themselves or gather everyone around the table, these menus are perfect for a morning when you want to take your time and pace the meal to the morning's activities. Each menu features a beverage, fruit and pastry, and egg course, so you can also mix and match dishes to create your own menu. Many of the recipes can be made in advance so you, too, can enjoy a relaxing Christmas morning.

Menu 1 – Bacon and Eggs
Holiday Morning Refresher, page 27
Christmas Breakfast Tea, page 27

Freezer Almond Cranberry Buns, page 28
Spiced Fruit Salad, page 29

Oven Scrambled Eggs, page 29
Maple Back Bacon, page 29

∼

Menu 2 – Sausage and Eggs
Holiday Morning Refresher, page 27
Eggnog Lattes, page 30

Fruity Mini Muffins, page 30
Christmas Morning Muesli, page 32

Turkey Cheddar Egg Cups, page 33
Cranberry Sausage Rolls, page 32

Timeline

Menu 1 – Bacon and Eggs

Up to One Month in Advance
Prepare and freeze almond cranberry buns

Day Before
Move almond cranberry buns from freezer to refrigerator
Assemble spice bundle for tea
Make fruit salad
Assemble back bacon
Chill ingredients for Holiday Morning Refresher

Day Of
When you wake up:
Remove almond cranberry buns from refrigerator
Make tea and Holiday Morning Refresher

An hour later:
Bake almond cranberry buns
Prepare scrambled eggs

After fruit and pastry are served:
Bake scrambled eggs
Bake back bacon

Menu 2 – Sausage and Eggs

Up to One Month in Advance
Bake and freeze muffins
Bake and freeze sausage rolls

Day Before
Assemble muesli
Assemble Turkey Cheddar Egg Cups
Chill ingredients for Holiday Morning Refresher

Day Of
When you wake up:
Make lattes and Holiday Morning Refresher
Reheat muffins
Sprinkle granola on muesli

After muesli and muffins are served:
Bake Turkey Cheddar Egg Cups
Reheat sausage rolls

Christmas Breakfast Tea, below

Christmas Breakfast Tea

Welcome Christmas morning with the aromatic warmth of a specially brewed tea. Serve with milk, sugar, lemon or honey, as desired.

Whole cloves	4	4
Cinnamon sticks (4 inches, 10 cm, each), broken up	2	2
Unpeeled orange quarter	1	1
Piece of gingerroot (1 inch, 2.5 cm, length), sliced thinly	1	1
English Breakfast tea bags	2	2
Boiling water	8 cups	2 L

Place first 4 ingredients on 5 inch (12.5 cm) square of double-layered cheesecloth. Draw up corners and tie with butcher's string.

Place spice bundle and tea bags in teapot. Pour boiling water over top. Let steep for 10 minutes. Discard spice bundle. Squeeze and discard tea bags. Makes about 8 cups (2 L).

1 cup (250 mL): 4 Calories; trace Total Fat (0 g Mono, trace Poly, trace Sat); 0 mg Cholesterol; 1 g Carbohydrate; trace Fibre; trace Protein; 3 mg Sodium

Pictured above.

Make Ahead: Assemble the spice bundle up to 24 hours ahead of time and store it in an airtight container in the refrigerator until ready to use.

Holiday Morning Refresher

This refreshing juice blend will bring a sparkle to sleepy eyes. Start with chilled ingredients for best results.

Orange juice	4 cups	1 L
Sparkling apple cider	3 cups	750 mL
Frozen concentrated cranberry cocktail, thawed	1/3 cup	75 mL

Combine all 3 ingredients in large pitcher. Makes about 8 cups (2 L).

1 cup (250 mL): 129 Calories; 0.4 g Total Fat (0.1 g Mono, 0.1 g Poly, 0.1 g Sat); 0 mg Cholesterol; 31 g Carbohydrate; trace Fibre; 1 g Protein; 5 mg Sodium

Pictured on page 24.

Tailored to Taste

The words "just for you" make all of us feel good, so customize a breakfast dish to suit the taste of each family member.

Menu 1: Adjust individual servings of Spiced Fruit Salad to include more of a preferred fruit (or conversely, less or even none of a less-liked fruit!).

Menu 2: In place of turkey and Cheddar cheese in the Turkey Cheddar Egg Cups, offer your family choices such as ham and Swiss cheese, lox and cream cheese, or a vegetarian combination. Add a little marker to flag which ramekin belongs to which person.

Freezer Almond Cranberry Buns

Fill your kitchen with the aroma of freshly baked sticky buns! You'll love this recipe, not only for Christmas but for anytime company's expected. Keep these in the freezer for up to one month. They'll need to thaw in the refrigerator overnight before baking.

Milk	1/2 cup	125 mL
Granulated sugar	1/4 cup	60 mL
Butter (or hard margarine)	2 tbsp.	30 mL
Salt	1/4 tsp.	1 mL
Warm water	1 cup	250 mL
All-purpose flour	2 1/2 cups	625 mL
Envelope of instant yeast (or 2 1/4 tsp., 11 mL)	1/4 oz.	8 g
Ground nutmeg	1/4 tsp.	1 mL
All-purpose flour	3/4 cup	175 mL
All-purpose flour, approximately	2 tbsp.	30 mL
ALMOND FILLING		
Butter (or hard margarine), softened	1/3 cup	75 mL
Brown sugar, packed	1/3 cup	75 mL
Ground almonds	1/3 cup	75 mL
All-purpose flour	2 tbsp.	30 mL
Large egg, fork-beaten	1	1
Almond extract	2 tsp.	10 mL
Dried cranberries	1 cup	250 mL
Slivered almonds	2/3 cup	150 mL
MAPLE GLAZE		
Butter (or hard margarine)	1/4 cup	60 mL
Brown sugar, packed	1/4 cup	60 mL
Maple (or maple-flavoured) syrup	2 tbsp.	30 mL

Combine first 4 ingredients in small saucepan. Heat and stir on medium until butter is melted and sugar is dissolved. Remove from heat.

Add warm water. Stir. Set aside.

Combine first amount of flour, yeast and nutmeg in large bowl. Make a well in centre. Add milk mixture. Stir well.

Add second amount of flour, 1/4 cup (60 mL) at a time, mixing well after each addition until soft dough forms. Turn out onto lightly floured surface. Knead for 5 to 10 minutes, adding third amount of flour, 1 tbsp. (15 mL) at a time if necessary to prevent sticking, until smooth and elastic. Place in separate greased large bowl, turning once to grease top. Cover with greased waxed paper and tea towel. Let stand in oven with light on and door closed for 30 minutes. Punch down dough. Turn out onto lightly floured surface. Knead for about 1 minute until smooth. Roll out to 9 × 14 inch (22 × 35 cm) rectangle.

Almond Filling: Beat first 4 ingredients in medium bowl until well combined. Add egg and extract. Beat until smooth. Makes about 1 cup (250 mL) filling. Spread filling on dough rectangle, leaving 1 inch (2.5 cm) edge on 1 long side.

Sprinkle cranberries and second amount of almonds over filling. Press down lightly. Roll up from covered long side, jelly-roll style. Press seam against roll to seal.

Maple Glaze: Measure all 3 ingredients into microwave-safe medium bowl. Microwave, covered, on high (100%) for about 45 seconds until butter is melted. Stir well. Makes about 1/2 cup (125 mL) glaze. Spread glaze in greased parchment paper-lined 9 × 13 inch (22 × 33 cm) pan (see Note). Cut roll into 12 equal slices using floured knife. Arrange, cut-side up, on top of glaze in pan. Cover tightly with greased plastic wrap and foil. Freeze immediately. When ready to thaw, remove foil and plastic wrap. Cover loosely with greased plastic wrap. Thaw in refrigerator for at least 8 hours or overnight. Let stand at room temperature for 1 hour. Bake, uncovered, in 350°F (175°C) oven for about 40 minutes until golden. Let stand in pan for 5 minutes before inverting onto serving platter. Makes 12 buns.

1 bun: 395 Calories; 17.5 g Total Fat (6.8 g Mono, 1.7 g Poly, 7.9 g Sat); 49 mg Cholesterol; 54 g Carbohydrate; 3 g Fibre; 7 g Protein; 183 mg Sodium

Pictured on page 24.

Note: Greasing the bottom and sides of the pan will help secure the parchment paper. Extend the parchment paper over both long sides for easy removal.

Spiced Fruit Salad

*Like many good things, this dish needs time.
So, while visions of sugarplums dance in your loved
ones' heads, let spices and fruit steep in their
natural juices for early-morning enjoyment.*

Halved seedless red grapes	2 cups	500 mL
Cubed honeydew	2 cups	500 mL
Can of pineapple chunks, drained	14 oz.	398 mL
Can of sliced peaches in juice, drained and juice reserved, chopped	14 oz.	398 mL
Reserved peach juice		
Vanilla extract	1 tsp.	5 mL
Ground ginger	1/2 tsp.	2 mL
Ground allspice	1/4 tsp.	1 mL

Combine first 4 ingredients in large bowl.

Combine remaining 4 ingredients in small bowl. Add to fruit. Stir until coated. Chill, covered, for at least 6 hours to blend flavours. Serves 6.

1 serving: 97 Calories; 0.3 g Total Fat (trace Mono, 0.1 g Poly, 0.1 g Sat); 0 mg Cholesterol; 25 g Carbohydrate; 2 g Fibre; 1 g Protein; 10 mg Sodium

Pictured on page 24.

Maple Back Bacon

Back bacon and maple syrup—a more Canadian combination has yet to be invented! With a hint of orange, this tender-sweet dish complements eggs of any style.

Back (Canadian) bacon, sliced	1 1/2 lbs.	680 g
Maple (or maple-flavoured) syrup	1/4 cup	60 mL
Orange juice	2 tbsp.	30 mL

Arrange bacon slices, slightly overlapping, in 9 inch (22 cm) deep-dish pie plate.

Drizzle syrup and orange juice over top. Bake, uncovered, in 375°F (190°C) oven for 20 to 25 minutes until heated through. Serves 6.

1 serving: 177 Calories; 5.9 g Total Fat (2.6 g Mono, 0.5 g Poly, 1.8 g Sat); 79 mg Cholesterol; 11 g Carbohydrate; trace Fibre; 21 g Protein; 1021 mg Sodium

Pictured on this page.

Make Ahead: Assemble the ingredients in the pie plate up to 24 hours ahead of time, cover and chill until ready to bake. Bake as directed.

Maple Back Bacon, this page   Oven Scrambled Eggs, below

Oven Scrambled Eggs

Quick and easy scrambled eggs baked in the oven. Tomato and green onion add a colourful, festive flair.

Large eggs	12	12
Block of cream cheese, softened and cut up	4 oz.	125 g
Milk	1/2 cup	125 mL
Salt	1/4 tsp.	1 mL
Pepper	1/8 tsp.	0.5 mL
Finely chopped tomato	1/2 cup	125 mL
Finely chopped green onion	1/4 cup	60 mL

Process first 5 ingredients in blender or food processor until smooth. Pour into well-greased 2 quart (2 L) shallow glass baking dish. Bake, uncovered, in 375°F (190°C) oven for 15 minutes. Stir. Bake for another 10 to 15 minutes until set.

Sprinkle with tomato and onion. Serves 6.

1 serving: 235 Calories; 17.6 g Total Fat (5.9 g Mono, 1.7 g Poly, 7.8 g Sat); 455 mg Cholesterol; 4 g Carbohydrate; trace Fibre; 15 g Protein; 299 mg Sodium

Pictured above.

Variation: Instead of plain cream cheese, use a flavoured cream cheese such as herb and garlic, or smoked salmon.

Breakfast Service with Style

On Christmas morning, even the food deserves to be wrapped in something special. Think about presenting the menu items in unique and interesting ways, for example:

❊ Ring in the start of breakfast: Serve the muffins or buns in a sleigh-shaped basket decorated with merry, jingling Christmas bells.

❊ Pull out those pretty cup-and-saucer sets hidden in your cupboard. Filling them with Christmas Breakfast Tea, page 27, is an obvious choice, but they'll also hold a delicious and nourishing serving of Christmas Morning Muesli, page 32.

❊ To show off the festive colours of the Spiced Fruit Salad, page 29, use a large punch bowl and include the matching glasses for service.

❊ Add simple little extras like a Christmas bow to the handle of your juice pitcher.

❊ Turkey Cheddar Egg Cups, page 33, are served straight from the oven and may be both hot and difficult for kids to manage on a flat plate. Here's a safe-serving trick with a festive touch: Create a "nest" inside individual bowls by scrunching up a decorative cloth or paper napkin. Set a ramekin into the centre where it will stay, nice and snug. Tuck in a sausage roll and fork, and this striking presentation is complete.

Fruity Mini Muffins

Great for snacking while unwrapping! The energy boost from these moist, fruity morsels will take you through the busy morning. Delicious warm or cold.

All-purpose flour	1 cup	250 mL
Brown sugar, packed	1/3 cup	75 mL
Baking powder	1 tsp.	5 mL
Baking soda	1/2 tsp.	2 mL
Salt	1/8 tsp.	0.5 mL
Quick-cooking rolled oats	3/4 cup	175 mL
Finely chopped peeled apple	2/3 cup	150 mL
Finely chopped dried apricot	1/3 cup	75 mL
Large egg	1	1
Peach yogurt	2/3 cup	150 mL
Cooking oil	3 tbsp.	50 mL
Milk	2 tbsp.	30 mL

Measure first 5 ingredients into large bowl. Stir.

Add next 3 ingredients. Stir until fruit is coated. Make a well in centre.

Combine remaining 4 ingredients in small bowl. Add to well. Stir until just moistened. Fill 24 greased mini muffin cups full (batter will be slightly mounded). Bake in 350°F (175°C) oven for about 17 minutes until golden and wooden pick inserted in centre of muffin comes out clean. Makes 24 mini muffins.

1 mini muffin: 77 Calories; 2.4 g Total Fat (1.2 g Mono, 0.7 g Poly, 0.3 g Sat); 9 mg Cholesterol; 13 g Carbohydrate; 1 g Fibre; 2 g Protein; 64 mg Sodium

Pictured on page 31.

Make Ahead: The muffins may be stored in an airtight container in the freezer for up to 3 months. To reheat from frozen, arrange the muffins on a lightly greased baking sheet. Cover them with foil and bake in a 350°F (175°C) oven for about 12 minutes or until warm.

Eggnog Lattes

Coffee-lovers and eggnog-lovers unite! Cozy up with a morning coffee that's made for slow sipping and savouring.

Eggnog	3 cups	750 mL
Hot strong prepared coffee	2 cups	500 mL
Coffee-flavoured liqueur (optional)	1/2 cup	125 mL
Ground cinnamon, sprinkle (optional)		
Ground nutmeg, sprinkle (optional)		

Heat eggnog in medium saucepan on medium for about 5 minutes, stirring occasionally, until hot but not boiling. Remove from heat. Add coffee. Stir.

Divide liqueur among 4 large mugs. Ladle eggnog mixture into each. Sprinkle with cinnamon and nutmeg. Serves 4.

1 serving: 400 Calories; 15.2 g Total Fat (4.5 g Mono, 0.7 g Poly, 9.0 g Sat); 118 mg Cholesterol; 45 g Carbohydrate; 0 g Fibre; 8 g Protein; 118 mg Sodium

Pictured on page 31.

IRISH EGGNOG LATTES: Use Irish cream liqueur instead of coffee-flavoured liqueur.

Top left: Christmas Morning Muesli, page 32
Top right: Fruity Mini Muffins, this page
Bottom: Eggnog Lattes, above

Christmas Morning Muesli

The first gift of the day—a beautiful breakfast!
Make this a day ahead to allow the granola to soften
into a traditional muesli texture. A little granola
sprinkled on top adds a satisfying crunch.

Granola, 1/2 cup (125 mL) reserved	3 1/2 cups	875 mL
Fresh strawberries, halved lengthwise (6 whole strawberries reserved for garnish)	1 lb.	454 g
Vanilla yogurt	3 cups	750 mL
Frozen blueberries	1 cup	250 mL
Kiwifruit, sliced	3	3
Can of mandarin orange segments, drained	10 oz.	284 mL

Layer all 6 ingredients in large glass bowl as follows:

1. 1 1/2 cups (375 mL) granola

2. Some strawberry halves, pressed cut-side out against inside of bowl to decorate. Layer remaining strawberry halves on top of granola.

3. 1 cup (250 mL) yogurt

4. 1/2 cup (125 mL) blueberries

5. 1 1/2 cups (375 mL) granola

6. Some kiwifruit slices, pressed cut-side out against inside of bowl to decorate. Layer any remaining kiwifruit slices on top of granola.

7. 1 cup (250 mL) yogurt

8. Remaining blueberries

9. Remaining yogurt

10. Some orange segments pressed against inside of bowl to decorate. Scatter any remaining orange segments on top of yogurt.

Garnish with reserved strawberries. Chill, covered, for at least 8 hours or overnight. Just before serving, sprinkle reserved granola over top. Makes about 8 cups (2 L).

3/4 cup (175 mL): 314 Calories; 13.3 g Total Fat (3.7 g Mono, 6.1 g Poly, 2.9 g Sat); 4 mg Cholesterol; 45 g Carbohydrate; 5 g Fibre; 9 g Protein; 48 mg Sodium

Pictured on page 31.

Cranberry Sausage Rolls

Cranberry sauce isn't just for turkey. Dress up
your sausage for the holidays, too! Delicious
either warm or at room temperature.

Package of puff pastry, thawed according to package directions	14 oz.	397 g
Whole cranberry sauce	2/3 cup	150 mL
Pork breakfast sausages (4 inches, 10 cm, each)	8	8
Large egg, fork-beaten	1	1

Roll out 1/2 (1 square) of puff pastry on lightly floured surface to 8 inch (20 cm) square. Cut in half to make 2 rectangles.

Spread 2 1/2 tbsp. (37 mL) cranberry sauce on each rectangle, leaving 1 inch (2.5 cm) edge on 1 long side. Cut each rectangle in half crosswise, for a total of 4 squares.

Place 1 sausage on each pastry square along edge that is opposite to uncovered edge. Brush uncovered edge with egg. Roll up each starting at sausage end, jelly-roll style. Press seam against roll to seal. Repeat with remaining pastry, cranberry sauce and sausages. Cut each roll into 3 equal pieces, for a total of 24 pieces. Arrange, seam-side down, in single layer on greased baking sheet. Brush with remaining egg. Bake in 375°F (190°C) oven for about 35 minutes until pastry is puffed and golden and meat thermometer inserted in centre of sausage reads 160°F (71°C). Let stand for 5 minutes before serving. Makes 24 rolls.

1 roll: 162 Calories; 11.0 g Total Fat (3.6 g Mono, 4.2 g Poly, 2.6 g Sat); 19 mg Cholesterol; 11 g Carbohydrate; trace Fibre; 5 g Protein; 259 mg Sodium

Pictured on page 33.

Make Ahead: The baked sausage rolls may be stored in an airtight container in the freezer for up to 1 month. To reheat from frozen, arrange them in a single layer on a parchment paper-lined baking sheet. Bake in a 375°F (190°C) oven for about 18 minutes or until heated through.

Turkey Cheddar Egg Cups, below

Cranberry Sausage Rolls, page 32

Turkey Cheddar Egg Cups

Baking this dish in individual ramekins allows you to customize fillings to suit individual tastes.

Chopped deli turkey breast (or ham)	1 cup	250 mL
Grated smoked Cheddar cheese	3/4 cup	175 mL
Chopped fresh chives (or green onion)	3 tbsp.	50 mL
Large eggs	9	9
Milk	2/3 cup	150 mL
Salt	1/4 tsp.	1 mL
Pepper	1/8 tsp.	0.5 mL

Combine turkey, cheese and chives in small bowl. Spoon into 6 greased 3/4 cup (175 mL) ramekins. Place ramekins in 9 × 13 inch (22 × 33 cm) pan.

Combine remaining 4 ingredients in medium bowl. Pour into ramekins until almost full. Carefully pour enough boiling water into pan until water comes halfway up sides of ramekins. Bake, uncovered, in 375°F (190°C) oven for about 20 minutes until set. Serves 6.

1 serving: 223 Calories; 14.3 g Total Fat (4.7 g Mono, 1.6 g Poly, 6.2 g Sat); 357 mg Cholesterol; 3 g Carbohydrate; trace Fibre; 20 g Protein; 599 mg Sodium

Pictured above.

Make Ahead: Fill the ramekins up to 12 hours ahead of time, cover and chill until ready to bake. Pour boiling water into the pan and bake as directed.

Family Breakfast

Family Fun Buffet

~

The holidays are all about family time. A day of doing something special together, maybe with another family or two, is always a wonderful and welcome break from our hectic schedules.

Whether you head out tobogganing, skating, bowling or to a movie, one thing's for sure: It's the kind of day you'll want to end by sharing supper together—without being the one who has to stay behind to prepare the meal.

Our two buffet menus are simple and ingenious solutions. Both can be made entirely ahead of time so almost everything that needs to be done is out of the way before your special activities begin—and whatever isn't, gets done while you're out having fun!

The dishes are deliberately uncomplicated because the evening is meant to be relaxing and enjoyable for all ages. Keeping food in its original pots and allowing guests to serve themselves makes the whole evening easy to host. We even suggest setting up your buffet in the coziest of all rooms—your kitchen. (We've included some decor ideas to bring a festive look to the room.) When it's time for cleanup, everyone can bring their plates back to the kitchen. What could be simpler? A perfect close to a day of happy holiday fun!

Left: Veggie Noodle Bake, page 38
Right: Lemony Chicken Caesar Salad, page 37

Family Fun Buffet

Make-Ahead Meal for 8

While you're out having fun, the hot dishes in these menus are slowly simmering and developing their flavours. Whether you're away for as little as two hours or as long as eight hours, you can have a full buffet dinner ready and waiting when you return home. You'll also find that none of these recipes requires guests to use a knife—good news for those who find it awkward to cut food on a plate perched atop their laps.

Menu 1 – Casserole

You can leave the noodle casserole cooking unattended for two to three hours. Even the drinks will sit warm and ready for everyone's return home.

Caramel Hot Chocolate, page 37
Lemony Chicken Caesar Salad, page 37
Veggie Noodle Bake, page 38
Snow Angel Trifle, page 39

~

Menu 2 – Stew

The stew can cook unattended for 4 to 10 hours. With such a flexible time frame, almost any family event you've planned can be accommodated.

Cranberry Apple Warmer, page 40
Meatball Stew, page 40
Tomato Pesto Swirl Bread, page 42
Pickle Platter, page 42
Coconut Snowball Sundaes, page 43

Timeline

Menu 1 – Casserole

Up to One Month in Advance
Assemble and freeze Veggie Noodle Bake

Day Before
Assemble salad
Make trifle
Assemble hot chocolate

Day Of
Up to 6 hours in advance:
Make hot chocolate

3 hours in advance:
Bake Veggie Noodle Bake

Just before serving:
Add syrup to hot chocolate
Toss salad

Menu 2 – Stew

Up to One Month in Advance
Bake and freeze bread
Prepare and freeze Coconut Snowballs

Day Before
Assemble stew

Day Of
Up to 9 hours in advance:
Prepare Cranberry Apple Warmer
Remove bread from freezer to thaw at room temperature
Arrange *Pickle Platter*
Cook stew

Just before serving:
Reheat Cranberry Apple Warmer
Slice bread
Heat peas and add to stew

After dinner:
Assemble sundaes

Caramel Hot Chocolate, below

Caramel Hot Chocolate

Life is short—have dessert first! Thick, creamy and oh-so-delicious! For an added treat, garnish with miniature multi-coloured marshmallows or splash a dash of your favourite nut-flavoured liqueur.

Water	6 cups	1.5 L
Skim milk powder	2 cups	500 mL
Can of sweetened condensed milk	11 oz.	300 mL
Cocoa, sifted if lumpy	3/4 cup	175 mL
Caramel syrup (such as Torani's)	1/2 cup	125 mL

Combine first 4 ingredients in 4 to 5 quart (4 to 5 L) slow cooker. Cook, covered, on Low for about 6 hours or on High for about 3 hours until boiling.

Add syrup. Stir until smooth. Makes about 8 cups (2 L). Serves 8.

1 serving: 290 Calories; 5.7 g Total Fat (1.6 g Mono, 0.2 g Poly, 3.5 g Sat); 23 mg Cholesterol; 48 g Carbohydrate; 3 g Fibre; 17 g Protein; 233 mg Sodium

Pictured above.

Make Ahead: Combine the first 4 ingredients in the slow cooker liner. Cover and chill overnight. Return the liner to the slow cooker and cook as directed.

Lemony Chicken Caesar Salad

Not the usual Caesar salad! The creamy dressing has an extra lemon-fresh tang that your guests are sure to love. Easily prepared the day before, the salad is ready to toss when you arrive home!

LEMONY CAESAR DRESSING

Mayonnaise	1/2 cup	125 mL
Grated Parmesan cheese	1/4 cup	60 mL
Italian dressing	2 tbsp.	30 mL
Lemon juice	1 tbsp.	15 mL
Grated lemon zest	1 1/2 tsp.	7 mL
Pepper	1/8 tsp.	0.5 mL
Chopped or torn romaine lettuce, lightly packed	8 cups	2 L
Chopped cooked chicken	2 cups	500 mL
Chopped green onion (optional)	1/4 cup	60 mL
Seasoned croutons	1 cup	250 mL
Bacon slices, cooked crisp and crumbled	6	6

Lemony Caesar Dressing: Combine first 6 ingredients in small bowl. Makes about 3/4 cup (175 mL) dressing.

Layer lettuce, chicken and onion, in order given, in large bowl. Spread dressing evenly on top to side of bowl to cover. Cover with plastic wrap. Chill for at least 2 hours to blend flavours.

Just before serving, sprinkle with croutons and bacon. Toss well. Makes about 9 cups (2.25 L). Serves 8.

1 serving: 292 Calories; 22.0 g Total Fat (11.0 g Mono, 6.0 g Poly, 4.0 g Sat); 58 mg Cholesterol; 6 g Carbohydrate; 1 g Fibre; 18 g Protein; 381 mg Sodium

Pictured on page 35.

LEMONY TURKEY CAESAR SALAD: Use cooked turkey instead of the chicken—a tasty way to use up holiday leftovers!

Entertaining Tip

Make It Easy on Yourself

With a menu that's mostly make-ahead, the cooking part of this party is already pretty easy, but it doesn't have to stop there.

For serving, bring the people to the kitchen rather than carrying everything to the table. If you use the vessel you cooked with to serve from, not only will the food stay hot for second helpings but you'll also have fewer dishes to wash.

Setting up the kitchen as your cooking and serving centre and asking everyone to bring in their plates and forks (or use disposables), makes final cleanup less of a chore.

Veggie Noodle Bake

Tender pasta topped with a spicy tomato sauce accented with smoky bacon. Omit the chilies if you prefer less heat.

Bacon slices, diced	8	8
Chopped onion	1 cup	250 mL
Finely chopped carrot	1 cup	250 mL
Finely chopped celery	1 cup	250 mL
Garlic cloves, minced (or 1/2 tsp., 2 mL, powder)	2	2
Can of diced tomatoes (with juice)	28 oz.	796 mL
Chopped unpeeled zucchini	3 cups	750 mL
Tomato pasta sauce	3 cups	750 mL
Sliced fresh white mushrooms	2 cups	500 mL
Bay leaves	2	2
Dried crushed chilies	1/2 tsp.	2 mL
Salt	1/2 tsp.	2 mL
Pepper	1/2 tsp.	2 mL
Fusilli pasta	4 cups	1 L
Grated Italian cheese blend	3 cups	750 mL

Cook bacon in large pot or Dutch oven on medium until almost crisp. Discard drippings, reserving about 1 tsp. (5 mL) in pot. Increase heat to medium-high.

Add next 4 ingredients. Cook for about 5 minutes, stirring occasionally, until carrot starts to soften.

Add next 8 ingredients. Stir. Bring to a boil. Reduce heat to medium. Boil gently, partially covered, for about 20 minutes, stirring occasionally, until thickened. Remove from heat. Discard bay leaves. Cover to keep warm.

Cook pasta in boiling salted water in separate large uncovered pot or Dutch oven for about 10 minutes, stirring occasionally, until tender but firm. Drain. Add to sauce. Toss until coated. Spread evenly in greased 3 quart (3 L) shallow baking dish.

Sprinkle with cheese. Bake in 350°F (175°C) oven for about 35 minutes until cheese starts to brown. Serves 8.

1 serving: 491 Calories; 19.1 g Total Fat (7.1 g Mono, 2.5 g Poly, 8.1 g Sat); 42 mg Cholesterol; 61 g Carbohydrate; 6 g Fibre; 21 g Protein; 1104 mg Sodium

Pictured on page 34.

Make Ahead: Assemble the casserole in the baking dish. Cover it with greased foil and store, unbaked, in the freezer for up to 1 month. Bake the casserole from frozen, covered, in a 300°F (150°C) oven for 3 hours. Remove the foil. Increase the heat to 400°F (205°C) and bake for another 5 to 10 minutes or until the cheese starts to brown.

Special Touch

Kitchen Wonderland

Don't ignore your kitchen as a convenient place for laying out a buffet: Assign some counter space or the island, and include the kitchen table if space is tight. Then transform this everyday room into a festive space with lights, flowers and ornaments. Here are a few ideas to get you started:

❋ Lay a lighted garland along the top of your cupboards and down the sides. Add wintry icicles and snowflakes, small Christmas ornaments or candy canes to your garland.

❋ String yarn across the front of a few cupboard doors, taping the ends to the inside of the door. Hang little mittens, snowflakes or Christmas wish cards on each clothesline with miniature clothespins.

❋ Hang snowflakes in the window, or use craft spray frost or snow to decorate the windows.

❋ Add fun, snowflake or Christmas stickers to your everyday mugs.

❋ Cover your serving counter with pretty seasonal paper (not only will it catch spills, but it makes for easy cleanup).

❋ Hang scented or unscented mini berry-boughs or wreaths from cupboard knobs or handles.

Snow Angel Trifle

Kids of all ages will love the mini cookies that garnish this festive dessert. Satisfying to the last spoonful!

Milk	4 cups	1 L
Boxes of instant white chocolate (or vanilla) pudding powder (4 serving size, each)	2	2
Commercial angel food cake, torn into 1 inch (2.5 cm) pieces	17 oz.	482 g
Package of cream-filled chocolate mini cookies, 12 cookies reserved for garnish	8 oz.	225 g
Sliced fresh strawberries	3 cups	750 mL
Frozen whipped topping, thawed	2 cups	500 mL

Beat milk and pudding powder on low in medium bowl for about 2 minutes until thickened.

Layer ingredients in large glass serving bowl as follows:

1. 1/2 of cake pieces

2. 1/2 of cookies

3. 1/2 of strawberry slices

4. 2 cups (500 mL) pudding, spread evenly

5. Remaining cake pieces

6. Remaining cookies

7. Remaining strawberry slices

8. Remaining pudding, spread evenly

Spread or pipe whipped topping in decorative pattern on top of pudding. Garnish with reserved cookies. Chill for at least 4 hours to blend flavours. Makes about 12 cups (3 L).

1 cup (250 mL): 344 Calories; 8.7 g Total Fat (2.8 g Mono, 0.9 g Poly, 4.3 g Sat); 3 mg Cholesterol; 62 g Carbohydrate; 2 g Fibre; 6 g Protein; 701 mg Sodium

Pictured above.

Cranberry Apple Warmer, below

Cranberry Apple Warmer

Deep amber colour and spicy apple aroma—brandy adds extra flavour for adults, but may be omitted for a party that includes children. If you prefer, make this in a slow cooker.

Cranberry cocktail	4 cups	1 L
Apple juice	4 cups	1 L
Water	2 cups	500 mL
Brown sugar, packed	1/4 cup	60 mL
Cinnamon sticks (4 inches, 10 cm, each)	3	3
Ground nutmeg	1/4 tsp.	1 mL
Brandy (optional)	1/2 cup	125 mL

Combine first 6 ingredients in large saucepan or Dutch oven. Bring to a boil on medium. Reduce heat to medium-low. Simmer, uncovered, for about 1 hour until fragrant. Discard cinnamon sticks. Makes about 10 cups (2.5 L).

Divide brandy among 8 mugs. Pour cranberry mixture over top. Stir. Serves 8.

1 serving: 167 Calories; 0.2 g Total Fat (trace Mono, trace Poly, trace Sat); 0 mg Cholesterol; 42 g Carbohydrate; trace Fibre; trace Protein; 12 mg Sodium

Pictured above.

Make Ahead: Bring the beverage to a boil then remove it from the heat. Instead of simmering it for 1 hour, let it stand at room temperature for up to 8 hours to infuse the flavours. Just before serving, return it to a boil on medium heat then discard the cinnamon sticks.

Meatball Stew

Ready-made meatballs make this stew a snap to put together. Making it in a slow cooker makes it even easier! If you prefer, use your favourite recipe for meatballs and freeze them ahead of time to use in this dish.

Chopped onion	1 1/2 cups	375 mL
Baby carrots	3 1/2 cups	875 mL
Baby potatoes, larger ones cut in half	2 lbs.	900 g
Dill weed	1 1/2 tsp.	7 mL
Pepper	1/2 tsp.	2 mL
Box of frozen cooked meatballs	2 1/4 lbs.	1 kg
Can of condensed cream of mushroom soup	10 oz.	284 mL
Prepared beef broth	1 cup	250 mL
Water	1/2 cup	125 mL
Worcestershire sauce	2 tsp.	10 mL
Frozen peas	1 1/2 cups	375 mL

Layer onion, carrots and potatoes, in order given, in 5 to 7 quart (5 to 7 L) slow cooker. Sprinkle with dill weed and pepper. Arrange meatballs on top.

Combine next 4 ingredients in medium bowl. Pour over meatballs. Cook, covered, on Low for 8 to 10 hours or on High for 4 to 5 hours.

Measure peas into small microwave-safe bowl. Microwave, covered, on high (100%) for 1 to 2 minutes until heated through. Add to stew. Stir. Serves 8.

1 serving: 349 Calories; 8.4 g Total Fat (0.6 g Mono, 1.5 g Poly, 0.9 g Sat); trace Cholesterol; 55 g Carbohydrate; 5 g Fibre; 14 g Protein; 803 mg Sodium

Pictured on page 41.

Make Ahead: Assemble the first 10 ingredients in the slow cooker liner. Cover and chill overnight. Return the liner to the slow cooker and cook as directed.

Top: Pickle Platter, page 42
Centre: Tomato Pesto Swirl Bread, page 42
Bottom: Meatball Stew, above

Tomato Pesto Swirl Bread

Only when sliced does the bread reveal the surprise spiral of flavourful, herbed pesto.

Milk	1 1/4 cups	300 mL
Granulated sugar	2 tsp.	10 mL
Envelope of active dry yeast (or 2 1/4 tsp., 11 mL)	1/4 oz.	8 g
All-purpose flour	3 cups	750 mL
Salt	1 tsp.	5 mL
Olive (or cooking) oil	1/4 cup	60 mL
All-purpose flour (optional)	1 tbsp.	15 mL
Sun-dried tomato pesto	1/2 cup	125 mL

Combine milk and sugar in small heavy saucepan. Heat and stir on medium until warm and sugar is dissolved. Pour into small bowl. Let stand for 5 minutes.

Sprinkle yeast over top. Let stand for 10 minutes. Stir until yeast is dissolved.

Measure first amount of flour and salt into large bowl. Stir. Make a well in centre. Add yeast mixture and olive oil to well. Mix until stiff dough forms. Turn out onto lightly floured surface. Knead for 5 to 10 minutes, adding second amount of flour if necessary to prevent sticking, until smooth and elastic. Place in greased large bowl, turning once to grease top. Cover with greased waxed paper and tea towel. Let stand in oven with light on and door closed for about 1 hour until doubled in bulk. Punch down dough. Turn out onto lightly floured surface. Knead for about 1 minute until smooth.

Roll out dough to 9 x 13 inch (22 x 33 cm) rectangle. Spread pesto on top, leaving 3/4 inch (2 cm) edge on each side. Roll up from long side, jelly-roll style. Press seam against roll to seal. Place roll, seam-side down, on greased baking sheet, tucking ends under. Using sharp knife, cut 6 slashes across top of roll, about 1/2 inch (12 mm) deep. Let stand, uncovered, in oven with light on and door closed for 45 to 60 minutes until doubled in size. Bake in 375°F (190°C) oven for about 35 minutes until golden brown and hollow sounding when tapped. Let stand for 5 minutes before removing to wire rack to cool. Cuts into 16 slices. Serves 8.

1 serving: 287 Calories; 9.2 g Total Fat (6.1 g Mono, 1.0 g Poly, 1.5 g Sat); 2 mg Cholesterol; 44 g Carbohydrate; 2 g Fibre; 7 g Protein; 338 mg Sodium

Pictured on page 41.

Make Ahead: The bread may be wrapped tightly with plastic wrap and foil and stored in the freezer for up to 3 months. Thaw for several hours at room temperature before serving.

Pickle Platter

A side dish of pickles brings zesty tastes and textures to the meal. Be considerate of your guests' preferences when you go shopping but be bold too, combine familiar favourites with a few new, adventurous and exotic varieties. Arrange a platter of pickles early in the day, cover with plastic wrap and chill.

Here are some helpful tips on assembling your platter:

❊ Cut larger pickles into spears or medallions.

❊ Leave bite-sized items whole.

❊ Drain pickles well.

❊ Use a serving dish with sides to collect any extra draining liquid.

❊ Keep beet pickles in a separate dish to avoid discolouring other pickles.

Any of these selections go with both menus, but they partner particularly well with the Meatball Stew and Tomato Pesto Swirl Bread:

Artichoke hearts

Banana peppers

Dill pickles

Dilled baby carrots

Gherkins

Large pickled onions

Mustard pickles

Olives

Pickled cocktail onions

Pickled garlic

Pickled green beans

Pickled green or white asparagus spears

Pickled mushrooms

Sweet mixed pickles

Coconut Snowball Sundaes

Cute and kid-friendly. Offer a selection of garnishes in small bowls so guests can help themselves and dress up their sundaes as they like.

COCONUT SNOWBALLS

Flake coconut	1 cup	250 mL
Vanilla ice cream	4 cups	1 L

SUGGESTED GARNISHES
Chocolate ice cream topping
Miniature marshmallows
Green and red jelly beans
Green and red candy-coated
   chocolate candies
Green and red jujubes
Crushed candy canes
Candy sprinkles

Coconut Snowballs: Measure coconut into small shallow dish. Working quickly, scoop ice cream into 8 balls. Roll balls in coconut until coated. Place on plastic wrap-lined baking sheet. Freeze until firm. Makes 8 snowballs.

Just before serving, put snowballs into 8 serving bowls. Garnish as desired. Serves 8.

1 serving: 187 Calories; 10.8 g Total Fat (2.3 g Mono, 0.3 g Poly, 7.5 g Sat); 31 mg Cholesterol; 21 g Carbohydrate; 1 g Fibre; 3 g Protein; 81 mg Sodium

Pictured above.

Make Ahead: Prepare the Coconut Snowballs ahead of time. Once frozen, transfer them from the baking sheet to an airtight container and store them in the freezer for up to 1 month.

Festive Brunch

~

Brunch buffets are a favourite entertaining choice for many of us. For the holiday season, though, we took our inspiration for this midday occasion from evening dinner parties: appetizers and cocktails in your living room, a conversational table setting during mealtime and, in between, the convenience of a buffet for food service.

Lay out the dining room table with your chosen selection of buffet items. In a separate area of your home—either in the living room or the room where your Christmas tree stands—set out three small tables with four chairs each, café-style.

Decorate the tables and include a place setting for each guest so everyone need only carry their plate from the buffet to the table where everything they need is close at hand. You have the intimacy of a sit-down meal without the worry of accommodating serving dishes.

Best of all, you don't need 12 of everything! Create your own fabulous bistro atmosphere by using coordinating, but not necessarily matching, dinnerware, cutlery and table linens. Your decor and tableware choices can make your brunch as upscale or as down-home as you like. Either way, your guests will enjoy lingering in conversation as morning turns to afternoon.

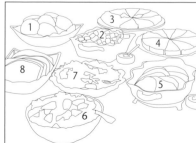

1. Gingerbread Muffins, page 48
2. Spiced Hash Brown Potatoes, page 56
3. Chicken And Leek Frittata, page 52
4. Spinach Salmon Tart, page 54
5. Baked Sweet Mustard Ham, page 56
6. Strawberry Citrus Salad, page 51
7. Lemon Fusilli Salad, page 52
8. Orange Eggnog Loaf, page 48

Festive Brunch

Elegant Brunch Buffet for 12

Buffets offer hosts the chance to set a bountiful table and guests get the chance to sample as little, or as much, as they would like of each dish. Serve all of the following recipes or serve brunch classics of your own in place of one or two items. Most of these dishes can be prepared in advance, including baked items that can be made ahead and frozen. We've included a generous provision of baking, so thaw only what will be used, keeping the rest for another occasion. We suggest you allow two pieces of baking per person.

Starters
Sparkling Peach Sipper, page 47
Sweet Onion Tartlets, page 47

Buffet
Strawberry Citrus Salad, page 51
Lemon Fusilli Salad, page 52

Spiced Hash Brown Potatoes, page 56
Baked Sweet Mustard Ham, page 56
Spinach Salmon Tart, page 54
Chicken And Leek Frittata, page 52

Chocolate And Pear Muffins, page 49
Gingerbread Muffins, page 48
Orange Eggnog Loaf, page 48

Cheese and Fruit
Cranberry Pepper Biscotti, page 57
Cheese Plate, page 52

Timeline

Up to One Month in Advance
Bake and freeze muffins and/or loaf
Bake and freeze tartlets
Bake and freeze biscotti

Day Before
Prepare peach purée and chill wine for
   Sparkling Peach Sipper
Prepare ingredients for fusilli salad
Bake salmon tart
Slice and arrange ham
Prepare ingredients for frittata
Remove baking from freezer to thaw at
   room temperature

Day Of
Up to 2 hours in advance:
Make strawberry salad

1 hour before guests arrive:
Prepare glaze for ham
Make hash brown potatoes
Arrange *Cheese Plate*

As guests arrive:
Reheat tartlets
Add wine to Sparkling Peach Sippers

30 minutes before serving:
Bake ham
Reheat salmon tart

Just before serving:
Cook frittata
Reheat muffins and loaf
Toss fusilli salad

Entertaining Tip

Small and Simple

If you're hosting a smaller crowd or a simpler affair, the menus are easy to adapt. Will you have fewer guests? Set out fewer buffet items, or serve smaller portions of each dish. Want to make the workload a little easier? Reduce the variety of dishes but increase the amount of what you choose to make and offer guests larger servings.

Sweet Onion Tartlets

Pressed for time? Use commercial tart shells instead of puff pastry for a quick-and-easy version of this recipe.

Olive (or cooking) oil	1 tbsp.	15 mL
Chopped onion	2 cups	500 mL
Garlic cloves, minced	2	2
(or 1/2 tsp., 2 mL, powder)		
Sweet chili sauce	2 tbsp.	30 mL
Balsamic vinegar	2 tsp.	10 mL
Large eggs	4	4
Half-and-half cream	3/4 cup	175 mL
Sour cream	1/2 cup	125 mL
Grated Parmesan cheese	1/2 cup	125 mL
Chopped fresh chives	3 tbsp.	50 mL
(or 2 1/4 tsp., 11 mL, dried)		
Chopped fresh thyme leaves	1 1/2 tsp.	7 mL
(or 1/4 tsp.,1 mL, dried)		
Package of puff pastry, thawed according to package directions	14 oz.	397 g

Heat olive oil in large frying pan on medium. Add onion and garlic. Cook for about 15 minutes, stirring occasionally, until onion is caramelized.

Add chili sauce and vinegar. Heat and stir for 1 minute. Remove from heat. Set aside.

Beat next 6 ingredients with whisk in medium bowl.

Roll out 1/2 (1 square) of puff pastry on lightly floured surface to 1/8 inch (3 mm) thickness. Cut out 18 circles using lightly floured 3 inch (7.5 cm) round cookie cutter. Press into greased mini muffin cups. Repeat with remaining 1/2 (1 square) of pastry. Spoon onion mixture into pastry shells. Spoon egg mixture over top until shells are almost full. Bake on bottom rack in 350°F (175°C) oven for 20 to 25 minutes until egg mixture is set. Makes 36 tartlets.

1 tartlet: 95 Calories; 6.6 g Total Fat (1.9 g Mono, 2.6 g Poly, 1.7 g Sat); 28 mg Cholesterol; 7 g Carbohydrate; trace Fibre; 3 g Protein; 79 mg Sodium

Pictured on this page.

Make Ahead: The tartlets may be stored in an airtight container in the freezer for up to 1 month. Reheat from frozen on an ungreased baking sheet in a 400°F (205°C) oven for about 20 minutes or until heated through.

Sparkling Peach Sipper, below

Sweet Onion Tartlets, left

Sparkling Peach Sipper

Brunch cocktails, sweet and velvety with a hint of sparkle, are a stylish start to any morning. Be sure to have the sparkling wine chilled.

Cans of sliced peaches (14 oz., 398 mL, each), drained	3	3
Peach schnapps	1/3 cup	75 mL
Bottle of sparkling white wine (or champagne)	26 oz.	750 mL

Process peaches and schnapps in blender or food processor until smooth. Pour into 12 champagne flutes.

Pour wine into flutes until almost full. Stir gently. Serves 12.

1 serving: 78 Calories; 0.1 g Total Fat (trace Mono, trace Poly, trace Sat); 0 mg Cholesterol; 8 g Carbohydrate; 1 g Fibre; 1 g Protein; 7 mg Sodium

Pictured above.

Variation: Use 3 cups (750 mL) lemon lime soft drink instead of sparkling wine.

Orange Eggnog Loaf

The traditional Christmas flavours of orange, cranberry and spice blend together in this finely textured loaf.

All-purpose flour	2 cups	500 mL
Baking powder	1 1/2 tsp.	7 mL
Ground cinnamon	1 tsp.	5 mL
Baking soda	1/2 tsp.	2 mL
Salt	1/2 tsp.	2 mL
Eggnog (or buttermilk plus 1/2 tsp., 2 mL, ground nutmeg)	1 cup	250 mL
Grated orange zest	2 tsp.	10 mL
Dried cranberries	1/2 cup	125 mL
Butter (or hard margarine), softened	1/3 cup	75 mL
Granulated sugar	2/3 cup	150 mL
Large eggs	2	2
Icing (confectioner's) sugar	3 tbsp.	50 mL
Frozen concentrated orange juice, thawed	2 tbsp.	30 mL

Measure first 5 ingredients into small bowl. Stir. Set aside.

Combine eggnog and orange zest in separate small bowl. Add cranberries. Stir well.

Cream butter and granulated sugar in medium bowl. Add eggs 1 at a time, beating well after each addition. Add flour mixture in 3 parts, alternately with eggnog mixture in 2 parts, stirring after each addition until just combined. Spread in greased 9 x 5 x 3 inch (22 x 12.5 x 7.5 cm) loaf pan. Bake in 350°F (175°C) oven for about 50 minutes until wooden pick inserted in centre comes out clean. Let stand in pan on wire rack.

Stir icing sugar and orange juice in separate small bowl until smooth. Brush on hot loaf. Let stand for 10 minutes before removing to wire rack to cool. Cuts into 16 slices.

1 slice: 237 Calories; 8.2 g Total Fat (2.4 g Mono, 0.5 g Poly, 4.6 g Sat); 64 mg Cholesterol; 37 g Carbohydrate; 2 g Fibre; 4 g Protein; 277 mg Sodium

Pictured on page 44.

Make Ahead: The loaf may be wrapped tightly with plastic wrap and foil and stored in the freezer for up to 3 months.

Gingerbread Muffins

A healthy addition to a holiday brunch. Crystallized ginger adds a special flair to these tender muffins.

All-purpose flour	1 cup	250 mL
Whole wheat flour	1 cup	250 mL
Minced crystallized ginger	1/3 cup	75 mL
Baking powder	1 tsp.	5 mL
Baking soda	1/2 tsp.	2 mL
Salt	1/2 tsp.	2 mL
Ground cinnamon	1/2 tsp.	2 mL
Ground ginger	1/2 tsp.	2 mL
Ground nutmeg	1/4 tsp.	1 mL
Butter (or hard margarine), softened	1/4 cup	60 mL
Brown sugar, packed	1/2 cup	125 mL
Large eggs	2	2
Vanilla yogurt	1 cup	250 mL
Fancy (mild) molasses	1/2 cup	125 mL

Measure first 9 ingredients into large bowl. Stir. Make a well in centre. Set aside.

Cream butter and brown sugar in medium bowl. Add eggs 1 at a time, beating well after each addition.

Add yogurt and molasses. Beat until smooth. Add to well in flour mixture. Stir until just moistened. Fill 12 greased muffin cups almost full. Bake in 375°F (190°C) oven for about 18 minutes until wooden pick inserted in centre of muffin comes out clean. Let stand in pan for 5 minutes before removing to wire rack to cool. Makes 12 muffins.

1 muffin: 236 Calories; 5.7 g Total Fat (1.7 g Mono, 0.4 g Poly, 3.1 g Sat); 48 mg Cholesterol; 43 g Carbohydrate; 2 g Fibre; 5 g Protein; 261 mg Sodium

Pictured on page 44.

Make Ahead: The muffins may be stored in an airtight container in the freezer for up to 3 months.

Entertaining Tip

Baking Advantages

There are plenty of good reasons for including baked goods in your buffet menu: They're easy to make ahead and freeze well, can be offered in single serving sizes and can be replenished fairly easily by simply pulling more from the freezer (to thaw at room temperature, or with a little help from the microwave, or to warm in the oven). Knowing that everyone enjoys the taste of homemade baking makes these extra touches well worth the effort.

Chocolate And Pear Muffins

Cinnamon is a subtle addition to this muffin full of pear and chocolate chunks.

All-purpose flour	2 cups	500 mL
Chopped peeled fresh pear	1 1/3 cups	325 mL
Brown sugar, packed	3/4 cup	175 mL
Milk chocolate bar, chopped	3 1/2 oz.	100 g
Baking powder	2 tsp.	10 mL
Ground cinnamon	1/4 tsp.	1 mL
Salt	1/4 tsp.	1 mL
Large egg	1	1
Buttermilk (or soured milk, see Tip)	3/4 cup	175 mL
Cooking oil	1/2 cup	125 mL

Combine first 7 ingredients in large bowl. Make a well in centre.

Beat remaining 3 ingredients with whisk in small bowl. Add to well. Stir until just moistened. Fill 12 greased muffin cups 3/4 full. Bake in 375°F (190°C) oven for about 25 minutes until wooden pick inserted in centre of muffin comes out clean. Let stand in pan for 5 minutes before removing to wire rack to cool. Makes 12 muffins.

1 muffin: 284 Calories; 12.9 g Total Fat (6.7 g Mono, 3.1 g Poly, 2.5 g Sat); 20 mg Cholesterol; 39 g Carbohydrate; 2 g Fibre; 4 g Protein; 147 mg Sodium

Pictured above.

Tip: To make sour milk, measure 2 tsp. (10 mL) white vinegar or lemon juice into 1 cup (250 mL) liquid measure. Add milk to make 3/4 cup (175 mL). Stir. Let stand for 1 minute.

Make Ahead: The muffins may be stored in an airtight container in the freezer for up to 3 months.

Compact Centrepiece

These fresh flower centrepieces take very little table space and will add a touch of class to your festive brunch. Make the arrangements the day before—you can do all three in under an hour. Use any colour roses and ribbon to suit your Christmas decor.

MATERIALS

* ❋ 3 small waterproof containers
* ❋ Decorative glass stones (enough for 3 containers)
* ❋ Waterproof florist tape
* ❋ Double-sided tape
* ❋ Red ribbon (the width of the double-sided tape)
* ❋ Fresh red roses (enough for 3 arrangements)
* ❋ Small pieces of Christmas greenery, such as cedar, pine or holly
* ❋ Baby's breath (or other filler flowers), optional

TOOLS AND SUPPLIES

lukewarm water, X-Acto knife, scissors, pruning shears

Fill the containers 1/2 full with glass stones. Add water until the containers are 2/3 full.

Make grids on top of the containers to support individual roses by crisscrossing waterproof florist tape tightly across the rims, securing the ends of the tape over the side of the containers (see photo).

Attach double-sided tape around the side of the container rims on top of the florist tape. Trim any florist tape that is below and not covered by the double-sided tape. Cut 3 lengths of ribbon, each 2 times the circumference of the container rim to which it will be attached. For each container, fold the ribbon in half to mark the centre. Attach the centre of the ribbon to the double-sided tape and continue pressing the ribbon to the tape along the rim to secure, leaving both ends of the ribbon free to tie a bow. Tie a bow. Trim the ends of the ribbon. Fill each container with roses and greenery, and baby's breath if desired, as follows, completing 1 arrangement before starting the next.

How to measure and trim stems of roses

Work with 1 rose at a time. Remove any leaves and thorns that will be below the water line. Trim the stem to the desired length and immediately insert into a grid opening. For a pretty dome-shaped arrangement, cut each row of rose stems progressively shorter than the last, inserting each row at a greater angle than the previous.

To easily measure the length of stem needed, place the container near the edge of the countertop. Hold a rose alongside the countertop at the angle in which it will be placed in the container so that you can see where to cut the stem. Cut the stem on an angle, and long enough to reach the bottom or side of the container for stability (see photo).

Place the longest stem in the centre of the grid so that it stands straight up in the container. Continue to work around the grid from the centre toward the rim, inserting 1 or 2 roses into each opening, depending on the size of the blooms. Turn the container as you work so that you can see the arrangement take shape. Insert the last row of roses so that they rest just above the rim of the container.

Insert small pieces of greenery between the roses and around the rim. Be sure to strip away any greenery from the stem that will be below the water line. For best results, keep the ends of the greenery the same length or shorter than the rose stems.

If you're using baby's breath, insert small sprigs among the roses.

Strawberry Citrus Salad

Enticing contrast and vibrant colour create a fresh and appealing salad. A hint of orange liqueur accents the pairing of strawberries and oranges. Large red seedless grapes can be substituted for the strawberries.

Medium oranges	5	5
Quartered fresh strawberries	5 cups	1.25 L
Orange liqueur	1/4 cup	60 mL
Liquid honey	3 tbsp.	50 mL

Cut small slice of peel from both ends of oranges so that flesh is exposed. Place oranges, cut-side down, on cutting board. Remove peel with sharp knife, cutting down and around flesh, leaving as little pith as possible (see photo). Cut oranges in half lengthwise. Place each half cut-side down. Cut into 1/4 inch (6 mm) slices. Put into large bowl.

Add strawberries. Toss gently.

Combine liqueur and honey in small cup. Drizzle over fruit. Toss gently until coated. Serves 12.

1 serving: 75 Calories; 0.3 g Total Fat (0.1 g Mono, 0.2 g Poly, trace Sat); 0 mg Cholesterol; 16 g Carbohydrate; 3 g Fibre; 1 g Protein; 1 mg Sodium

Pictured above and on page 44.

Make Ahead: The salad may be made up to 2 hours ahead of time and stored in an airtight container in the refrigerator. Toss gently before serving.

Chicken And Leek Frittata

Applewood-smoked Cheddar is a flavourful variety to use in this frittata. It melts beautifully and has a distinct smoky flavour.

Cooking oil	1 tbsp.	15 mL
Boneless, skinless chicken breast halves, chopped	12 oz.	340 g
Thinly sliced leek (white part only)	1 1/2 cups	375 mL
Large eggs	10	10
Grated smoked Cheddar cheese	1/2 cup	125 mL
Chopped fresh basil	3 tbsp.	50 mL
Salt	1/4 tsp.	1 mL
Pepper	1/4 tsp.	1 mL
Grated smoked Cheddar cheese	1/2 cup	125 mL

Heat cooking oil in large non-stick frying pan on medium. Add chicken and leek. Cook for about 10 minutes, stirring occasionally, until chicken is no longer pink inside.

Beat next 5 ingredients with whisk in medium bowl. Pour over chicken mixture. Spread egg mixture evenly in pan. Cook, covered, for about 4 minutes until bottom is golden and top is almost set. Remove from heat.

Sprinkle with second amount of cheese. Broil on top rack in oven for about 2 minutes until cheese is melted and frittata is set (see Note). Let stand for 5 minutes. Cuts into 12 wedges.

1 wedge: 157 Calories; 9.2 g Total Fat (3.3 g Mono, 1.2 g Poly, 3.6 g Sat); 206 mg Cholesterol; 4 g Carbohydrate; 1 g Fibre; 14 g Protein; 168 mg Sodium

Pictured on pages 45 and 53.

Note: To avoid damaging the frying pan handle in the oven, wrap the handle with foil before placing under the broiler.

Make Ahead: Prepare the uncooked chicken, leek and cheese up to 24 hours ahead of time and store them in separate airtight containers in the refrigerator. Cook as directed.

Lemon Fusilli Salad

Green spinach and red pepper add a festive touch to this pasta and mushroom salad. The creamy, sweet citrus dressing is a refreshing twist.

Fusilli pasta	4 cups	1 L
Fresh spinach, stems removed, lightly packed	3 cups	750 mL
Sliced fresh white mushrooms	2 1/2 cups	625 mL
Chopped red pepper	3/4 cup	175 mL
LEMON HONEY DRESSING		
Mayonnaise	1/2 cup	125 mL
Lemon juice	2 tbsp.	30 mL
Liquid honey	1 tbsp.	15 mL
Grated lemon zest	1/2 tsp.	2 mL
Salt	1/2 tsp.	2 mL
Pepper	1/4 tsp.	1 mL
Ground ginger	1/4 tsp.	1 mL

Freshly ground pepper, for garnish

Cook pasta in boiling salted water in large uncovered pot or Dutch oven for 8 to 10 minutes, stirring occasionally, until tender but firm. Drain. Rinse with cold water. Drain well. Transfer to extra-large bowl.

Add next 3 ingredients. Toss.

Lemon Honey Dressing: Combine first 7 ingredients in small bowl. Makes about 2/3 cup (150 mL) dressing. Drizzle over salad. Toss well.

Garnish with pepper. Serves 12.

1 serving: 197 Calories; 8.4 g Total Fat (4.4 g Mono, 2.8 g Poly, 0.8 g Sat); 6 mg Cholesterol; 26 g Carbohydrate; 2 g Fibre; 5 g Protein; 164 mg Sodium

Pictured on pages 44 and 53.

Make Ahead: Prepare the pasta, vegetables and dressing up to 24 hours ahead of time and store them in separate airtight containers in the refrigerator. Toss together just before serving.

1. Gingerbread Muffins, page 48
2. Chicken And Leek Frittata, this page
3. Lemon Fusilli Salad, above

Spinach Salmon Tart

Sweet caramelized onion, mild spinach and rich, mellow cheese raise canned salmon to the level of exceptional. A beautiful and flavourful brunch dish.

All-purpose flour	1 1/4 cups	300 mL
Granulated sugar	1 tbsp.	15 mL
Dill weed	1/2 tsp.	2 mL
Salt	1/4 tsp.	1 mL
Cold butter (or hard margarine), cut up	1/3 cup	75 mL
Egg yolks (large), fork-beaten	2	2
Ice water	3 tbsp.	50 mL
Butter (or hard margarine)	2 tbsp.	30 mL
Sliced onion	3 cups	750 mL
Dijon mustard	2 tbsp.	30 mL
Can of skinless, boneless pink salmon, drained and flaked	6 oz.	170 g
Box of frozen chopped spinach, thawed and squeezed dry	10 oz.	300 g
Large eggs	3	3
Sour cream	1/2 cup	125 mL
Grated Parmesan cheese	1/4 cup	60 mL
Lemon pepper	1/2 tsp.	2 mL
Grated havarti cheese	1/2 cup	125 mL

Process first 5 ingredients in food processor until mixture resembles coarse crumbs (see Note).

Add egg yolk and ice water. Pulse with on/off motion until mixture just starts to come together. Do not over-process. Turn out onto lightly floured surface. Press pastry into ball. Flatten slightly into disc. Wrap with plastic wrap. Chill for 30 minutes. Roll out pastry on lightly floured surface to fit ungreased 9 inch (22 cm) tart pan with fluted sides and removable bottom. Carefully lift pastry and press into bottom and up side of tart pan. Trim edge. Place pan on baking sheet (see Note). Chill, covered, for 1 hour. Cover pastry with parchment paper, bringing paper up over edge. Fill halfway up side with dried beans. Bake on bottom rack in 375°F (190°C) oven for 15 minutes. Remove from oven. Carefully remove parchment paper and beans, reserving beans for next time you bake pastry. Bake crust for another 10 minutes until golden. Let stand on baking sheet on wire rack for 10 minutes.

Melt second amount of butter in large frying pan on medium. Add onion. Cook for about 15 minutes, stirring often, until caramelized. Remove from heat.

Spread mustard on bottom of crust. Scatter with salmon and spinach. Scatter caramelized onion on top.

Beat next 4 ingredients in medium bowl until frothy. Carefully pour over onion.

Sprinkle with havarti cheese. Bake in 375°F (190°C) oven for 35 to 40 minutes until cheese is golden. Let stand for 5 minutes before serving. Cuts into 12 wedges.

1 wedge: 230 Calories; 14.2 g Total Fat (4.3 g Mono, 1.2 g Poly, 7.6 g Sat); 123 mg Cholesterol; 17 g Carbohydrate; 2 g Fibre; 9 g Protein; 360 mg Sodium

Pictured on pages 45 and 55.

Note: If you don't have a food processor, combine flour, sugar, dill weed and salt in a medium bowl. Cut in the butter until mixture resembles coarse crumbs. Stir in the egg yolk and water with a fork until mixture just starts to come together. Continue as directed.

Note: Placing the tart pan on a baking sheet provides a safe way to remove the hot pan from the oven.

Make Ahead: The tart may be baked 24 hours ahead of time, covered and stored in the refrigerator overnight. To reheat, cover with foil and bake in a 400°F (205°C) oven for about 20 minutes or until heated through.

Entertaining Tip

Seating by Design

Deciding who sits where can be a little more challenging when you're dealing with three tables. If all your guests know each other well it's certainly easier. Quite often, however, not everyone knows everyone else and the tables of four will encourage small circles of conversation during the meal. Here are a few suggestions to help you with seating arrangements:

❋ Know a little bit about each guest: Bring together those with shared interests, hobbies, plans or personalities that might hit it off.

❋ Mix up friends: Instead of visiting with the same people, everyone can meet someone new.

❋ Be careful about seating co-workers together: Now is not the time to discuss work!

❋ Don't worry about the ratio of men to women: Focus on inviting people you want at your brunch and who you think will enjoy each other's company.

❋ If you find planned seating stressful, make a game out of it: Have guests randomly draw lots from three different Christmas-themed tags or ornaments, then match each group to a table.

Clockwise from left:
Spiced Hash Brown Potatoes, page 56
Spinach Salmon Tart, this page
Baked Sweet Mustard Ham, page 56

Baked Sweet Mustard Ham

Glazed ham is a brunch classic, but sweet pepper, orange and mustard are an especially inviting complement to the smoky flavour of this dish. By slicing the ham in advance, it bakes more quickly and is easier to serve hot.

ORANGE GLAZE

Red jalapeño jelly	1/2 cup	125 mL
Frozen concentrated orange juice, thawed	2 tbsp.	30 mL
Dijon mustard (with whole seeds)	2 tbsp.	30 mL
Prepared mustard	2 tbsp.	30 mL
Fully cooked boneless ham	3 lbs.	1.4 kg

Orange Glaze: Measure jelly into small microwave-safe bowl. Microwave on high (100%) for about 20 seconds until softened. Add next 3 ingredients. Stir until smooth. Makes about 1 cup (250 mL) glaze.

Cut ham in half lengthwise. Cut each half crosswise into 1/4 inch (6 mm) slices. Arrange ham slices, slightly overlapping, in 9 × 13 inch (22 × 33 cm) baking dish. Brush 1/2 of glaze over ham. Bake, uncovered, in 400°F (205°C) oven for 10 minutes. Brush with remaining glaze. Bake for another 10 to 12 minutes until ham is heated through. Makes twelve 3 oz. (85 g) servings.

1 serving: 245 Calories; 10.6 g Total Fat (5.2 g Mono, 1.7 g Poly, 3.6 g Sat); 67 mg Cholesterol; 11 g Carbohydrate; trace Fibre; 26 g Protein; 1776 mg Sodium

Pictured on pages 45 and 55.

Make Ahead: Slice and arrange the ham in the baking dish up to 24 hours ahead of time, cover and store in the refrigerator until ready to bake. Prepare the glaze and brush it over the ham then bake as directed.

Spiced Hash Brown Potatoes

The secret is in the spices. Made-from-scratch potatoes—golden crisp on the outside, tender on the inside—don't get any better than these.

Olive (or cooking) oil	2 tbsp.	30 mL
Chopped fresh thyme leaves (or 3/4 tsp., 4 mL, dried)	1 tbsp.	15 mL
Ground cumin	1/2 – 1 tsp.	2 – 5 mL
Paprika	1 tsp.	5 mL
Salt	1 tsp.	5 mL
Pepper	1/2 tsp.	2 mL
Cayenne pepper	1/4 tsp.	1 mL
Unpeeled potatoes, cut into 1/2 inch (12 mm) cubes	3 lbs.	1.4 kg

Put first 7 ingredients into large bowl. Stir.

Add potato. Toss until coated. Spread in single layer on greased baking sheet with sides. Bake in 400°F (205°C) oven for about 50 minutes, stirring occasionally, until golden and crisp. Makes about 6 cups (1.5 L).

1/2 cup (125 mL): 106 Calories; 2.5 g Total Fat (1.7 g Mono, 0.3 g Poly, 0.3 g Sat); 0 mg Cholesterol; 19 g Carbohydrate; 2 g Fibre; 3 g Protein; 206 mg Sodium

Pictured on pages 44 and 55.

Special Touch

Space Matters

The café-style layout is on a smaller scale but it still allows room for table decorations. We've included a Special Project, page 50, that describes a compact design for creating a high-impact centrepiece. To prevent a crowded look, avoid adorning the table with charger plates or fixed-size placemats and consider instead a few of these decor ideas that won't overwhelm the tabletop.

Creative placemats
Use festive, all-natural cedar boughs to indicate each person's place (cedar is best as it lays flat and holds no sap). Set the plates right on top of the greenery as a beautiful frame. Tuck some greenery underneath the dishes on your buffet table to tie everything together.

Creative place cards
* Cut store-bought place cards in half (so they still stand but are narrower) before adding names.

* Use Christmas gift tags tied with ribbon around napkins.

* Attach tags to ornaments, miniature stockings or candy canes and hang them on the backs of chairs.

* Use the centrepiece as a paperweight. Display names on one half of a folded place card and slide the other half of the card under the centrepiece container.

Cheese Plate, page 52

Cranberry Pepper Biscotti, below

Cranberry Pepper Biscotti

This savoury biscotti is best served with a creamy cheese such as Brie or Gorgonzola. A dab of jalapeño jelly adds a sweet-hot kick. A delicious option to crackers on a cheese tray.

All-purpose flour	1 3/4 cups	425 mL
Dried cranberries	1 cup	250 mL
Coarsely chopped walnuts	1/2 cup	125 mL
Coarse ground pepper	1 tsp.	5 mL
Baking powder	1/2 tsp.	2 mL
Salt	1/8 tsp.	0.5 mL
Butter (or hard margarine), softened	1/4 cup	60 mL
Granulated sugar	1/2 cup	125 mL
Large eggs	2	2

Put first 6 ingredients into large bowl. Stir. Make a well in centre.

Cream butter and sugar in medium bowl. Add eggs 1 at a time, beating well after each addition. Add to well. Stir until soft dough forms. Turn out onto lightly floured surface. Knead 6 times. Divide dough in half. Shape each half into 8 inch (20 cm) long log. Place logs crosswise on greased baking sheet about 3 inches (7.5 cm) apart. Flatten logs slightly to 3/4 inch (2 cm) thickness. Bake in 350°F (175°C) oven for about 25 minutes until edges are golden. Remove from oven. Let stand for about 10 minutes until cool enough to handle. Using serrated knife, cut logs diagonally into 1/2 inch (12 mm) slices. Arrange, cut-side down, on greased baking sheet. Reduce heat to 275°F (140°C). Bake for about 20 minutes until bottoms are golden. Turn slices over. Turn oven off. Let stand in oven for about 30 minutes until dry and crisp. Makes about 2 dozen (24) biscotti.

1 biscotti: 102 Calories; 4.2 g Total Fat (1.1 g Mono, 1.2 g Poly, 1.5 g Sat); 23 mg Cholesterol; 14 g Carbohydrate; 1 g Fibre; 2 g Protein; 47 mg Sodium

Pictured above.

Make Ahead: The biscotti may be baked up to 2 weeks ahead of time and stored in an airtight container at room temperature. For longer storage time, these freeze well for up to 3 months.

Dessert Buffet

~

Candy canes to sugarplums, Christmas pudding to mincemeat tarts, and anything chocolate—for many of us, this is the time of year when we permit ourselves indulgence in the sweets of the season. Revel in the tradition and host a lavish dessert buffet. Invite friends over after a concert, community event or even late-night shopping, or after supper for an hour or two of visiting once the children are tucked in their beds.

Our approach to this menu is simple: Focus only on dessert and set everything out at once in a stunning presentation. Preparation is mostly make-ahead, so there's little to do during party time—especially if guests serve themselves. As well, cleanup duties are much lighter than for other entertaining occasions.

We've included a selection of 10 desserts so you have plenty of choice in creating your own customized dessert menu. Following our guidelines will ensure you have variety in taste, texture and visual appeal for your party of 12. The menu is also adaptable for a smaller circle of friends or even an intimate evening for two.

For those who love desserts, 'tis the season to share sweet times in good company.

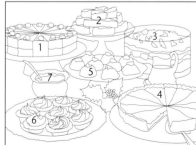

1. Heavenly Eggnog Cheesecake, page 64
2. Almond Ginger Triangles, page 62
3. Blueberry Lemon Trifle, page 69
4. Pear Tart With Maple Sauce, page 68
5. Glistening Brownie Bombes, page 62
6. Lemon Cherry Tartlets, page 70
7. Cranberry Orange Sauce, page 64

Dessert Buffet

Fancy Late-Evening Buffet for 12

This selection of recipes categorizes desserts for creative mixing and matching. Each yields smaller, buffet-sized servings rather than full-sized, single-dessert portions. Some recipes yield more pieces than you may need for the buffet. To calculate the number of dessert portions you need, we suggest you count on five to six small pieces per person.

For a party of 12, select one dessert from each of the five categories and one more—of your choice—for a total of six items at the buffet table. Some desserts need to be sliced before serving, while others are already single-serving size. It's nice to have some of each, both for visual presentation and guest preference. A seasonal fresh fruit tray is always a colourful and appealing addition to any buffet.

Menu Choices
Chocolate
Chocolate Silk Fondue, page 61
Glistening Brownie Bombes, page 62

Citrus
Blueberry Lemon Trifle, page 69
Lemon Cherry Tartlets, page 70

Cream
Heavenly Eggnog Cheesecake, page 64
Peppermint Cream Puffs, page 66

Fruit
Pear Tart With Maple Sauce, page 68
Caramel Apple Bites, page 66

Nuts
Walnut Raisin Tart, page 63
Almond Ginger Triangles, page 62

Specialty Beverages
Chocolate Martini, page 72
Kris Kringle Kaffee, page 70

Timeline

All of the menu items are included in this timeline so you can easily see what needs to be done and when, no matter which combination of recipes you choose to make.

Up to One Month in Advance
Make and freeze:
Glistening Brownie Bombes
Lemon Cherry Tartlets
Heavenly Eggnog Cheesecake
Peppermint Cream Puffs
Caramel Apple Bites
Walnut Raisin Tart
Almond Ginger Triangles

Up to Two Days in Advance
Make sauce for cheesecake
Make Pfeffernuss Cream for Kris Kringle Kaffee

Day Before
Make Blueberry Lemon Trifle
Bake Pear Tart
Make Maple Sauce for Pear Tart
Move Almond Ginger Triangles from freezer
    to refrigerator
Set up beverage stations

Day Of
4 hours in advance:
Chop chocolate and cut cake for fondue
Mix liquor and liqueurs for martini

2 hours in advance:
Remove desserts (that require slicing) from freezer
    to thaw slightly at room temperature
Remove Pear Tart from refrigerator

1 1/2 hours in advance:
Portion whole desserts, arrange on serving trays

1 hour before guests arrive:
Take out individual frozen desserts and arrange
    on serving trays
Heat sauce for Pear Tart and brush on pears

30 minutes before guests arrive:
Make chocolate fondue

Just before guests arrive:
Cut fruit for fondue
Transfer fondue to fondue pot
Brew coffee
Make tea

Chocolate Silk Fondue

Smooth, dark and delicious! Good-quality chocolate makes the difference between special and extra-special. Provide your guests with small plates for the sauce to prevent double-dipping.

Dark chocolate bars (3 1/2 oz., 100 g, each), chopped	2	2
Whipping cream	1 cup	250 mL

SUGGESTED DIPPERS
Ladyfingers
White or yellow cake
Angel food cake
Marshmallows
Assorted fruit

Heat chocolate and whipping cream in small heavy saucepan on lowest heat, stirring often until chocolate is almost melted. Do not overheat. Remove from heat. Stir until smooth. Pour into fondue pot. Keep warm over low flame.

Serve with your choice of dippers. Makes about 1 2/3 cups (400 mL) fondue.

2 tbsp. (30 mL) fondue: 124 Calories; 10.1 g Total Fat (3.1 g Mono, 0.3 g Poly, 6.2 g Sat); 21 mg Cholesterol; 10 g Carbohydrate; 1 g Fibre; 1 g Protein; 8 mg Sodium

Pictured above.

Variation: Add 1 oz. (2 tbsp., 30 mL) of your favourite liqueur to melted chocolate mixture.

Make Ahead: Chop the chocolate ahead of time to speed up last-minute preparation. Cut the cake into cubes and store them in an airtight container at room temperature until serving time. The fruit is best cut just before serving.

Almond Ginger Triangles

An intriguing balance of almond, ginger and chocolate makes these treats pleasingly unique.

Butter (or hard margarine)	1/2 cup	125 mL
Finely crushed vanilla wafers (9 oz., 250 g, package of wafers)	2 cups	500 mL
Butter (or hard margarine), softened	3/4 cup	175 mL
Granulated sugar	3/4 cup	175 mL
Vanilla extract	1 tsp.	5 mL
Large eggs	3	3
Ground almonds	1 1/2 cups	375 mL
Minced crystallized ginger	1/4 cup	60 mL
All-purpose flour	3 tbsp.	50 mL
Ground nutmeg	1/4 tsp.	1 mL
Semi-sweet chocolate baking squares (1 oz., 28 g, each), grated	2	2
Salt	1/4 tsp.	1 mL
Sliced blanched almonds	1/3 cup	75 mL

Icing (confectioner's) sugar, for dusting

Melt first amount of butter in medium saucepan. Remove from heat. Add wafer crumbs. Mix well. Press firmly into greased 9 x 13 inch (22 x 33 cm) pan.

Cream second amount of butter and granulated sugar in medium bowl. Add extract. Stir. Add eggs 1 at a time, beating well after each addition.

Add next 6 ingredients. Stir. Spread evenly on top of crust.

Sprinkle with second amount of almonds. Bake in 350°F (175°C) oven for about 35 minutes until golden and wooden pick inserted in centre comes out clean. Let stand in pan on wire rack until cooled. Cut into 20 rectangles. Cut each in half diagonally, for a total of 40 triangles.

Dust with icing sugar. Makes 40 triangles.

1 triangle: 126 Calories; 9.4 g Total Fat (3.5 g Mono, 0.8 g Poly, 4.5 g Sat); 35 mg Cholesterol; 10 g Carbohydrate; trace Fibre; 2 g Protein; 96 mg Sodium

Pictured on pages 58 and 67.

Make Ahead: The triangles may be stored in an airtight container in the freezer for up to 3 months. Thaw them in the refrigerator overnight. Dust them with icing sugar just before arranging them on the platter.

Glistening Brownie Bombes

Store-bought brownies are magically transformed into decadent petits fours! A simple, easy recipe that will really wow your guests.

Package of commercial 2-bite brownies (about 16 brownies)	10 1/2 oz.	300 g
Orange liqueur	2 tbsp.	30 mL
Whipping cream	1/4 cup	60 mL
Semi-sweet chocolate baking squares (1 oz., 28 g, each), cut up	3	3
Orange liqueur	2 tsp.	10 mL
Candy orange slices, each cut into 4 wedges	4	4

Poke bottom of brownies in several places with wooden pick. Place, bottom-side up, on wire rack set on baking sheet with sides. Brush with first amount of liqueur. Set aside.

Measure whipping cream into small heavy saucepan. Bring to a boil on medium. Remove from heat.

Add chocolate and second amount of liqueur. Stir until smooth. Slowly spoon over brownies, allowing glaze to run down sides.

Top with orange wedges. Chill for about 1 hour until glaze is set. Makes about 16 brownie bombes.

1 brownie bombe: 123 Calories; 5.9 g Total Fat (2.5 g Mono, 0.6 g Poly, 2.5 g Sat); 8 mg Cholesterol; 17 g Carbohydrate; trace Fibre; 1 g Protein; 61 mg Sodium

Pictured on page 58.

Make Ahead: The brownie bombes may be stored in a single layer in an airtight container in the freezer for up to 1 month.

Walnut Raisin Tart

Sweet juicy raisins and tangy sour cream fill a crunchy, nutty crust. Lovely with fresh fruit and whipped cream. You'll need a food processor to grind the walnuts fine for the crust. If serving the tart as a regular dessert—not as a dessert buffet selection—cut it into eight wedges.

Chopped walnuts	1 cup	250 mL
All-purpose flour	3/4 cup	175 mL
Icing (confectioner's) sugar	1/4 cup	60 mL
Cocoa	3 tbsp.	50 mL
Cold butter (or hard margarine), cut up	1/2 cup	125 mL
Sour cream	1 cup	250 mL
Granulated sugar	1/2 cup	125 mL
Brown sugar, packed	1/2 cup	125 mL
Dark raisins	2/3 cup	150 mL
Chopped walnuts	1/3 cup	75 mL
Large eggs, fork-beaten	2	2
White vinegar	1 tbsp.	15 mL
Vanilla extract	1 tsp.	5 mL
Salt	1/2 tsp.	2 mL
Ground cinnamon	1/4 tsp.	1 mL
Ground nutmeg	1/8 tsp.	0.5 mL

Whipped cream, for garnish

Process first 4 ingredients in food processor for 5 seconds. Add butter. Pulse with on/off motion until mixture resembles fine crumbs. Press into bottom and up side of lightly greased 9 inch (22 cm) tart pan with fluted sides and removable bottom. Place pan on baking sheet (see Note).

Combine sour cream, granulated sugar and brown sugar in large bowl. Fold in raisins, walnuts and egg.

Add next 5 ingredients. Stir. Spread evenly on pastry shell. Bake on centre rack in 350°F (175°C) oven for about 1 hour until wooden pick inserted in centre comes out clean. Let stand in pan on wire rack until cool. Remove to serving plate.

Garnish with whipped cream. Cuts into 12 wedges.

1 wedge: 345 Calories; 20.4 g Total Fat (5.4 g Mono, 6.1 g Poly, 7.8 g Sat); 66 mg Cholesterol; 38 g Carbohydrate; 2 g Fibre; 7 g Protein; 206 mg Sodium

Pictured above.

Note: Placing the tart pan on a baking sheet provides a safe way to remove the hot pan from the oven.

Make Ahead: The baked tart may be stored in an airtight container in the freezer for up to 1 month.

Heavenly Eggnog Cheesecake

Smooth and light, this no-bake cheesecake needs only a dollop of whipped cream and a cranberry on each slice to be ready for your dessert buffet. If you're serving the cheesecake as a regular dessert—rather than on a dessert buffet with other choices—cut it into 12 wedges.

ORANGE GRAHAM CRUST

Butter (or hard margarine)	1/2 cup	125 mL
Graham cracker crumbs	1 3/4 cups	425 mL
Grated orange zest	1 tsp.	5 mL
Milk	3/4 cup	175 mL
Dark (navy) rum	1/4 cup	60 mL
Envelopes of unflavoured gelatin (about 1 1/2 tbsp., 25 mL)	1 1/2	1 1/2
Blocks of cream cheese (8 oz., 250 g, each), softened	2	2
Eggnog	2 cups	500 mL
Box of instant vanilla pudding powder (4 serving size)	1	1
Ground cinnamon	1/4 tsp.	1 mL
Ground nutmeg	1/4 tsp.	1 mL
Whipping cream	1 cup	250 mL

CRANBERRY ORANGE SAUCE

Fresh (or frozen) cranberries	1 cup	250 mL
Cranberry cocktail	2/3 cup	150 mL
Granulated sugar	2/3 cup	150 mL
Orange juice	3 tbsp.	50 mL
Cornstarch	2 tbsp.	30 mL
Butter (or hard margarine)	2 tbsp.	30 mL
Grated orange zest	2 tsp.	10 mL
Salt	1/8 tsp.	0.5 mL

Orange Graham Crust: Melt butter in medium saucepan. Remove from heat. Add graham crumbs and orange zest. Mix well. Press firmly into bottom and 1 inch (2.5 cm) up side of greased 9 inch (22 cm) springform pan. Chill for 1 hour.

Combine milk and rum in small saucepan. Sprinkle gelatin over top. Let stand for 1 minute. Heat and stir on medium-low for about 1 minute until gelatin is dissolved. Remove from heat. Let stand for 5 minutes.

Beat cream cheese in large bowl for about 3 minutes until smooth. Slowly add gelatin mixture, beating constantly until smooth. Add next 4 ingredients. Beat well.

Beat whipping cream in medium bowl until soft peaks form. Fold into eggnog mixture. Spread evenly in crust. Chill for about 3 hours until set.

Cranberry Orange Sauce: Combine first 3 ingredients in small saucepan. Heat on medium for about 5 minutes, stirring occasionally, until boiling and cranberries are softened.

Stir orange juice into cornstarch in small cup until smooth. Add to cranberry mixture. Heat and stir for 1 to 2 minutes until boiling and thickened.

Add butter, orange zest and salt. Stir well. Cool. Makes about 1 2/3 cups (400 mL) sauce. Spoon over individual servings of cheesecake. Cuts into 16 wedges.

1 wedge with 1 1/2 tbsp. (25 mL) sauce: 398 Calories; 27.2 g Total Fat (8.0 g Mono, 1.1 g Poly, 16.5 g Sat); 93 mg Cholesterol; 32 g Carbohydrate; 1 g Fibre; 6 g Protein; 370 mg Sodium

Pictured on pages 58 and 65.

Make Ahead: The cheesecake may be stored in an airtight container in the freezer for up to 1 month. The sauce may be stored in an airtight container in the refrigerator for up to 2 days.

Special Touch

Presenting: Dessert!

❋ Show off these spectacular desserts to greatest advantage with a dazzling display of colour and decor.

❋ Because a dessert buffet features just one course with the food available over a period of several hours, it's not necessary to have a table layout that requires guests to move from one end to the other. Arrange your table—a round one works especially well—away from the walls, and let guests approach from any direction.

❋ Set plates and cutlery at two or three different places around the table so that guests can see all of the dessert at once—and proceed directly to their first choice!

❋ Place your dessert items against contrasting colours, patterns and textures to create the desired impression. A contemporary approach, for example, might include modern black and white styling, while a traditional setting might feature richer shades of dark green, gold and maroon. Blend in deep, rich blues and purples with shining silver, stars and angels for a lighter, seasonal mood.

❋ Create steps or tiers for your desserts by overturning ramekins or small bowls, and setting your platters on top.

❋ Delicate white doilies add a fresh, dressed-up look to any style of serving plate. Tip: Use double-sided tape to hold the doilies in place.

❋ Transform non-seasonal or well-worn platters with overlapping paper napkins in a pretty seasonal pattern topped with a large gold- or silver-foil doily.

Peppermint Cream Puffs

Petite puffs with mint green filling are a pretty holiday sweet, and they freeze beautifully for easy, as-needed replenishment of your dessert tray. Dust with icing sugar or drizzle with chocolate for an even more spectacular presentation.

Milk	1/2 cup	125 mL
Butter (or hard margarine)	2 tbsp.	30 mL
Salt, just a pinch		
All-purpose flour	2/3 cup	150 mL
Large eggs	2	2
Milk	1 cup	250 mL
Box of instant vanilla pudding powder (4 serving size)	1	1
Peppermint extract	1/8 tsp.	0.5 mL
Drops of liquid green food colouring	1 – 2	1 – 2
Whipping cream	1/2 cup	125 mL

Combine first 3 ingredients in small saucepan. Heat and stir on medium-high until butter is melted. Reduce heat to medium.

Add flour all at once. Stir vigorously for about 1 minute until mixture pulls away from side of saucepan to form soft dough. Remove from heat. Transfer to medium bowl.

Add eggs 1 at a time, beating after each addition until well combined and dough is thick and glossy. Spoon dough into piping bag fitted with large star tip. Pipe twenty-four 1 1/2 inch (3.8 cm) rosettes about 1 inch (2.5 cm) apart onto greased baking sheet. Bake in 425°F (220°C) oven for about 10 minutes until puffed. Reduce heat to 350°F (175°C). Bake for another 10 minutes until golden and dry. Transfer to wire rack to cool.

Beat second amount of milk and pudding powder on low in separate medium bowl for about 2 minutes until thickened. Add extract and food colouring, 1 drop at a time until a pretty green. Beat well.

Beat whipping cream in separate medium bowl until stiff peaks form. Fold into peppermint mixture. Trim 1/4 inch (6 mm) slice from top of each cream puff. Set tops aside. Fill separate piping bag fitted with large star tip with peppermint mixture. Pipe into cream puffs. Cover with tops. Makes 24 cream puffs.

1 cream puff: 66 Calories; 3.3 g Total Fat (1.0 g Mono, 0.2 g Poly, 1.9 g Sat); 27 mg Cholesterol; 8 g Carbohydrate; trace Fibre; 2 g Protein; 86 mg Sodium

Pictured on page 67.

Make Ahead: The cream puffs may be stored in an airtight container in the freezer for up to 1 month. Thaw them at room temperature for 1 hour before serving.

Entertaining Tip

Serving Up Sweets

❋ Arrange sweets, especially crumbly or gooey ones, in decorative baking cups to keep trays and fingers neat and clean. Use patterned or foil versions to dress things up.

❋ Varied shapes—square, triangular, round—make for a more interesting dessert tray. Keep the pieces about the same size.

❋ Petits fours and tarts are arranged more easily on trays while frozen or partially frozen.

❋ Many cakes cut best when partially frozen. This is especially good to keep in mind when cutting slender portions for a buffet. Use a knife with a long, thin blade that has been heated in hot water. Wipe it dry with a clean cloth then make your cut. Repeat until all the slices are cut.

Caramel Apple Bites

Eat these tempting, dainty cookies right away or allow to stand a few hours for a softer, biscuit-like texture.

Finely chopped dried apple	1 cup	250 mL
Ground cinnamon	1/2 tsp.	2 mL
Ground nutmeg, just a pinch		
Brandy (or apple juice)	2 tbsp.	30 mL
Caramels	20	20
Whipping cream	1 tbsp.	15 mL
Vanilla wafers	36	36

Put first 3 ingredients into medium bowl. Toss until apple is coated. Add brandy. Stir.

Heat and stir caramels and whipping cream in small heavy saucepan on medium-low for about 15 minutes until smooth. Pour over apple mixture. Stir well.

Arrange wafers, upside-down, on waxed paper-lined baking sheet. Spoon about 1 tsp. (5 mL) apple mixture onto each wafer. Makes 3 dozen (36) apple bites.

1 apple bite: 44 Calories; 1.1 g Total Fat (0.3 g Mono, 0.2 g Poly, 0.5 g Sat); 3 mg Cholesterol; 8 g Carbohydrate; trace Fibre; trace Protein; 26 mg Sodium

Pictured on page 67.

Make Ahead: The apple bites may be stored in an airtight container at room temperature for up to 1 week, or in the freezer for up to 1 month.

1. Almond Ginger Triangles, page 62
2. Lemon Cherry Tartlets, page 70
3. Peppermint Cream Puffs, this page
4. Caramel Apple Bites, above

Pear Tart With Maple Sauce

This delicious dessert is sure to impress! If you're serving the tart as a regular dessert—not on a dessert buffet with other choices—cut it into eight wedges.

Pastry for 9 inch (22 cm) pie shell, your own or a mix		
Butter (or hard margarine), softened	1/4 cup	60 mL
Granulated sugar	1/3 cup	75 mL
Large egg	1	1
Almond extract	1/2 tsp.	2 mL
Ground almonds	2/3 cup	150 mL
All-purpose flour	3 tbsp.	50 mL
Seedless raspberry jam (not jelly)	1/4 cup	60 mL
Can of pear halves, drained, blotted dry, cut into thin wedges	28 oz.	796 mL
Brown sugar, packed	3 tbsp.	50 mL
MAPLE SAUCE		
Maple (or maple-flavoured) syrup	1/2 cup	125 mL
Whipping cream	1/3 cup	75 mL
Butter	1/3 cup	75 mL

Roll out pastry on lightly floured surface to fit ungreased 9 inch (22 cm) tart pan with fluted sides and removable bottom. Carefully lift pastry and press into bottom and up side of pan. Trim edge. Place pan on ungreased baking sheet (see Note).

Cream butter and granulated sugar in medium bowl. Add egg and extract. Beat well.

Add almonds and flour. Stir until mixture resembles fine paste.

Spread jam evenly on bottom of pastry shell. Spread almond mixture on top of jam.

Arrange pear wedges, slightly overlapping, in fan pattern on top of almond mixture to cover.

Sprinkle with brown sugar. Bake on bottom rack in 375°F (190°C) oven for about 1 1/4 hours until pastry is golden and pear just starts to brown. Let stand in pan on wire rack to cool.

Maple Sauce: Combine all 3 ingredients in small saucepan on medium. Heat and stir until butter is melted and mixture is boiling. Boil gently for about 3 minutes, stirring occasionally, until thickened. Makes about 1 cup (250 mL) sauce. Brush 1/4 cup (60 mL) on top of tart. Spoon remaining sauce over individual servings. Cuts into 12 wedges.

1 wedge with 1 tbsp. (15 mL) sauce: 228 Calories; 13.2 g Total Fat (4.9 g Mono, 1.0 g Poly, 6.5 g Sat); 39 mg Cholesterol; 27 g Carbohydrate; 1 g Fibre; 2 g Protein; 135 mg Sodium

Pictured on page 59.

Note: Placing the tart pan on a baking sheet provides a safe way to remove the hot pan from the oven.

Variation: Omit the Maple Sauce. Heat 1/4 cup (60 mL) of seedless raspberry jam in a small microwave-safe bowl on medium (50%) until melted. Brush on top of the tart before cutting it into wedges.

Make Ahead: The baked tart may be covered and stored in the refrigerator for up to 24 hours. Bring to room temperature before serving. The sauce may be stored in an airtight container in the refrigerator for up to 24 hours. Reheat it in a medium saucepan on low heat before brushing over the tart.

Entertaining Tip

Dessert by Design

For a party that serves 12 guests, we recommend six desserts, with at least one chosen from each of the five categories that are used by professional pastry chefs. These categories focus on the main flavour or ingredient:

* Chocolate
* Citrus
* Cream
* Fruit
* Nuts

Other considerations that pastry chefs take into account include:

* Variety in colour, flavour, shape and texture
* Balancing rich desserts with light
* Combining warm with cold

By choosing one dessert from each category, plus another one that complements or contrasts nicely with your first choices—or one that just strikes your fancy—you can create dozens of different menus.

To help you plan like a pro, here are a few other tips:

* Check ahead of time to make sure you have all the equipment you require: tart pans, trifle bowl, springform pan, fondue pot and so on.

* Arrange serving utensils and platters in advance; you may need to borrow a pie lifter or two, or additional fondue forks.

* Place small plates or bowls under the sauce pitchers to catch drips and protect your tablecloth.

* Consider the size of your portions when choosing the size of plates you set out. Slices of cheesecake and Pear Tart will require a larger plate than just petits fours.

* Take advantage of recipes that can do double-duty: a second batch of the Pfeffernuss Cream from the Kris Kringle Kaffee recipe is a wonderful topping for fresh fruit or the Walnut Raisin Tart.

Blueberry Lemon Trifle

Quick and easy to prepare, this attractive layered trifle is a refreshing contrast to heavier desserts.

Frozen pound cake, thawed and cubed	10 1/2 oz.	298 g
Can of lemon pie filling	19 oz.	540 mL
Flake coconut, toasted (see Tip)	1 cup	250 mL
Frozen blueberries	2 cups	500 mL
Frozen whipped topping, thawed	3 cups	750 mL

Cover bottom of extra-large glass bowl with 1/2 of cake cubes.

Combine pie filling and 1/2 of coconut in small bowl. Spread 1/2 of mixture evenly over cake in bowl.

Sprinkle with blueberries. Spread 1/2 of whipped topping over blueberries. Layer remaining cake, lemon mixture and whipped topping, in order given, over blueberries. Sprinkle with remaining coconut. Chill, covered, for at least 4 hours to blend flavours. Makes about 14 cups (3.5 L).

1 cup (250 mL): 356 Calories; 20.1 g Total Fat (8.1 g Mono, 1.0 g Poly, 9.7 g Sat); 114 mg Cholesterol; 43 g Carbohydrate; 1 g Fibre; 4 g Protein; 523 mg Sodium

Pictured above and on page 59.

Tip: To toast the coconut, place it in an ungreased frying pan. Heat on medium for 2 to 4 minutes, stirring often, until it is golden.

Lemon Cherry Tartlets

These sweet tarts have a surprise cherry filling hidden beneath a silky lemon custard. Even with a whipped cream topping, they freeze beautifully. For added sparkle, dust with a sprinkle of golden sanding sugar just before serving.

Frozen mini tart shells	36	36
Cherry jam, fruit finely chopped	6 tbsp.	100 mL
Large eggs	3	3
Granulated sugar	1 cup	250 mL
Grated lemon zest	1 tsp.	5 mL
Lemon juice	1/4 cup	60 mL
Butter (or hard margarine), cut up	1/4 cup	60 mL
Whipping cream	1 cup	250 mL
Instant vanilla pudding powder	1 tbsp.	15 mL

Arrange tart shells on 2 baking sheets with sides. Bake on separate racks in 375°F (190°C) oven for about 15 minutes, switching position of baking sheets at halftime, until golden.

Spoon 1/2 tsp. (2 mL) jam into each shell. Set aside.

Beat eggs and sugar in medium bowl until thick and pale. Transfer to heavy medium saucepan.

Add next 3 ingredients. Heat and stir on medium for about 10 minutes until thickened and just starting to boil. Transfer to 4 cup (1 L) heatproof liquid measure. Pour into tart shells. Chill for about 1 hour until set.

Beat whipping cream and pudding powder in separate medium bowl for about 5 minutes until stiff peaks form. Spoon into piping bag fitted with large star tip. Pipe on custard in tarts. Chill until ready to serve. Makes 36 tartlets.

1 tartlet: 120 Calories; 7.1 g Total Fat (2.7 g Mono, 0.6 g Poly, 3.4 g Sat); 30 mg Cholesterol; 13 g Carbohydrate; trace Fibre; 1 g Protein; 90 mg Sodium

Pictured on pages 58 and 67.

Make Ahead: The tartlets may be stored (with the piped whipped cream on top) in a single layer in an airtight container in the freezer for up to 1 month. Thaw them at room temperature for about 1 hour before serving.

Kris Kringle Kaffee

A sophisticated adaptation of the traditional German cookie Pfeffernuss (pronounced FEHF-fuhr-noos)—in a mug! Guests will enjoy sipping the warm Kaffee (pronounced KAHF-fee) while sampling your dessert buffet.

PFEFFERNUSS CREAM

Whipping cream	1 cup	250 mL
Instant vanilla pudding powder	1 tbsp.	15 mL
Brown sugar, packed	1 tbsp.	15 mL
Grated lemon zest	1/2 tsp.	2 mL
Ground cinnamon	1/4 tsp.	1 mL
Ground allspice	1/8 tsp.	0.5 mL
Ground nutmeg, just a pinch		
Ground cloves, just a pinch		
Pepper, sprinkle		
Almond liqueur	1 1/2 cups	375 mL
Hot strong prepared coffee	12 cups	3 L
Sliced natural almonds, toasted (see Tip)	1/4 cup	60 mL

Pfeffernuss Cream: Beat first 9 ingredients on low in medium bowl until stiff peaks form. Makes about 1 2/3 cups (400 mL) cream.

Divide liqueur among 12 large mugs (see Note). Add coffee. Top with Pfeffernuss Cream. Sprinkle with almonds. Serves 12.

1 serving: 229 Calories; 8.2 g Total Fat (2.8 g Mono, 0.5 g Poly, 4.3 g Sat); 24 mg Cholesterol; 20 g Carbohydrate; trace Fibre; 1 g Protein; 38 mg Sodium

Pictured on page 71.

Tip: To toast the almonds, place them in an ungreased frying pan. Heat on medium for 3 to 5 minutes, stirring often, until they are browned.

Note: For self-service, pour about 1 oz. (2 tbsp., 30 mL) liqueur into large mug, fill with coffee and top with Pfeffernuss Cream and almonds.

Make Ahead: The Pfeffernuss Cream may be stored in an airtight container in the refrigerator for up to 2 days.

Kris Kringle Kaffee, above

Chocolate Martini

The ultimate chocolate beverage.
Smooth, sophisticated and stunning.

Vodka	1 3/4 cups	425 mL
Chocolate liqueur	1 3/4 cups	425 mL
Irish cream liqueur	1 cup	250 mL
Ice cubes	36	36
Chocolate sticks with orange filling (such as Ovation), for garnish	12	12

Put first 3 ingredients into large pitcher. Stir. Pour about 3/4 cup (175 mL) of mixture into cocktail shaker. Add 6 ice cubes. Replace lid. Hold firmly and shake vigorously until cold. Strain through sieve into 2 chilled martini glasses. Repeat 5 more times with remaining vodka mixture and ice cubes.

Garnish each with 1 chocolate "stir stick." Serves 12.

1 serving: 291 Calories; 10.0 g Total Fat (2.9 g Mono, 0.4 g Poly, 6.2 g Sat); 9 mg Cholesterol; 16 g Carbohydrate; 0 g Fibre; 2 g Protein; 56 mg Sodium

Pictured above.

Make Ahead: Combine the vodka and liqueurs in the pitcher and store it in the refrigerator for up to 4 hours. Shake with the ice cubes just before serving.

Entertaining Tip

Beverage Stations
To avoid congestion, create two separate designated areas away from the dessert buffet: one for coffee and tea, and one for liqueur and wine.

Coffee and Tea
A warming selection of good-quality tea or coffee is a natural partner with dessert. Avoid blends that overwhelm delicate dessert tastes but do choose full-flavoured varieties. Medium to dark roast coffees and black tea blends such as Earl Grey, or an herbal mint tea, are good choices. Remember to include decaffeinated versions of both beverages.

Coffee is best served right after brewing, so remove it from any heating element and serve from a thermos-style carafe. Tea can be steeped in the same pot in which it will be served—pre-warming the pot with a little boiling water and covering it with a tea cozy will help keep the tea hot. Set a carafe of hot water out for any guests who would like to adjust the strength of their beverages.

People take their cup of tea or coffee in different ways. If you're going all-out on a dessert buffet, give your guests a similar range of choices at the coffee and tea bar. Here are some extras to set out in decorative pitchers and bowls:

* Half-and-half and coffee cream
* 2% and skim milk
* Superfine white, demerara brown and raw sugar, loose and/or cubed
* Honey
* Fresh lemon wedges
* Artificial creamer and sweetener

Clearly label carafes or containers with colourful Christmas place cards and lay out enough cups and saucers or mugs to serve everyone. If space is limited, set out about half, then restock if and when needed. Also remember to set out a generous supply of spoons and a container in which to deposit used ones.

Wine and Liqueur
As only desserts are being served, sweeter wines and liqueurs are recommended. A small selection is all you need, and you don't necessarily have to give guests a choice of both. Here are some suggestions:

* Dessert wines, such as ice wine or late harvest vidal
* Fortified wines, such as port or shooting sherry
* Orange-flavoured liqueur, such as Grand Marnier or Cointreau
* Cream-based liqueur, such as Bailey's Irish Cream
* Brandy

While a decanter is often recommended for fortified wine, which is more likely to have sediment in the bottom of the bottle, consider serving some of the liqueurs in decanters as an added dazzling touch to the evening.

Have the appropriate styles of glassware on hand to serve all of your guests, but set out only a small selection at first, restocking as needed. This is an event where you may want to borrow or rent extra glasses, or limit the selection of wine or liqueur to what you can accommodate with your own personal supply.

Sit-Down Meals

Sit-Down Meal Guide

A sit-down meal is one of the easiest and most natural ways to entertain family and friends. After all, it's the way we eat most of the time. However, a well-planned sit-down meal can be a truly memorable occasion.

Sit-down meals are usually most comfortable with a smaller number of guests. This style of gathering encompasses a breadth of possibilities from super-casual family style to ultra-formal restaurant style—and everything in-between. Menus can easily accommodate your personal taste, budget and available time.

Perhaps of greatest importance, a well-planned sit-down meal enables the host to be part of the intimate gathering around the table.

Sit-Down Serving Style

A sit-down meal that gathers everyone around the table immediately creates a communal and intimate atmosphere. Family-style service, in which everyone helps themselves from communal serving dishes, is the most casual. Plated or restaurant-style service, in which each guest receives his or her own plate of food directly from the kitchen, is the most formal.

Beyond whether a casual or formal serving style best suits your party plans, other considerations might be:

✳ Is there sufficient room on the table, or a nearby sideboard, to hold the serving vessels?

✳ Do you have enough serving bowls, platters and utensils?

✳ Do you wish to show off your tablecloth, centrepiece or dinnerware with an uncluttered table?

✳ Do you want to control portion size by plating each course?

✳ Would a combination service, with courses presented in both styles, be an option?

Planning a Menu

No matter how casual or formal, large or small, the right recipe choices and a timeline are your best help for planning your menu. Plan your sit-down dinner based on courses, selecting some or all of the following: hors d'oeuvres or appetizers, salad, soup, main course, dessert and cheese plate. Also plan any accompanying beverages. Think about the following when deciding on a menu:

✳ Make sure that the courses, and the dishes within the courses, complement each other in colour, texture and flavour.

✳ Coordinate cooking times and methods for easy preparation and service.

✳ Add a simple garnish to each course to make the whole meal special.

✳ Make sure your guests will have room for dessert by taking into account the number of courses and the serving sizes.

Seating Arrangements

As your guests approach the table, there is often that uncomfortable moment of hesitation as they try to decide where to sit. Often they will look to the host for direction. For the comfort of your guests, it's worth thinking about seating arrangements ahead of time.

If you choose to let guests decide on their own, most will likely sit near people they are comfortable around. Guests who don't know others may feel left out, and the group as a whole will be denied an opportunity to mingle and converse throughout dinner.

With a little forethought and planning, you can smoothly seat guests and create a convivial gathering. Here are a few suggestions:

✳ Know who's talkative, who's shy, who's acquainted with everyone, who's a stranger to most, and strategically seat your guests around the table to encourage conversation.

✳ Direct guests to the seats you've pre-assigned in your mind. As soon as you guide the first guest, the others will wait for your cue.

✳ Set out place cards. Write the names on both sides of the cards to help guests who are meeting each other for the first time remember names. Place cards can also work nicely as a table decor element.

Keep in mind: It's a good idea to seat yourself—and any helper—closest to the kitchen.

Tips for Plated Service

Plating
✳ Create "layered" place settings—for example, soup bowls or salad plates on top of dinner plates on top of chargers—for a more elegant and formal presentation. This will also make serving and cleanup easier.

✳ Arrange your tableware in the kitchen in advance, with a note identifying which course goes on which plate.

✳ For each course, make a list of all the foods that go on that plate—including the garnish—and refer to it as you prepare each plate.

✳ Keep the rim of the plate clear of food and garnishes. Use a clean damp cloth to clean any smudges or spills on the rim before serving.

Serving
✳ For courses served hot, warm the plates just before use: Place them in the oven on the lowest heat for two minutes then turn off the heat.

✳ Serve food from the left and pick up empty plates and cutlery from the right.

✳ Serve women before men and, in both cases, from the eldest to the youngest.

✳ Ask someone to pour the wine while you're serving the different courses.

✳ As you're serving each course, tell your guests a little about the dishes, the ingredients and the wine you've chosen as an accompaniment.

✳ After the main course, clear everything, including the salt and pepper shakers, off the table. With the plated dessert, bring in coffee and tea, creamer, sugar bowl, cups and saucers.

Place Settings
For a formal, multi-course dinner, set out your china, crystal and cutlery according to the following diagram. Omit unneeded items for fewer courses or less formality. There's no need for cutlery anxiety: Think about the order in which courses will be served and set the spoons, forks and knives so guests start from the outside and move in.

1. Salad fork
2. Dinner fork
3. Dinner knife
4. Soup spoon
5. Dessert fork
6. Teaspoon
7. Butter knife
8. Water glass
9. Wine glass

Table Decor

During a sit-down meal, the table becomes a focal point of preparation in your home. A beautifully set table is a feast for the eyes and whets the appetite as surely as the wonderful aroma of food cooking. Consider some of the following ideas to set the mood and create eager anticipation about the meal to come:

Table covering As a rule of thumb, the more formal the dinner, the more coverage on the table. Placemats are great for a casual family meal, but you might want to use your good damask tablecloth for a special dinner. Creative options include using a table runner and placemats, or layering them with a tablecloth.

Dishes, glasses and cutlery Finest china or rugged stoneware, identical or mix-and-match—all look terrific. Have everything in place when the guests come to the table, or simplify the setting by bringing items out when needed, for example, the dessert plate and cutlery.

Charger plates For an easy touch of elegance, set a larger plate at each setting to hold and frame the plate for each course. Leave it in place for the whole meal, clearing it off with the dinner plate after the main course. With a charger, your table still looks set even while bowls and plates are being taken away and brought back throughout dinner.

Table centrepiece Family-style or plated service might affect the amount of table space available for your centrepiece, or whether you might opt for several smaller arrangements down the length of the table. Always keep in mind that you want to keep items low enough that people can talk across the table without ducking and weaving.

Candles As the only illumination, candles create a warm, intimate setting. Light them just before guests come to the table. If your room has a chandelier, use the dimmer to create ambience.

Menu cards Follow the lead of fine dining restaurants: Write tempting descriptions of your menu, course-by-course, and print out cards for your guests.

Place cards Functional place cards can be fun or formal depending on your party plan—and imagination.

Napkins A versatile accent that comes in many varieties and can be wrapped, rolled, folded and placed in numerous ways. There's sure to be a napkin that's right for your chosen style.

Step back and look at your pre-set table. It should be inviting and approachable, with breathing space for people and food to be part of the setting. If it already looks overcrowded, simplify. Final touches shouldn't overpower the table and overshadow the food.

Friendship Lunch

~

Holiday entertaining isn't just for evenings. Take advantage of winter daylight hours and host a luncheon for a small group. Think about inviting friends and acquaintances you see regularly throughout the year: the book or social club, golf gang, bridge partners, church or parents' group.

This is a busy time of year, so guests will appreciate a host who can plan a two-hour lunch that gives time to eat, visit and maybe even share in a special activity. (A cookie exchange, for example, is a wonderful, fun tradition that sends everyone home with a wide selection of treats and one less thing to do on their Christmas lists.) Service is quick with all the dessert items laid out ahead of time so that anyone who needs to leave early can take a sweet to go.

One special feature of this delightful menu is the recipe for Friendship Tea Mix. It makes enough mix to serve a pot of tea at lunch and to give as take-home gifts. In our Special Project, we show you how to make Poinsettia Friendship Favours, a decorative way to "wrap" the tea mix and decorate your table at the same time!

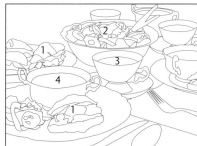

1. Shrimp Brie Croissants, page 80
2. Fresh Garden Salad, page 80
3. Friendship Tea, page 84
4. Creamy Onion Soup, page 79

Friendship Lunch

Quick Lunch for 6

This luncheon menu includes a selection of soup, salad and sandwich recipes that can be mixed and matched, plus three desserts. We recommend three main course luncheon items per person:

❋ *soup, one salad and one sandwich, or*
❋ *soup and two sandwiches, or*
❋ *one salad and two sandwiches.*

The dessert recipes yield more than you will need for this luncheon but are handy to freeze and take out for any other holiday functions. You can also use any extras as part of a cookie exchange.

The Friendship Tea Mix recipe makes enough to serve everyone at your luncheon plus create five take-home gifts.

Menu Choices

Soup
Creamy Onion Soup, page 79

Salads
Mandarin Poppy Seed Salad, page 79
Fresh Garden Salad, page 80

Sandwiches
Shrimp Brie Croissants, page 80
Artichoke Croissants, page 81
Chutney Egg Croissants, page 81
Smoked Salmon Avocado Bagels, page 82

Sweets
Shortbread Macaroons, page 82
Chocolate Fruit Squares, page 83
Mincemeat Bites, page 84

Beverage/Gift
Friendship Tea, mix on page 84

Timeline

All of the menu items are included in this timeline so you can easily see what needs to be done and when, no matter which combination of recipes you choose to make.

Up to One Month in Advance
Make Friendship Tea Mix
Bake and freeze sweets

Up to Two Days in Advance
Make soup
Make salad dressing

Day Before
Make croissant filling(s)

Day Of
Up to 4 hours in advance:
Wash greens, cut vegetables or fruit for salad
Arrange frozen sweets on tray

Up to 1 hour before serving:
Assemble sandwiches

Up to 30 minutes before serving:
Heat soup

Just before serving:
Make Friendship Tea in pitcher (heatproof if serving hot)
Toss salad

Creamy Onion Soup

Caramelized onion and cream are a delicious pairing in this rich, luscious soup. As an even more decadent treat, you may choose to serve this with a sprinkle of blue cheese. Worthy of being listed on any bistro menu.

Cooking oil	2 tbsp.	30 mL
Butter (or hard margarine)	2 tbsp.	30 mL
Chopped onion	4 cups	1 L
Chopped leek (white part only)	2 cups	500 mL
Garlic cloves, minced (or 1/2 tsp., 2 mL, powder)	2	2
Dried thyme	1/2 tsp.	2 mL
Medium sherry	3/4 cup	175 mL
Prepared chicken broth	1 cup	250 mL
Prepared chicken broth	2 cups	500 mL
Salt	1/4 tsp.	1 mL
Pepper	1/4 tsp.	1 mL
Half-and-half cream	1 cup	250 mL
Blue cheese, crumbled (optional)	2 1/2 oz.	70 g

Heat cooking oil and butter in large frying pan on medium. Add next 4 ingredients. Cook for about 20 minutes, stirring often, until onion is caramelized.

Add sherry. Cook for 2 to 3 minutes, stirring occasionally, until liquid is evaporated.

Add first amount of broth. Stir. Process in 2 batches in blender or food processor until smooth. Transfer to large saucepan.

Add next 3 ingredients. Stir. Bring to a boil on medium. Remove from heat.

Add cream. Stir well. Makes about 6 cups (1.5 L).

Sprinkle individual servings with cheese. Serves 6.

1 serving: 236 Calories; 13.8 g Total Fat (5.4 g Mono, 2.0 g Poly, 5.7 g Sat); 24 mg Cholesterol; 18 g Carbohydrate; 3 g Fibre; 6 g Protein; 579 mg Sodium

Pictured on page 76.

Make Ahead: Prepare the soup without adding the half-and-half cream or cheese. Store it in an airtight container in the refrigerator for up to 2 days. Reheat it in a large saucepan on medium heat for about 15 minutes, stirring occasionally, until boiling. Stir in the cream. Sprinkle each serving with cheese.

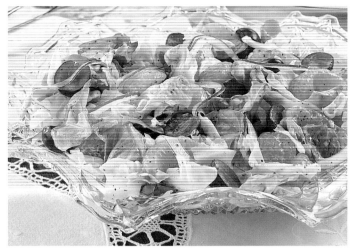

Mandarin Poppy Seed Salad, below

Mandarin Poppy Seed Salad

Delicate lettuce and luscious fruit topped with a creamy dressing—a refreshing combination!

Chopped or torn butter lettuce leaves (or mixed salad greens), lightly packed	8 cups	2 L
Can of mandarin orange segments, drained and syrup reserved	10 oz.	284 mL
Seedless red grapes, halved	1 cup	250 mL
Thinly sliced red onion	1/4 cup	60 mL
ORANGE POPPY SEED DRESSING		
Liquid honey	3 tbsp.	50 mL
Apple cider vinegar	2 tbsp.	30 mL
Cooking oil	2 tbsp.	30 mL
Reserved mandarin orange syrup	2 tbsp.	30 mL
Dijon mustard	1 tbsp.	15 mL
Poppy seeds	1 tsp.	5 mL
Pepper, sprinkle		

Put first 4 ingredients into large bowl. Toss gently.

Orange Poppy Seed Dressing: Process all 7 ingredients in blender or food processor for about 3 minutes until smooth. Makes about 1/2 cup (125 mL) dressing. Drizzle over salad. Toss gently. Serves 6.

1 serving: 120 Calories; 5.2 g Total Fat (2.8 g Mono, 1.7 g Poly, 0.4 g Sat); 0 mg Cholesterol; 19 g Carbohydrate; 1 g Fibre; 2 g Protein; 42 mg Sodium

Pictured above.

Make Ahead: The dressing may be stored in an airtight container in the refrigerator for up to 2 days.

Fresh Garden Salad

Taste the variety in every bite—from soft mushrooms to crunchy peppers and almonds. Combined with a light, fresh dressing, this salad is sure to charm your friends!

Head of romaine lettuce, chopped or torn	1	1
Cherry (or grape) tomatoes, larger ones cut in half	1 cup	250 mL
Sliced fresh white mushrooms	1 cup	250 mL
Thinly sliced red pepper	1/2 cup	125 mL
Whole natural almonds, toasted (see Tip) and coarsely chopped	1/2 cup	125 mL
Sliced green onion	1/4 cup	60 mL
Shaved Parmesan cheese	1/4 cup	60 mL

HONEY MUSTARD SOY DRESSING

Olive (or cooking) oil	2 tbsp.	30 mL
Red wine vinegar	1 tbsp.	15 mL
Liquid honey	1 tbsp.	15 mL
Dijon mustard	2 tsp.	10 mL
Soy sauce	2 tsp.	10 mL
Small garlic clove, minced (or 1/8 tsp., 0.5 mL, powder)	1	1
Pepper, just a pinch		

Put first 7 ingredients into large bowl. Toss.

Honey Mustard Soy Dressing: Combine all 7 ingredients in jar with tight-fitting lid. Shake well. Makes about 1/3 cup (75 mL) dressing. Drizzle over salad. Toss. Serves 6.

1 serving: 173 Calories; 12.8 g Total Fat (8.0 g Mono, 2.0 g Poly, 2.1 g Sat); 3 mg Cholesterol; 10 g Carbohydrate; 3 g Fibre; 6 g Protein; 235 mg Sodium

Pictured on page 76.

Tip: To toast the almonds, place them in an ungreased frying pan. Heat on medium for 3 to 5 minutes, stirring often, until they are browned.

Make Ahead: The dressing may be stored in a jar with a tight-fitting lid in the refrigerator for up to 2 days.

Shrimp Brie Croissants

Soft pieces of Brie add a touch of sophistication to this delicious shrimp filling. Perfect size for a light lunch.

Frozen cooked shrimp (peeled and deveined), thawed, blotted dry, chopped	3 1/4 oz.	91 g
Chopped Brie cheese	1 1/2 oz.	43 g
Mayonnaise	1 tbsp.	15 mL
Seafood cocktail sauce	1 tbsp.	15 mL
Mini croissants, split	6	6
Lettuce leaves (your choice), halved	3	3

Combine first 4 ingredients in small bowl.

Spread shrimp mixture on bottom half of each croissant.

Place lettuce on shrimp mixture. Cover with top halves of croissants. Makes 6 croissants.

1 croissant: 192 Calories; 10.9 g Total Fat (3.5 g Mono, 1.2 g Poly, 5.3 g Sat); 62 mg Cholesterol; 16 g Carbohydrate; 1 g Fibre; 7 g Protein; 367 mg Sodium

Pictured on page 76.

Make Ahead: The shrimp mixture may be stored in an airtight container in the refrigerator for up to 24 hours.

The sandwiches may be assembled up to 1 hour ahead of time and stored in an airtight container in the refrigerator until ready to serve.

Entertaining Tip

Keep a Time-Sensitive Meal Moving Along

* Stay aware of the time. Sit where you can easily see a clock.

* Build in flexibility. Take smaller servings so you can tend to hosting and still finish eating when your guests do.

* Set an example. Divide your time between eating and talking, and encourage your guests to do the same.

* Help your guests. If there's a slow eater make sure that person is served first. Encourage everyone to start eating immediately and not to wait for everyone else.

* Speak up. Gentle, polite verbal cues are acceptable and effective. If guests know that you're gathering for a fixed length of time, there's nothing wrong with a reminder that it's time to serve the next course. Guests can relax, not worry and take comfort in knowing that you're keeping an eye on the clock.

Artichoke Croissants

Often combined as a dip, cream cheese and artichokes make an equally tasty sandwich filling with the crunchy addition of fresh vegetables.

Jar of marinated artichoke hearts, drained and finely chopped	6 oz.	170 mL
Cream cheese, softened	1/4 cup	60 mL
Finely chopped celery	1 tbsp.	15 mL
Finely chopped red pepper	1 tbsp.	15 mL
Salt, sprinkle (optional)		
Pepper, sprinkle (optional)		
Mini croissants, split	6	6
Lettuce leaves (your choice), halved	3	3

Combine first 6 ingredients in small bowl.

Spread artichoke mixture on bottom half of each croissant.

Place lettuce on artichoke mixture. Cover with top halves of croissants. Makes 6 croissants.

1 croissant: 182 Calories; 10.7 g Total Fat (2.9 g Mono, 0.6 g Poly, 6.2 g Sat); 36 mg Cholesterol; 18 g Carbohydrate; 2 g Fibre; 4 g Protein; 340 mg Sodium

Pictured below.

Make Ahead: The artichoke mixture may be stored in an airtight container in the refrigerator for up to 24 hours. The sandwiches may be assembled up to 1 hour ahead of time and stored in an airtight container in the refrigerator until ready to serve.

Chutney Egg Croissants

Mango chutney adds flair to an all-time favourite filling—proving egg sandwiches need not be boring. This filling is especially good in buttery mini croissants.

Large hard-cooked eggs	2	2
Mayonnaise	2 tbsp.	30 mL
Mango chutney, larger pieces chopped	1 tbsp.	15 mL
Chopped fresh parsley (or 1/4 tsp., 1 mL, flakes)	1 tsp.	5 mL
Mini croissants, split	6	6
Lettuce leaves (your choice), halved	3	3

Mash eggs with fork in small bowl. Add next 3 ingredients. Mix well.

Spread egg mixture on bottom half of each croissant.

Place lettuce on egg mixture. Cover with top halves of croissants. Makes 6 croissants.

1 croissant: 198 Calories; 12.6 g Total Fat (4.7 g Mono, 1.9 g Poly, 4.8 g Sat); 100 mg Cholesterol; 16 g Carbohydrate; 1 g Fibre; 5 g Protein; 294 mg Sodium

Pictured below.

Make Ahead: The egg mixture may be stored in an airtight container in the refrigerator for up to 24 hours. The sandwiches may be assembled up to 1 hour ahead of time and stored in an airtight container in the refrigerator until ready to serve.

Artichoke Croissants, above   Smoked Salmon Avocado Bagels, page 82   Chutney Egg Croissants, above

Smoked Salmon Avocado Bagels

Lovely layers of flavour in this open-faced sandwich. Any leftover avocado can be added to the Fresh Garden Salad, page 80, or to the Mandarin Poppy Seed Salad, page 79.

Dill spreadable cream cheese	3 tbsp.	50 mL
Lemon juice	1 1/2 tsp.	7 mL
Drops of hot pepper sauce (optional)	2	2
Multi-grain (or plain) mini bagels, split	3	3
Thinly sliced smoked salmon	2 1/2 oz.	70 g
Thin ripe avocado slices	12	12
Paper-thin red onion slices, halved and separated	3	3

Combine cream cheese, lemon juice and hot pepper sauce in small bowl.

Spread cream cheese mixture on bagel halves.

Layer salmon on cream cheese mixture. Arrange 2 avocado slices on each. Top with onion. Makes 6 bagel halves.

1 bagel half: 124 Calories; 7.3 g Total Fat (3.9 g Mono, 0.8 g Poly, 1.8 g Sat);
7 mg Cholesterol; 11 g Carbohydrate; 1 g Fibre; 5 g Protein; 355 mg Sodium

Pictured on page 81.

Make Ahead: The bagels may be assembled up to 1 hour ahead of time and stored in an airtight container in the refrigerator until ready to serve.

Shortbread Macaroons

Sweet toasted coconut in a bite-sized cookie that's been rolled in even more coconut! A terrific and tempting variation on an old favourite.

Icing (confectioner's) sugar	1/4 cup	60 mL
Fine coconut, toasted (see Tip)	1/4 cup	60 mL
Butter (or hard margarine), softened	1/2 cup	125 mL
Granulated sugar	1/2 cup	125 mL
Large egg	1	1
Vanilla extract	1/4 tsp.	1 mL
All-purpose flour	1 1/4 cups	300 mL
Fine coconut, toasted (see Tip)	2 tbsp.	30 mL
Baking powder	1/4 tsp.	1 mL
Salt	1/4 tsp.	1 mL

Combine icing sugar and first amount of coconut in small shallow dish. Set aside.

Cream butter and granulated sugar in large bowl. Add egg and extract. Beat until smooth.

Combine remaining 4 ingredients in small bowl. Add to butter mixture. Stir until combined. Roll into 1 inch (2.5 cm) balls. Arrange about 1 inch (2.5 cm) apart on greased cookie sheets. Chill for 10 minutes. Bake in 350°F (175°C) oven for 10 to 12 minutes until edges are golden. Let stand on cookie sheets for 2 minutes to cool slightly. While still warm, roll each cookie in coconut mixture until coated. Transfer to wire racks to cool. Makes about 3 dozen (36) cookies.

1 cookie: 64 Calories; 3.5 g Total Fat (0.9 g Mono, 0.2 g Poly, 2.3 g Sat);
13 mg Cholesterol; 8 g Carbohydrate; trace Fibre; 1 g Protein; 49 mg Sodium

Pictured on page 83.

Tip: To toast the coconut, place it in an ungreased frying pan. Heat on medium for 1 to 2 minutes, stirring often, until it is golden.

Make Ahead: The cookies may be stored in an airtight container in the freezer for up to 1 month.

Special Touch

Poinsettia Table Posies

A simple way to dress up your table. After covering the table, gather up the tablecloth at each corner of the table and secure it with an elastic band. Tie a medium width ribbon slightly above the elastic band, letting the tails of the ribbon trail down. Make or buy a bow slightly bigger than the poinsettia, secure it to the ribbon, then tuck the poinsettia inside the bow. Instant pretty.

Chocolate Fruit Squares

A rich, no-bake treat with a pretty marbled top. Use a foil-lined pan for easy removal and cutting. Cut into small squares before freezing for ready-to-use convenience (or to have on hand when guests stop by during the holidays).

Graham cracker crumbs	1 1/2 cups	375 mL
Chopped mixed glazed fruit	1 cup	250 mL
Orange juice	1/2 cup	125 mL
Semi-sweet chocolate baking squares (1 oz., 28 g, each), chopped	12	12
Butter (or hard margarine)	1/4 cup	60 mL
Semi-sweet chocolate baking squares (1 oz., 28 g, each), chopped	3	3
Butter (or hard margarine)	1 1/2 tsp.	7 mL
White candy melting wafers (about 10 large wafers)	2 1/2 tbsp.	37 mL
Red candy melting wafers (about 10 large wafers)	2 1/2 tbsp.	37 mL

Combine graham crumbs, fruit and orange juice in large bowl. Let stand for about 20 minutes until juice is absorbed.

Heat first amounts of chocolate and butter in heavy medium saucepan on lowest heat, stirring often until almost melted. Do not overheat. Remove from heat. Stir until smooth. Add to fruit mixture. Mix well. Spread evenly in foil-lined 9 × 9 inch (22 × 22 cm) pan. Set aside.

Heat second amounts of chocolate and butter in same heavy medium saucepan on lowest heat, stirring often until almost melted. Do not overheat. Remove from heat. Stir until smooth. Set aside.

Microwave white candy wafers in small uncovered microwave-safe bowl on medium-high (70%), stirring every 15 seconds, until melted. Stir until smooth. Microwave red candy wafers in separate small uncovered microwave-safe bowl on medium-high (70%), stirring every 15 seconds, until melted. Stir until smooth. Spread chocolate mixture evenly on fruit mixture in pan. Drizzle white and red candy over chocolate mixture. Swirl wooden pick through top to create marbled effect. Chill for about 1 hour until firm. Cuts into 64 squares.

1 square: 64 Calories; 3.3 g Total Fat (1.1 g Mono, 0.1 g Poly, 1.9 g Sat); 3 mg Cholesterol; 9 g Carbohydrate; 1 g Fibre; 1 g Protein; 25 mg Sodium

Pictured on this page.

Make Ahead: The squares may be stored in an airtight container in the freezer for up to 1 month.

Top: Chocolate Fruit Squares, this page
Centre: Shortbread Macaroons, page 82
Bottom: Mincemeat Bites, page 84

Friendship Tea Mix

A subtle mix of orange and cloves in a refreshing beverage that tastes great hot or cold. This recipe will make enough for lunch and then some! Store any extra in an airtight container to keep on hand for the holidays—or better yet, send some home with your guests as party favours (see Special Project, page 85).

Powdered iced tea mix, with lemon	3 cups	750 mL
Granulated sugar	3 cups	750 mL
Envelopes of sweetened powdered orange drink crystals (3 1/2 oz., 98 g, each)	3	3
Ground cinnamon	1 tbsp.	15 mL
Ground cloves	1 tbsp.	15 mL

Combine all 5 ingredients in large bowl. Makes about 6 cups (1.5 L).

1 1/2 tbsp. (25 mL) mix: 87 Calories; 0.1 g Total Fat (0 g Mono, trace Poly, trace Sat); 0 mg Cholesterol; 22 g Carbohydrate; trace Fibre; 1 g Protein; 59 mg Sodium

Friendship Tea for 1: Combine 1 1/2 tbsp. (25 mL) Friendship Tea Mix and 1 cup (250 mL) boiling or ice-cold water until dissolved. Makes 1 cup (250 mL).

Friendship Tea for Friendship Lunch: Combine 1 cup (250 mL) Friendship Tea Mix and 10 1/2 cups (2.6 L) boiling or ice-cold water until dissolved. Makes 10 1/2 cups (2.6 L).

Pictured on page 76.

Make Ahead: The Friendship Tea Mix may be made up to 1 month ahead of time and stored in an airtight container.

Mincemeat Bites

Coated with pecans, these delicate thimble cookies are filled with just a dab of mincemeat and accented with a hint of cinnamon and nutmeg. Absolutely perfect for any Christmas gathering.

Butter (or hard margarine), softened	1/2 cup	125 mL
Granulated sugar	1/2 cup	125 mL
Egg yolk (large)	1	1
Rum extract	1 tsp.	5 mL
All-purpose flour	1 1/4 cups	300 mL
Baking powder	1/4 tsp.	1 mL
Salt	1/4 tsp.	1 mL
Ground pecans	2/3 cup	150 mL
Granulated sugar	3 tbsp.	50 mL
Egg white (large)	1	1
Ground cinnamon	1/8 tsp.	0.5 mL
Ground nutmeg, sprinkle		
Mincemeat, approximately	3 tbsp.	50 mL

Cream butter and first amount of sugar in medium bowl. Add egg yolk and extract. Beat until smooth.

Measure next 3 ingredients into small bowl. Stir. Add to butter mixture. Stir until combined. Roll into 1 inch (2.5 cm) balls.

Combine pecans and second amount of sugar in small shallow dish.

Beat next 3 ingredients with fork in separate small bowl. Dip 1 ball into egg white mixture. Roll in pecan mixture until coated. Repeat with remaining balls, egg white mixture and pecan mixture. Arrange about 2 inches (5 cm) apart on well-greased cookie sheets. Dent each ball with thumb.

Spoon about 1/4 tsp. (1 mL) mincemeat into each dent. Bake in 325°F (160°C) oven for 18 to 20 minutes until edges are golden. Let stand on cookie sheets for 5 minutes before removing to wire racks to cool. Makes about 3 dozen (36) cookies.

1 cookie: 76 Calories; 4.5 g Total Fat (1.8 g Mono, 0.5 g Poly, 1.9 g Sat); 13 mg Cholesterol; 9 g Carbohydrate; trace Fibre; 1 g Protein; 51 mg Sodium

Pictured on page 83.

Make Ahead: The cookies may be stored in an airtight container in the freezer for up to 1 month.

Poinsettia Friendship Favours

You can make these favours, filled with Friendship Tea Mix, in 30 minutes or less. Cluster them together for a showy table centrepiece, then give one to each guest as a parting gift. Be sure to include a card with the directions for making the tea.

MATERIALS

5 resealable sandwich bags
5 terra cotta pots (3 inch, 7.5 cm, diameter)
5 cups (1.25 L) Friendship Tea Mix, page 84
5 elastic bands
5 silk poinsettias (about 5 inch, 12.5 cm, diameter), with stems
10 sheets of green tissue paper (20 × 26 inches, 50 × 65 cm, each)
5 pieces of 1/8 inch (3 mm) ribbon (22 inch, 55 cm, length, each)

Note: Even though the terra cotta pots will be wrapped and hidden, using the correct size will create the proper proportion for the poinsettia. Small silk poinsettias are often sold as bushes in craft stores, although they may also be available individually for purchase.

TOOLS AND SUPPLIES

dry measure, wire cutter, scissors

Open a sandwich bag in each terra cotta pot. Fill each bag with 1 cup (250 mL) of Friendship Tea Mix. Seal.

Wrap an elastic band tightly around the top of each bag. Trim the stem of each poinsettia to a 1/2 inch (12 mm) length. Tuck a poinsettia stem into each elastic band so that the base of the flower sits securely on top of the bag.

Cut each sheet of tissue paper into a 14 inch (35 cm) square. Lay 2 sheets on top of each other. Give the top one a quarter-turn so the sheets are staggered. Place a terra cotta pot on the centre of the squares. Bring up the sides of the paper around the pot to cover.

Tie a piece of ribbon around the paper, just above the rim of the pot. Tie just tightly enough to hold the paper in place, being careful not to tear it. Tie a decorative bow. Arrange the tissue paper around the poinsettia to resemble leaves. Repeat to make 5 friendship favours.

The Poinsettia

The poinsettia, named for Joel R. Poinsett who brought the plant to the U.S. in the late 1820s, is native to Mexico and South America. Its Christmas connection comes from the story of a poor Mexican girl who was heartbroken because she had no gift to set before the altar of the Virgin and Child. She gathered weeds from along the road and laid them around the church, where they suddenly blossomed into a beautiful array of red flowers. In Spanish, the poinsettia is called "flor de nochebuene" or "flower of Christmas Eve."

The colourful part of the poinsettia is its leaves or bracts, with the tiny yellow cluster in the centre being the actual flower. If the plant has red bracts with green-tinged edges, the plant was probably shipped before fully maturing. When purchasing, avoid plants that are droopy, dry or crowded together. Plants with tightly closed flowers will last longer. When transporting, keep the poinsettia sheltered from the cold in a large paper bag or sleeve.

Once home, punch holes through any foil covering the pot so that water can drain completely. Poinsettias like sandy, drained, moist soil. Keep your plant in a warm, bright spot that isn't in direct sunlight, and try to add a bit of humidity. Poinsettias should not be fertilized during their blooming period. With a little attention these beautiful plants can be enjoyed for many months.

Simply Elegant Dinner Party

~

This gathering is ideal for early in the Christmas season. Intimate and understated, it's a quietly elegant beginning to the often bigger and busier entertaining to come.

Two menus offer a taste of the exotic and a nod to the ancient flavours of the Middle Eastern world where the Christmas story began. From the before-dinner Meze Platter or Star Consommé waiting at each place setting to the gift box of sweetmeats sent home with each guest, this is an evening of leisurely indulgence from start to finish.

Think about reflecting the simple beauty of the first Christmas in your decor with an array of stars, candlelight and white and gold trimmings. Create a dazzling welcome in your dining room with your best china, cutlery, crystal, serving pieces and table linens. The theme of refinement should continue in your living room where the evening will wrap up in pleasant conversation.

This more formal, plated sit-down dinner is simple to manage. Both menus offer make-ahead recipes, with main course dishes needing only to be finished in the oven before arranging on individual plates. Not only will you have stunning results, but your hosting duties will remain relaxed, allowing you to enjoy time with your guests.

1. Tomato Crowns, page 92
2. Confetti Beans, page 91
3. Sweet Saffron Pilaf, page 91
4. Spinach-Stuffed Chicken, page 90
5. Citrus Herb Butter, page 90

Simply Elegant Dinner Party

Contemporary Dinner Party for 6

These two menus deliver stylish cuisine with select exotic touches. Follow the make-ahead suggestions and purchase some ready-made items for the appetizer (meze) platter to ensure you're relaxed and ready when it comes to serving each course. Plated service allows you to portion the food per guest, present the main course beautifully and serve everyone at once. Our photos are a good reference on how to place the food items on the plate, taking into account variation in shape and height.

Menu 1 – Chicken
Star Consommé, page 89

Spinach-Stuffed Chicken, page 90
Citrus Herb Butter, page 90
Sweet Saffron Pilaf, page 91
Confetti Beans, page 91
Tomato Crowns, page 92

Raspberry Sundae, page 91
Baklava, page 91

❧

Menu 2 – Beef
Meze Platter, page 91

Herbed Chèvre Steaks, page 92
Light Tomato Sauce, page 94
Golden Potato Cups, page 94
Confetti Beans, page 91

Spiced Mango Pears, page 95
Raspberry Liqueur Sauce, page 95

Special Project – Confection Gift Box
To celebrate the gift of friendship, we've assembled a delightful assortment of sweetmeats for your guests to take home.
Almond-Stuffed Dates, page 96
Petite Pears, page 96
Jewelled Fruit Bites, page 97

Timeline

Menu 1 – Chicken

Up to Five Days in Advance
Make herb butter
Make raspberry sauce

Up to Two Days in Advance
Make croutons for soup

Day Before
Prepare Tomato Crowns

Day Of
Up to 8 hours in advance:
Prepare chicken mixture for soup
Prepare beans
Prepare pilaf

Up to 4 hours in advance:
Prepare and stuff chicken
Arrange *baklava* on platter

30 minutes before serving soup:
Heat soup

Just before serving soup:
Bake chicken and pilaf

Just before serving main course:
Bake tomatoes
Cook beans

Menu 2 – Beef

Up to Five Days in Advance
Make raspberry sauce

Up to Two Days in Advance
Make tomato sauce

Day Before
Assemble mango pears
Prepare potato cups

Day Of
Up to 8 hours in advance:
Prepare beans
Prepare steaks

Up to 4 hours in advance:
Cut vegetables for *Meze Platter*

Up to 1 hour before serving:
Arrange *meze* items on platter

Just before serving:
Bake potato cups   Warm pita bread
Bake steaks   Heat tomato sauce
Bake mango pears

Star Consommé

This soup is sure to be a stellar start to your elegant dinner. A clear broth filled with star-shaped pasta and vegetables—with Star Croutons on the side! For best presentation, serve in shallow bowls to show off the twinkling colours in the soup.

STAR CROUTONS

Melted butter (or hard margarine)	2 tbsp.	30 mL
Chopped fresh chives (or 3/4 tsp., 4 mL, dried)	1 tbsp.	15 mL
Garlic clove, minced (or 1/4 tsp., 1 mL, powder)	1	1
White bread slices, lightly toasted	6	6
Stellini (tiny star-shaped) pasta	1/4 cup	60 mL
Finely diced cooked chicken	1/3 cup	75 mL
Finely diced red pepper	1/3 cup	75 mL
Chopped fresh chives (or 1 1/2 tsp., 7 mL, dried)	2 tbsp.	30 mL
Prepared chicken broth	8 cups	2 L
Dry sherry	1/4 cup	60 mL

Star Croutons: Combine first 3 ingredients in small bowl.

Brush both sides of toast slices with butter mixture. Cut out 3 to 4 stars from each slice, using 2 inch (5 cm) star-shaped cookie cutter. Arrange in single layer on greased baking sheet. Broil on centre rack in oven for 1 to 2 minutes per side until golden. Set aside. Makes 18 to 24 croutons.

Cook pasta in boiling salted water in small uncovered saucepan for 8 to 10 minutes, stirring occasionally, until tender but firm. Drain. Transfer to medium bowl.

Add next 3 ingredients. Stir.

Bring broth to a boil in large saucepan on high. Reduce heat to medium. Add chicken mixture and sherry. Bring to a boil. Ladle into 6 soup bowls. Set bowls on dinner plates. Arrange 3 to 4 croutons around each bowl. Serves 6.

1 serving: 210 Calories; 7.6 g Total Fat (2.6 g Mono, 0.9 g Poly, 3.4 g Sat); 20 mg Cholesterol; 20 g Carbohydrate; 1 g Fibre; 13 g Protein; 1277 mg Sodium

Pictured below.

Make Ahead: The croutons may be stored in an airtight container at room temperature for up to 2 days.

The chicken mixture may be prepared up to 8 hours ahead of time and stored in an airtight container in the refrigerator.

Spinach-Stuffed Chicken

Moist chicken breasts stuffed with a delicately spiced spinach filling make this a dish worthy of any fine dining restaurant. This main course goes well with Citrus Herb Butter, this page, or Light Tomato Sauce, page 94, depending on your taste preference. For best presentation, slice each chicken breast on a sharp angle.

Cooking oil	1 tsp.	5 mL
Finely chopped onion	1/2 cup	125 mL
Garlic clove, minced (or 1/4 tsp., 1 mL, powder)	1	1
Ground cumin	1/2 tsp.	2 mL
Ground nutmeg, just a pinch		
Box of frozen chopped spinach, thawed and squeezed dry	10 oz.	300 g
Crumbled feta cheese	1/2 cup	125 mL
Boneless, skinless chicken breast halves (4 – 6 oz., 113 – 170 g, each)	6	6
Cooking oil	2 tsp.	10 mL

Heat first amount of cooking oil in large frying pan on medium. Add onion. Cook for 5 to 10 minutes, stirring often, until softened and just starting to brown.

Add next 3 ingredients. Heat and stir for about 1 minute until fragrant.

Add spinach. Cook for about 2 minutes, stirring occasionally, until liquid is evaporated. Remove from heat.

Add cheese. Stir until melted. Transfer to small bowl. Chill, covered, for about 1 hour until cold.

Cut deep pocket in thickest part of chicken breast halves, almost but not quite through to other side. Spoon filling into pockets.

Heat second amount of cooking oil in separate large frying pan on medium-high. Add chicken. Cook for 2 to 3 minutes per side until browned. Transfer to greased baking sheet with sides. Bake in 375°F (190°C) oven for about 20 minutes until chicken is no longer pink inside and meat thermometer inserted into centre of stuffing reads 165°F (74°C). Remove from oven. Cover with foil. Let stand for 5 minutes before serving. Serves 6.

1 serving: 229 Calories; 7.8 g Total Fat (2.6 g Mono, 1.4 g Poly, 2.9 g Sat); 94 mg Cholesterol; 4 g Carbohydrate; 2 g Fibre; 35 g Protein; 184 mg Sodium

Pictured on page 86.

Make Ahead: Stuff the chicken breast halves up to 4 hours ahead of time and store in an airtight container in the refrigerator.

Citrus Herb Butter

Serve this delicious mixture atop Spinach-Stuffed Chicken, this page, or put in a pretty dish on the table for guests to use for buttering warm dinner rolls.

Butter (or hard margarine), softened	1/2 cup	125 mL
Chopped fresh chives	1 tbsp.	15 mL
Chopped fresh parsley	1 tbsp.	15 mL
Grated orange zest	2 tsp.	10 mL
Grated lime zest	2 tsp.	10 mL
Lime juice	1 tsp.	5 mL

Cream butter in small bowl until smooth.

Add remaining 5 ingredients. Beat well. Chill, covered, for about 40 minutes until butter is firm but not hard. Roll into 6 inch (15 cm) long log. Wrap with plastic wrap. Chill until ready to serve. Cuts into twelve 1/2 inch (12 mm) slices.

1 slice: 73 Calories; 8.1 g Total Fat (2.3 g Mono, 0.3 g Poly, 5.1 g Sat); 22 mg Cholesterol; trace Carbohydrate; trace Fibre; trace Protein; 83 mg Sodium

Pictured on page 86.

Make Ahead: The butter may be wrapped with plastic wrap and foil and stored in the refrigerator for up to 5 days, or in the freezer for up to 3 months.

Entertaining Tip

Charger Plates

Adding a more formal, elegant touch to any sit-down table setting can be easy with charger plates. A charger plate is simply a large, decorative plate usually made of heavy china, metal or plastic. It acts as an attractive frame for the dinner plate that sits on top of it and adds a colourful touch to the entire table setting.

For this dinner, a table setting that includes charger plates can be laid out in this order: charger plate, followed by the dinner plate, a napkin or doily, then the soup bowl. The napkin creates a non-slip surface, allowing you to deliver and remove the dinner plate and soup bowl simultaneously and with greater ease. After the soup course is finished, this arrangement enables you to bring your dinner plates to the kitchen, add the main course and place them back on the charger plates in front of your guests.

Sweet Saffron Pilaf

Saffron adds so much to this aromatic rice dish making it worth the extra cost. The rice is first cooked like you would pasta, then baked in the oven to a golden finish.

Warm water	1 tbsp.	15 mL
Saffron threads (or turmeric)	1/4 tsp.	1 mL
Water	8 cups	2 L
Salt	2 tsp.	10 mL
White basmati (or long grain) rice	1 1/2 cups	375 mL
Butter (or hard margarine)	2 tbsp.	30 mL
Finely chopped onion	1/2 cup	125 mL
Chopped pistachios	1/2 cup	125 mL
Chopped dried apricot	1/4 cup	60 mL
Dried cranberries	1/4 cup	60 mL
Liquid honey	1/4 cup	60 mL
Grated orange zest	1 tbsp.	15 mL

Stir warm water into saffron in small bowl. Set aside.

Combine second amount of water and salt in large pot or Dutch oven. Bring to a boil. Add rice. Stir. Reduce heat to medium. Cook, uncovered, for about 15 minutes, stirring occasionally, until rice is tender. Drain. Rinse with cold water. Drain well. Set aside.

Melt butter in large frying pan on medium. Add onion. Cook for 5 to 10 minutes, stirring often, until softened.

Add saffron mixture and remaining 5 ingredients. Heat and stir for 1 minute. Remove from heat. Add rice. Stir well. Spread rice mixture evenly in greased 2 quart (2 L) shallow baking dish (see Note). Bake, uncovered, in 375°F (190°C) oven for about 25 minutes until rice is heated through and edges are golden. Serves 6.

1 serving: 360 Calories; 9.8 g Total Fat (4.9 g Mono, 1.1 g Poly, 3.2 g Sat); 11 mg Cholesterol; 64 g Carbohydrate; 3 g Fibre; 6 g Protein; 45 mg Sodium

Pictured on page 86.

Note: Greasing the baking dish with butter will result in a delicious, crusty browned rice edge.

Make Ahead: Assemble the pilaf in the baking dish up to 8 hours ahead of time, cover and chill until ready to bake. Bake as directed for an additional 10 minutes.

Meze Platter

Meze (pronounced meh-ZAY) is Turkish for "hors d'oeuvre" or "appetizer." Tempt your guests with an impressive and easy-to-prepare first course that introduces the Middle Eastern flavours of your dinner menu. Arrange a pretty array of purchased dips, such as baba ghanouj (roasted eggplant dip), hummus (chickpea dip) and tzatziki (yogurt dip), a variety of olives, a selection of dippers, such as romaine lettuce hearts, cherry tomatoes, English cucumber spears (or your favourite raw vegetables), and fresh pita bread.

Raspberry Sundae

For a delicious, quick dessert, pour Raspberry Liqueur Sauce, page 95, over vanilla frozen yogurt and sprinkle with chopped pistachios.

Baklava

Set out a selection of purchased baklava to enjoy with coffee. This phyllo and chopped nut pastry is available in Middle Eastern and Mediterranean specialty stores as well as some grocery stores.

Confetti Beans

Elegance is often just something simple presented with flair. Whole green beans, a popular vegetable choice, become upscale when accented with festive flecks of colour.

Fresh (or frozen) whole green beans	4 cups	1 L
Butter (or hard margarine)	2 tbsp.	30 mL
Finely diced red pepper	1/4 cup	60 mL
Finely diced yellow pepper	1/4 cup	60 mL
Finely chopped fresh chives	2 tbsp.	30 mL

Cook green beans in salted water in large saucepan for about 5 minutes until just tender-crisp. Drain.

Melt butter in large frying pan on medium. Add green beans and red and yellow pepper. Heat and stir for 2 to 3 minutes until pepper is softened. Remove to medium serving bowl.

Sprinkle with chives. Serves 6.

1 serving: 62 Calories; 4.0 g Total Fat (1.1 g Mono, 0.2 g Poly, 2.5 g Sat); 11 mg Cholesterol; 6 g Carbohydrate; 2 g Fibre; 2 g Protein; 45 mg Sodium

Pictured on pages 86 and 93.

Make Ahead: Trim the beans and dice the peppers up to 8 hours ahead of time and store them in separate airtight containers in the refrigerator.

Tomato Crowns

The zigzag cut gives these tomatoes a regal appearance, and is easier to do than you might think! Just follow our step-by-step directions. Crunchy crumbs seasoned with garlic add a crowning touch.

Medium Roma (plum) tomatoes	3	3
Fine dry bread crumbs	1/4 cup	60 mL
Olive (or cooking) oil	1 tbsp.	15 mL
Chopped fresh parsley (or 3/4 tsp., 4 mL, flakes)	1 tbsp.	15 mL
Small garlic clove, minced (or 1/8 tsp., 0.5 mL, powder)	1	1
Seasoned salt	1/8 tsp.	0.5 mL

Trim thin slice from both ends of each tomato. Using small sharp knife, carefully cut zigzag (W-shaped pattern) crosswise around circumference of each tomato (see photo), cutting through tomato skin to centre of flesh. Carefully split each tomato in half, for a total of 6 crowns. Arrange in greased 1 quart (1 L) shallow baking dish.

Combine remaining 5 ingredients in small bowl. Spoon about 1 tbsp. (15 mL) crumb mixture on top of zigzag on each crown. Bake, uncovered, in 375°F (190°C) oven for about 15 minutes until crumb mixture is golden. Makes 6 Tomato Crowns.

1 Tomato Crown: 53 Calories; 2.8 g Total Fat (1.8 g Mono, 0.4 g Poly, 0.4 g Sat); 0 mg Cholesterol; 7 g Carbohydrate; 1 g Fibre; 1 g Protein; 73 mg Sodium

Pictured on page 86.

Make Ahead: Assemble the Tomato Crowns up to 24 hours ahead of time and store in an airtight container in the refrigerator. Bake as directed.

Special Touch

Fresh Pear Centrepiece

This arrangement is simplicity itself. Start with a shallow glass bowl or plate. Position firm, unblemished green pears in an unstructured, eye-pleasing arrangement, then wind gold star garland around the fruit. Check your centrepiece from all angles. For a smaller table with less surface area, use these same elements but create a higher, three-tiered "cone" of pears.

Herbed Chèvre Steaks

Beef tenderloin and elegant presentation—accomplished with minimal fuss. This dish needs only a garnish of fresh thyme and chives to let guests know they're in for a treat. Serve with Light Tomato Sauce, page 94.

HERBED CHÈVRE TOPPING

Peppercorn goat (chèvre) cheese, cut up	5 oz.	140 g
Egg yolk (large)	1	1
Prepared horseradish	1 1/2 tsp.	7 mL
Chopped fresh chives	1 1/2 tsp.	7 mL
Chopped fresh thyme leaves	1 tsp.	5 mL
Cooking oil	1/2 tsp.	2 mL
Beef tenderloin steaks (each about 4 oz., 113 g, and at least 1 inch, 2.5 cm, thick)	6	6

Herbed Chèvre Topping: Combine first 5 ingredients in medium bowl. Makes about 3/4 cup (175 mL) topping.

Heat cooking oil in large frying pan on medium-high. Add steaks. Cook for 2 to 3 minutes per side until browned. Transfer to ungreased baking sheet with sides. Spread about 2 tbsp. (30 mL) topping on each steak. Bake in 375°F (190°C) oven for about 8 minutes for medium, or until desired doneness, and topping starts to brown. Serves 6.

1 serving: 227 Calories; 13.8 g Total Fat (4.2 g Mono, 0.6 g Poly, 7.2 g Sat); 98 mg Cholesterol; 1 g Carbohydrate; trace Fibre; 24 g Protein; 163 mg Sodium

Pictured on page 93.

Make Ahead: Brown the steaks and spread them with the topping up to 8 hours ahead of time and store them in an airtight container in the refrigerator. Cook the chilled steaks as directed, allowing a few extra minutes of baking time for medium doneness.

Clockwise from left:
Golden Potato Cups, page 94
Confetti Beans, page 91
Herbed Chèvre Steaks, above
Light Tomato Sauce, page 94

Golden Potato Cups

The presentation of these stuffed, baked potatoes creates a contemporary look for an old favourite! If you don't have a pastry bag, spoon the stuffing into the shells.

Large unpeeled baking potatoes	3	3
Cooking oil	1 tsp.	5 mL
Large unpeeled yam (or sweet potato), about 1 lb. (454 g), halved	1	1
Chopped fresh chives	1 tbsp.	15 mL
Salt	1/4 tsp.	1 mL
Pepper	1/8 tsp.	0.5 mL
Ground nutmeg, just a pinch		
Melted butter (or hard margarine)	2 tsp.	10 mL
Chopped fresh chives	1 tbsp.	15 mL

Brush potatoes with cooking oil. Poke several holes randomly with fork in potatoes and yam halves. Place on ungreased baking sheet. Bake in 350°F (175°C) oven for about 1 1/2 hours until tender. Let stand for about 10 minutes until cool enough to handle. Scoop out flesh from yam into large bowl. Discard peels. Cover yam to keep warm.

Cut potatoes in half crosswise (see photo). Trim thin slice from bottom of each half so it will stand upright. Scoop out flesh from each half into small bowl, leaving shells about 1/4 inch (6 mm) thick. Add potato flesh to yam.

Add next 4 ingredients. Mash until smooth. Spoon into pastry bag fitted with large star tip. Place potato shells on greased baking sheet. Pipe potato mixture into shells.

Brush with butter. Bake in 375°F (190°C) oven for about 20 minutes until filling is heated through.

Sprinkle with second amount of chives. Makes 6 potato cups.

1 potato cup: 182 Calories; 2.4 g Total Fat (0.8 g Mono, 0.4 g Poly, 0.9 g Sat); 4 mg Cholesterol; 37 g Carbohydrate; 4 g Fibre; 4 g Protein; 130 mg Sodium

Pictured on page 93.

Make Ahead: Assemble the potato cups up to 24 hours ahead of time and store in an airtight container in the refrigerator. Bake as directed for an additional 10 minutes.

Light Tomato Sauce

Vibrant and versatile, this sauce is lovely served with Spinach-Stuffed Chicken, page 90, or Herbed Chèvre Steaks, page 92.

Olive (or cooking) oil	1 tsp.	5 mL
Finely chopped onion	1/2 cup	125 mL
Finely chopped leek (white part only)	1/2 cup	125 mL
Garlic clove, minced (or 1/4 tsp., 1 mL, powder)	1	1
Salt, just a pinch		
Can of diced tomatoes (with juice)	14 oz.	398 mL
Dry (or alcohol-free) white wine	1/2 cup	125 mL
Bay leaf	1	1
Pepper	1/8 tsp.	0.5 mL

Heat olive oil in large saucepan on medium. Add next 4 ingredients. Cook for 5 to 10 minutes, stirring often, until onion is softened.

Add remaining 4 ingredients. Stir. Bring to a boil. Reduce heat to medium-low. Simmer, uncovered, for 10 to 15 minutes until slightly thickened and vegetables are softened. Discard bay leaf. Cool slightly. Process in blender or food processor until smooth. Makes about 2 cups (500 mL).

1/3 cup (75 mL): 46 Calories; 1.0 g Total Fat (0.6 g Mono, 0.2 g Poly, 0.1 g Sat); 0 mg Cholesterol; 6 g Carbohydrate; 1 g Fibre; 1 g Protein; 113 mg Sodium

Pictured on page 93.

Make Ahead: The sauce may be stored in an airtight container in the refrigerator for up to 2 days, or in the freezer for up to 1 month.

Spiced Mango Pears With Raspberry Liqueur Sauce, below

Spiced Mango Pears

Served alone or with Raspberry Liqueur Sauce, this page, this sophisticated finale to dinner can warm in the oven while you and your guests are enjoying the main course. Also delicious with vanilla ice cream.

Can of sliced mango in syrup, drained and syrup reserved, chopped	14 oz.	398 mL
Grated lime zest	1 tsp.	5 mL
Ground cinnamon	1/4 tsp.	1 mL
Ground cardamom	1/8 tsp.	0.5 mL
Reserved mango syrup		
Lime juice	1 tbsp.	15 mL
Can of pear halves in light syrup, drained	28 oz.	796 mL
Brown sugar, packed	2 tbsp.	30 mL
Chopped pistachios	1/4 cup	60 mL

Combine first 4 ingredients in medium bowl.

Combine reserved mango syrup and lime juice in ungreased 9 inch (22 cm) deep-dish pie plate. Arrange pear halves, cut-side up, on top of syrup mixture. Spoon mango mixture into centre of pear halves.

Sprinkle brown sugar and pistachios over mango mixture. Bake in 375°F (190°C) oven for about 15 minutes until heated through and pistachios are toasted. Serves 6.

1 serving: 123 Calories; 2.9 g Total Fat (1.9 g Mono, 0.5 g Poly, 0.4 g Sat); 0 mg Cholesterol; 25 g Carbohydrate; 4 g Fibre; 2 g Protein; 7 mg Sodium

Pictured above.

Make Ahead: Assemble the dessert in the pie plate up to 24 hours ahead of time, cover and chill. Bake as directed.

Raspberry Liqueur Sauce

This jewel-toned sauce is wonderful for drizzling on dessert plates or spooning over ice cream for a simple ending to a fabulous meal. Orange juice—ideally fresh-squeezed, and added at the very end—adds a fabulous burst of tangy flavour.

Container of frozen raspberries in syrup, thawed	15 oz.	425 g
Raspberry liqueur	2 tbsp.	30 mL
Cornstarch	1 tbsp.	15 mL
Orange juice	1/4 cup	60 mL

Press raspberries with syrup through sieve into medium saucepan. Discard seeds. Bring raspberry mixture to a boil on medium.

Stir liqueur into cornstarch in small cup until smooth. Slowly add to raspberry mixture, stirring constantly. Heat and stir for about 1 minute until boiling and thickened. Remove from heat.

Add orange juice. Stir. Cool. Makes about 1 1/2 cups (375 mL).

1/4 cup (60 mL): 94 Calories; 0.2 g Total Fat (trace Mono, 0.1 g Poly, 0 g Sat); 0 mg Cholesterol; 21 g Carbohydrate; 3 g Fibre; 1 g Protein; 1 mg Sodium

Pictured above.

Make Ahead: The sauce may be stored in an airtight container in the refrigerator for up to 5 days.

Special Project

Confection Gift Box

Each individually labelled, beautifully decorated box holds a selection of sweet confections. Arrange the boxes as part of your table place setting, or offer them to guests at the end of the evening as they leave.

Start with small purchased cardboard boxes or tin containers—all the same or each different—then adorn creatively. Tied with ribbon, sealed with wax or sparkling with rhinestones, guests will know something special rests within.

Our suggestion is three lovely little single-portion sweetmeats per box, each carrying through the Middle Eastern theme of the dinner menu. Make them all or use one or two to complement other holiday treats you have on hand such as chocolates, truffles, specialty candy or your own shortbread.

Almond-Stuffed Dates

Simple, satisfying and a change from the usual holiday baking. The Medjool date featured in this recipe is considered to be the "King of Dates" due to its large size, soft flesh and extreme sweetness.

Medjool fresh whole dates	6	6
Almond paste, cut into 6 equal pieces, room temperature	1 1/2 oz.	43 g
Whole natural almonds, toasted (see Tip)	6	6

Cut 1 inch (2.5 cm) slit lengthwise in each date. Discard pits.

Roll each piece of almond paste into 3/4 inch (2 cm) long log. Insert 1 log lengthwise into each date. Press 1 almond, flat-side down, into centre of almond paste in each. Dates will remain open. Makes 6 stuffed dates.

1 stuffed date: 61 Calories; 2.5 g Total Fat (1.6 g Mono, 0.5 g Poly, 0.2 g Sat); 0 mg Cholesterol; 9 g Carbohydrate; 2 g Fibre; 1 g Protein; 1 mg Sodium

Pictured on page 97.

Tip: To toast the almonds, place them in an ungreased frying pan. Heat on medium for 3 to 5 minutes, stirring often, until they are browned.

Make Ahead: The stuffed dates may be stored in an airtight container in the refrigerator for up to 1 month.

Petite Pears

Hand-sculpted little pears with a sweet almond flavour are a beautiful colour and decorative shape. Truly an elegant and decadent treat.

Drops of yellow liquid food colouring	2	2
Cocoa, sifted if lumpy	1/4 tsp.	1 mL
Almond paste, room temperature	3 oz.	85 g
Cocoa, sifted if lumpy, just a pinch		
Pieces of shoestring licorice, any colour (1/4 inch, 6 mm, each)	6	6

Knead food colouring and first amount of cocoa into almond paste in small bowl until evenly distributed (see Note). Roll mixture into 6 inch (15 cm) long log. Cut into 6 equal pieces. Roll 1 piece into a ball. Pinch ball to form pear shape. Flatten bottom slightly so pear will stand upright. Repeat with remaining pieces, for a total of 6 pears.

Lightly brush tops of pears with finger dipped in second amount of cocoa. Insert 1 licorice piece in top of each for stem. Makes 6 pears.

1 pear: 65 Calories; 3.9 g Total Fat (2.5 g Mono, 0.8 g Poly, 0.4 g Sat); 0 mg Cholesterol; 7 g Carbohydrate; 2 g Fibre; 2 g Protein; 2 mg Sodium

Pictured on page 97.

Note: To avoid staining your hands with the food colouring, wear disposable plastic gloves when kneading the almond paste.

Make Ahead: The pears may be stored in an airtight container at room temperature for up to 1 month.

Clockwise from top left: Petite Pears, page 96; Jewelled Fruit Bites, below; Almond-Stuffed Dates, page 96

Jewelled Fruit Bites

Sparkly sugar and colourful bits of glazed fruit give these sweet Marsala wine and chocolate treats the look of diamonds and jewels! The recipe makes extras, so include some on your dessert trays throughout the holiday season.

Finely crushed vanilla wafers (about 36 wafers)	1 cup	250 mL
Marsala wine	1/4 cup	60 mL
White chocolate baking squares (1 oz., 28 g, each), coarsely chopped	3	3
Finely chopped mixed glazed fruit	1 3/4 cups	425 mL
White sanding (decorating) sugar (see Note)	1/2 cup	125 mL

Combine wafer crumbs and wine in medium bowl. Let stand, covered, for 1 hour.

Heat chocolate in small heavy saucepan on lowest heat, stirring often until almost melted. Do not overheat. Remove from heat. Stir until smooth. Add to crumb mixture. Mix well. Chill, uncovered, for about 15 minutes until firm enough to roll into balls. Roll into balls, using about 1 tsp. (5 mL) for each.

Roll balls in glazed fruit in small bowl, then in sanding sugar in small shallow dish until coated. Makes about 40 balls.

1 ball: 67 Calories; 1.2 g Total Fat (0.4 g Mono, 0.2 g Poly, 0.5 g Sat); 3 mg Cholesterol; 14 g Carbohydrate; trace Fibre; trace Protein; 19 mg Sodium

Pictured above.

Note: Sanding sugar is a coarse decorating sugar that comes in white and various colours and is available at specialty kitchen stores.

Make Ahead: The fruit bites may be stored in an airtight container in the freezer for up to 1 month. Thaw them, uncovered, at room temperature for 30 minutes before serving.

Christmas Eve Feast

~

With the coming of dusk, the day before Christmas becomes Christmas Eve, and a sense of peace and calm settles on our world. The early closing of shops and wrapping of last-minute gifts seem to signal an end to the pre-holiday hustle and bustle. Christmas is almost here.

The traditions associated with Christmas Eve are as diverse as the people who celebrate them. For some, it's a time when children don their Christmas best and families head to candlelight church services. French-Canadian families might hold a traditional midnight "réveillon." Others simply appreciate the chance to bring together far-flung family and friends for a night of festivity. And of course, children young and old eagerly await the late-night arrival of old St. Nick.

Part of many Christmas Eve traditions is a special meal. We've taken our menu inspiration from one of the many different customs associated with this evening: the serving of a meatless meal. The vegetarian menu is a bountiful and satisfying banquet, while the elegant seafood menu is inspired by the Italian Feast of Seven Fishes.

Whether you choose one of these menus as the celebration of a custom, as the complement to a traditional Christmas Day dinner or as the chance to serve something new, your Christmas Eve gathering will be spectacular.

1. Sweet Sautéed Scallops, page 101
2. Meatless Antipasto Platter, page 101
3. Tuna Crostini, page 102

Christmas Eve Feast

Sumptuous Meatless Dinner for 8

These menus may seem complex but they are both very manageable, with plenty of make-ahead suggestions to simplify preparations. (Only your guests will think you worked hard.) Serve this plated dinner at a relaxed, even pace. If you like, take a couple of hours—as you might at a fine dining restaurant—to enjoy both a multi-course dinner and the company around the table.

Menu 1 – Seafood
Meatless Antipasto Platter, page 101
Tuna Crostini, page 102
Sweet Sautéed Scallops, page 101

Tomato Shrimp Soup, page 103
Basil Vinaigrette, page 102

Lobster-Stuffed Pasta Shells, page 104
Lemon Basil Sea Trout, page 106
Vegetable Medley, page 106

Cinnamon Panna Cotta, page 110
Cranberry Pear Compote, page 111

∼

Menu 2 – Vegetarian
Meatless Antipasto Platter, page 101

Tomato Fennel Soup, page 103

Basil Tossed Salad, page 108
Basil Vinaigrette, page 102

Pastry-Wrapped Lentil Loaf, page 108
Baked Fennel Flower, page 109
Vegetable Medley, page 106

Cinnamon Panna Cotta, page 110
Cranberry Pear Compote, page 111
Tartufi, page 112

Timeline

Menu 1 – Seafood

Up to One Month in Advance
Make and freeze soup

Up to Three Days in Advance
Make panna cotta
Make compote
Make vinaigrette

Day Before
Clean scallops
Make tuna mixture for crostini
Remove soup from freezer to refrigerator to thaw

Day Of
Up to 8 hours in advance:
Assemble stuffed pasta shells

Up to 4 hours in advance:
Toast baguette slices
Prepare sea trout
Prepare Vegetable Medley
Assemble *antipasto platter*

Note the cooking time required for each dish. Determine the pace of your dinner and set your cooking timeline accordingly.

Menu 2 – Vegetarian

Up to One Month in Advance
Make and freeze soup
Make and freeze Tartufi

Up to Three Days in Advance
Make panna cotta
Make compote
Make vinaigrette

Day Before
Prepare lentil loaf
Remove soup from freezer to refrigerator to thaw

Day Of
Up to 8 hours in advance:
Assemble fennel flower
Wash and cut salad greens

Up to 4 hours in advance:
Prepare Vegetable Medley
Assemble *antipasto platter*
Arrange frozen Tartufi on serving plate

Note the cooking time required for each dish. Determine the pace of your dinner and set your cooking timeline accordingly.

Meatless Antipasto Platter

Many antipasto platters feature a variety of cold cuts but there are plenty of meatless options as well. Choose a good deli; these days it might be right in your grocery store. Select items that offer a pleasing balance of flavours, colours and textures, such as:

* ❋ A variety of cheeses
* ❋ Marinated vegetables
* ❋ Canned hearts of palm
* ❋ Olives in a variety of colours, sizes and flavours
* ❋ Marinated artichoke hearts
* ❋ Cherry tomatoes
* ❋ Slices of raw fennel
* ❋ Cheese-stuffed hot peppers

Sweet Sautéed Scallops

Delicate scallops are heavenly with this light citrus glaze. Include cocktail picks with the platter of scallops so guests can help themselves. Or try them atop mixed salad greens tossed with Basil Vinaigrette, page 102.

Olive (or cooking) oil	2 tsp.	10 mL
Butter (or hard margarine)	2 tsp.	10 mL
Fresh (or frozen, thawed) large sea scallops (see Note)	1 lb.	454 g
Seasoned salt	1/4 tsp.	1 mL
Orange juice	3/4 cup	175 mL
Grated orange zest	1 tsp.	5 mL

Heat olive oil and butter in large non-stick frying pan on medium-high until butter is melted. Add scallops. Sprinkle with seasoned salt. Cook for about 5 minutes, turning scallops once, until browned on both sides. Transfer to large plate. Cover to keep warm.

Measure orange juice into same pan. Bring to a boil. Reduce heat to medium. Boil gently for about 5 minutes until reduced by 3/4. Return scallops to pan. Heat and stir for about 1 minute until glazed. Remove to large serving plate.

Sprinkle with orange zest. Serves 8.

1 serving: 80 Calories; 2.6 g Total Fat (1.2 g Mono, 0.3 g Poly, 0.8 g Sat); 21 mg Cholesterol; 4 g Carbohydrate; trace Fibre; 10 g Protein; 140 mg Sodium

Pictured on page 98.

Note: Some scallops may have a thin, tough, white muscle loosely attached to the side. Pull them off and discard. Rinse the scallops in cold water to remove any sand, then blot dry with paper towels.

Tuna Crostini

*A step up from tuna salad, this delicious mixture
adds an elegant touch to your appetizer tray.
Cut diagonal baguette slices for added appeal.*

Can of solid albacore tuna, drained	6 oz.	170 g
Finely diced tomato	2 tbsp.	30 mL
Chopped black olives	2 tbsp.	30 mL
Chopped green onion	1 tbsp.	15 mL
Olive oil	2 tsp.	10 mL
Lemon juice	2 tsp.	10 mL
Garlic clove, minced (or 1/4 tsp., 1 mL, powder)	1	1
Dried oregano	1/4 tsp.	1 mL
Pepper	1/8 tsp.	0.5 mL
Baguette bread slices (1/2 inch, 12 mm, thick)	24	24
Olive oil	2 tbsp.	30 mL

Combine first 9 ingredients in medium bowl. Chill, covered, for at least 4 hours to blend flavours.

Lightly brush both sides of baguette slices with second amount of olive oil. Place on baking sheet. Broil on centre rack in oven for 2 to 3 minutes, turning once, until golden. Just before serving, spoon tuna mixture onto baguette slices. Makes 24 crostini.

*1 crostini: 92 Calories; 2.5 g Total Fat (1.5 g Mono, 0.4 g Poly, 0.4 g Sat);
3 mg Cholesterol; 13 g Carbohydrate; 1 g Fibre; 4 g Protein; 182 mg Sodium*

Pictured on page 98.

Make Ahead: Prepare the tuna mixture and store it in an airtight container in the refrigerator for up to 24 hours. Broil the baguette slices up to 4 hours ahead of time and store them, uncovered, at room temperature until ready to serve.

Basil Vinaigrette

*So versatile. Toss with fresh greens for a light
salad or use as an attractive garnish for
Tomato Shrimp Soup, page 103.*

Fresh basil, lightly packed	1 cup	250 mL
Olive (or cooking) oil	1/2 cup	125 mL
White wine vinegar	3 tbsp.	50 mL
Liquid honey	1 tbsp.	15 mL
Salt, just a pinch		
Pepper, just a pinch		

Process all 6 ingredients in blender or food processor until smooth. Makes about 1 cup (250 mL).

*2 tbsp. (30 mL): 131 Calories; 13.7 g Total Fat (10.1 g Mono, 1.2 g Poly, 1.9 g Sat);
0 mg Cholesterol; 3 g Carbohydrate; 0 g Fibre; trace Protein; trace Sodium*

Pictured on page 103.

Make Ahead: The vinaigrette may be stored in an airtight container in the refrigerator for up to 3 days. Stir before using.

Entertaining Tip

Serving Suggestions

In pacing your dinner consider the length of time guests will be sitting at the dining table. You might want to offer first-course appetizers in the living room, then return there after the meal for coffee and conversation.

You can plan this dinner as a combination of both plated and family-style service. Offer a plated appetizer, ladle soup at the table, pass serving vessels for the main course and end with a plated dessert.

Family members can be enlisted to help serve the courses. If a younger child is helping with one of the plated courses, use easy-to-manage shallow bowls rather than flat plates.

Tomato Shrimp Soup, below, With Basil Vinaigrette, page 102

Tomato Shrimp Soup

Rich red soup with a hint of licorice-flavoured liqueur. Drizzle with Basil Vinaigrette, page 102, for an added burst of colour and a lively flavour accent. (For better control use a squeeze bottle.)

Olive (or cooking) oil	1 tsp.	5 mL
Frozen uncooked small shrimp (peeled and deveined), thawed	1 lb.	454 g
Olive (or cooking) oil	1 tsp.	5 mL
Finely chopped onion	1 cup	250 mL
Finely chopped fennel bulb (white part only)	1/2 cup	125 mL
Garlic clove, minced (or 1/4 tsp., 1 mL, powder)	1	1
Licorice-flavoured liqueur	2 tbsp.	30 mL
Cans of crushed tomatoes (28 oz., 796 mL, each)	2	2
Prepared chicken broth	3 3/4 cups	925 mL
Water	1 1/4 cups	300 mL

Heat first amount of olive oil in large pot or Dutch oven on medium-high. Add shrimp. Heat and stir for about 1 minute until shrimp turn pink. Transfer to large bowl. Set aside. Reduce heat to medium.

Heat second amount of olive oil in same pot. Add next 3 ingredients. Cook for about 5 minutes, stirring often, until onion is softened.

Add liqueur. Heat and stir for 1 minute.

Add tomatoes, broth and water. Stir. Bring to a boil on medium-high. Reduce heat to medium-low. Simmer, covered, for about 20 minutes, stirring occasionally, until fennel is tender. Add shrimp. Heat for about 2 minutes until shrimp is heated through. Serves 8.

1 serving: 140 Calories; 3.3 g Total Fat (1.4 g Mono, 0.8 g Poly, 0.6 g Sat); 86 mg Cholesterol; 12 g Carbohydrate; 2 g Fibre; 16 g Protein; 801 mg Sodium

Pictured above.

TOMATO FENNEL SOUP: Omit shrimp and first amount of olive oil.

Make Ahead: The soup may be stored in an airtight container in the refrigerator for up to 3 days, or in the freezer for up to 1 month.

Lobster-Stuffed Pasta Shells

Lobster is an extravagance, but if there is an occasion for such an indulgence, Christmas Eve is it. This dish is a bit time-consuming but it can all be done in advance. An impressive course for your holiday table and a sure hit with your guests.

Cans of frozen lobster meat (11 1/3 oz., 320 g, each), thawed, drained and liquid reserved, squeezed dry	2	2
Jumbo shell pasta	24	24
Water	1 cup	250 mL
Dry (or alcohol-free) white wine	1/2 cup	125 mL
Medium lemon, quartered	1/2	1/2
Bay leaf	1	1
Boneless, skinless sole fillets	1 lb.	454 g
Butter (or hard margarine)	3 tbsp.	50 mL
Finely chopped shallots (or green onion)	1/2 cup	125 mL
All-purpose flour	1/4 cup	60 mL
Reserved lobster liquid		
Whipping cream	1 cup	250 mL
Brandy (optional)	2 tbsp.	30 mL
Chopped fresh chives	1/4 cup	60 mL
Crushed buttery crackers (such as Ritz), about 22 crackers	3/4 cup	175 mL
Finely diced red pepper	1/4 cup	60 mL
Chopped fresh chives	3 tbsp.	50 mL

Remove any cartilage from lobster meat. Coarsely chop larger meat pieces. Set aside.

Cook pasta in boiling salted water in large uncovered pot or Dutch oven for about 10 minutes, stirring occasionally, until tender but firm. Drain. Rinse with cold water. Drain well. Set aside.

Combine next 4 ingredients in medium saucepan. Bring to a boil on medium.

Add fillets. Reduce heat to medium-low. Simmer, uncovered, for about 4 minutes until fish flakes easily when tested with fork. Remove fillets with slotted spoon to large bowl. Break into small pieces. Set aside. Pour liquid from pan through sieve into 4 cup (1 L) liquid measure. Discard solids. Set aside.

Melt butter in same saucepan on medium. Add shallots. Cook for about 5 minutes, stirring occasionally, until softened.

Add flour. Heat and stir for 1 minute. Gradually add next 3 ingredients and pan liquid, stirring constantly until smooth. Heat and stir until boiling and thickened. Reduce heat to medium-low. Simmer for 10 minutes, stirring often, to blend flavours. Remove from heat.

Add lobster meat and first amount of chives to fish. Add 1 cup (250 mL) sauce. Mix well. Pour remaining sauce into ungreased 9 × 13 inch (22 × 33 cm) baking dish. Spread evenly. Spoon lobster mixture into cooked pasta. Arrange on top of sauce. Bake, covered, in 350°F (175°C) oven for 30 minutes.

Sprinkle cracker crumbs over pasta. Bake, uncovered, for another 10 to 15 minutes until lobster mixture is heated through and crumbs are golden. Arrange pasta on 8 dinner plates. Spoon sauce from dish around shells.

Sprinkle individual servings with red pepper and second amount of chives. Serves 8.

1 serving: 466 Calories; 19.0 g Total Fat (5.7 g Mono, 1.9 g Poly, 9.9 g Sat); 130 mg Cholesterol; 38 g Carbohydrate; 2 g Fibre; 32 g Protein; 485 mg Sodium

Pictured on page 105.

Make Ahead: Stuff the pasta and arrange it on the sauce in the dish up to 8 hours ahead of time, cover and chill. Remove the pasta from the refrigerator 20 minutes before baking.

Vegetable Medley

*A colourful, no-fuss medley of potatoes and vegetables.
For ease and convenience in meal preparation and service,
everything is cut the same size for even baking.*

Olive (or cooking) oil	1/4 cup	60 mL
Chopped fresh rosemary leaves	1 tbsp.	15 mL
Dried oregano	2 tsp.	10 mL
Salt	1/2 tsp.	2 mL
Pepper	1/4 tsp.	1 mL
Baby potatoes, halved	1 lb.	454 g
Butternut squash, cut into 1 1/2 inch (3.8 cm) cubes	1 lb.	454 g
Large unpeeled zucchini, cut into 1 1/2 inch (3.8 cm) pieces	1	1
Large red pepper, cut into 1 1/2 inch (3.8 cm) pieces	1	1
Small red onion, cut into 1 1/2 inch (3.8 cm) pieces	1	1

Combine first 5 ingredients in large bowl.

Add remaining 5 ingredients. Toss until vegetables are coated. Spread in greased 9 × 13 inch (22 × 33 cm) baking dish. Bake, uncovered, in 350°F (175°C) oven for 1 to 1 1/4 hours, stirring occasionally, until potatoes are tender. Serves 8.

1 serving: 144 Calories; 7.4 g Total Fat (5.3 g Mono, 0.7 g Poly, 1.0 g Sat); 0 mg Cholesterol; 19 g Carbohydrate; 3 g Fibre; 2 g Protein; 156 mg Sodium

Pictured on pages 107 and 109.

Make Ahead: Cut and toss the vegetables with the olive oil mixture up to 4 hours ahead of time. Put the vegetables into the baking dish, cover and chill. Remove from the refrigerator 20 minutes before baking. Bake as directed.

Lemon Basil Sea Trout

*Steelhead trout has a beautiful pink colour
and delicate, moist texture. If it's not available,
rainbow trout or salmon is a good substitute.*

Liquid honey	1 tbsp.	15 mL
Lemon juice	1 tbsp.	15 mL
Salt	1/4 tsp.	1 mL
Pepper	1/8 tsp.	0.5 mL
Finely chopped red pepper	1/4 cup	60 mL
Chopped fresh basil	3 tbsp.	50 mL
Grated lemon zest	1 tbsp.	15 mL
Chopped capers (optional)	2 tbsp.	30 mL
Boneless, skinless steelhead trout fillets (about 4 oz., 113 g, each)	8	8

Combine first 4 ingredients in small bowl. Set aside.

Combine next 4 ingredients in separate small bowl. Set aside.

Arrange fillets on greased baking sheet with sides. Brush with honey mixture. Broil on centre rack in oven for 8 to 10 minutes until golden and fish flakes easily when tested with fork. Remove to large serving platter. Spoon red pepper mixture on fillets. Serves 8.

1 serving: 178 Calories; 7.5 g Total Fat (3.7 g Mono, 1.7 g Poly, 1.3 g Sat); 66 mg Cholesterol; 3 g Carbohydrate; trace Fibre; 24 g Protein; 133 mg Sodium

Pictured on page 107.

Make Ahead: Arrange the fillets on the baking sheet and brush with the honey mixture up to 4 hours ahead of time. Cover and chill until ready to broil. Broil as directed.

Top right: Vegetable Medley, this page
Bottom: Lemon Basil Sea Trout, above

Pastry-Wrapped Lentil Loaf

Wrapped in golden puff pastry, this vegetarian entrée is a dish even meat lovers will enjoy.

Olive (or cooking) oil	1 tbsp.	15 mL
Finely chopped onion	1 cup	250 mL
Finely chopped celery	1 cup	250 mL
Finely chopped carrot	1 cup	250 mL
Garlic cloves, minced (or 1/2 tsp., 2 mL, powder)	2	2
Can of lentils, rinsed and drained	19 oz.	540 mL
Cooked long grain brown rice (about 2/3 cup, 150 mL, uncooked)	2 cups	500 mL
Finely chopped walnuts	1 cup	250 mL
Finely chopped red pepper	1 cup	250 mL
Fine dry bread crumbs	1/2 cup	125 mL
Finely chopped fresh chives	1/2 cup	125 mL
Chopped fresh sage (or 1 1/2 tsp., 7 mL, dried)	2 tbsp.	30 mL
Salt	1 1/2 tsp.	7 mL
Pepper	1/4 tsp.	1 mL
Large eggs, fork-beaten	2	2
Package of puff pastry, thawed according to package directions	14 oz.	397 g
Large egg, fork-beaten	1	1

Heat olive oil in large frying pan on medium. Add next 4 ingredients. Cook for about 15 minutes, stirring occasionally, until vegetables are softened.

Add lentils. Heat and stir for 5 minutes. Transfer to large bowl.

Add next 8 ingredients. Stir.

Add first amount of egg. Mix well.

Roll out puff pastry on lightly floured surface to 12 × 15 inch (30 × 37.5 cm) rectangle. Trim 1 inch (2.5 cm) from each corner (see diagram). Reserve trimmings. Spoon lentil mixture lengthwise along centre of pastry rectangle. Press mixture into 4 × 10 inch (10 × 25 cm) mound, leaving about 2 1/2 inches (6.4 cm) pastry uncovered on both short sides. Fold 1 long side of pastry over lentil mixture. Brush opposite long pastry edge with some of second amount of egg. Fold opposite long side of pastry over lentil mixture. Pinch edges together to seal. Brush 1 short side of pastry with egg. Bring up to enclose lentil mixture, trimming any excess pastry if necessary. Pinch edges together to seal. Repeat with opposite short side. Carefully roll pastry loaf, seam-side down, onto sheet of parchment paper. Place parchment paper with roll on baking sheet with sides. Cut out shapes from reserved pastry trimmings using small Christmas-themed cookie cutter. Brush bottom side of cut-outs with egg and arrange on top of roll to decorate. Brush with egg. Cut 6 to 8 small vents in top of roll to allow steam to escape. Bake in 350°F (175°C) oven for about 45 minutes until pastry is golden and lentil mixture is heated through. Let stand for 15 minutes before serving. Cuts into 8 slices. Serves 8.

1 serving: 571 Calories; 33.0 g Total Fat (8.8 g Mono, 17.9 g Poly, 4.4 g Sat); 81 mg Cholesterol; 55 g Carbohydrate; 5 g Fibre; 16 g Protein; 770 mg Sodium

Pictured on page 109.

Make Ahead: Assemble the loaf up to 24 hours ahead of time and attach cut-outs. Do not brush exterior with egg. Cover and chill until ready to bake. Brush exterior with egg and bake as directed.

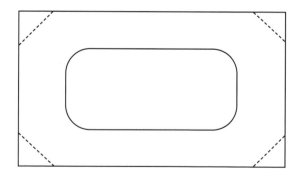

Baked Fennel Flower

Fennel, finocchio *in Italian, is a winter treat in that cuisine. Although we've suggested this dish for the vegetarian menu, the sweet licorice-like flavour of fennel is also a delightful pairing with the seafood menu.*

Large fennel bulbs (white part only), quartered	2	2
Olive (or cooking) oil	1 tsp.	5 mL
Roasted red peppers, drained, blotted dry, cut into 24 long, thin triangles	1 cup	250 mL
Grated Parmesan cheese	1/4 cup	60 mL
Olive (or cooking) oil	1 tsp.	5 mL
Chopped fresh parsley	1 tbsp.	15 mL

Cook fennel in boiling salted water in large saucepan until tender-crisp. Drain. Let stand until cool enough to handle. Cut each lengthwise into 3 wedges, for a total of 24 wedges.

Grease 9 inch (22 cm) round shallow baking dish or pie plate with first amount of olive oil. Arrange fennel and red pepper alternately in dish, slightly overlapping, with pointed ends toward centre of dish to make flower shape.

Sprinkle with Parmesan cheese. Drizzle with second amount of olive oil. Bake in 350°F (175°C) oven for 30 to 35 minutes until cheese is golden and fennel is tender.

Sprinkle with parsley. Serves 8.

1 serving: 67 Calories; 2.4 g Total Fat (1.1 g Mono, 0.1 g Poly, 0.8 g Sat); 3 mg Cholesterol; 10 g Carbohydrate; trace Fibre; 3 g Protein; 122 mg Sodium

Pictured below.

Make Ahead: Assemble everything, except parsley, in the baking dish up to 8 hours ahead of time, cover and chill. Remove from the refrigerator 20 minutes before baking.

Pastry-Wrapped Lentil Loaf, page 108   Vegetable Medley, page 106   Baked Fennel Flower, above

Christmas Eve Feast

Meatless Traditions

Christmas Eve marks the final day of Advent, historically observed in the Eastern Orthodox, Roman Catholic and other churches as a period of fasting that included abstinence from meat, eggs and dairy products. Today, many cultures continue to celebrate this holy day with a meatless meal.

In parts of central and southern Italy, Christmas Eve marks the Feast of the Seven Fishes, though some regions celebrate with nine, 11 or even 13 fish selections.

In the Ukrainian tradition, 12 meatless courses are offered in dedication to the 12 apostles on *Svyata Vechera* (Holy Supper). A *kolach* (braided ring of Christmas bread) is placed in the centre of the table.

Poland celebrates with *Wigilia*, beginning with a shared bit of *oplatek* (a Christmas wafer), followed by a 12-course meatless meal that might include such traditional dishes as pickled herring, fried fish and pierogi. Lithuanian culture refers to Christmas Eve supper as *Kucios* and holds many customs that are similar to those of Poland.

In some areas of Greece, rice-stuffed cabbage leaves, representing Christ wrapped in the manger, are eaten. The rice is considered a sign of blessings of prosperity.

Cinnamon Panna Cotta

A refreshing, light-tasting dessert that's perfect after a holiday feast. Serve with Cranberry Pear Compote, page 111.

Cold water	3 tbsp.	50 mL
Unflavoured gelatin	4 tsp.	20 mL
Whipping cream	1 1/3 cups	325 mL
Granulated sugar	1/3 cup	75 mL
Strips of orange zest (about 1 × 3 inches, 2.5 × 7.5 cm, each), see Note	2	2
Ground cinnamon	1/2 tsp.	2 mL
Vanilla yogurt	2 2/3 cups	650 mL

Measure cold water into small bowl. Sprinkle gelatin over top. Let stand for 1 minute.

Heat next 4 ingredients in small saucepan on medium for about 6 minutes, stirring occasionally, until boiling and sugar is dissolved. Remove from heat. Add gelatin mixture. Stir until gelatin is dissolved. Let stand for 15 minutes to allow flavours to blend. Pour through fine sieve into medium bowl. Discard solids.

Add yogurt. Stir until smooth. Spoon into 8 greased 3/4 cup (175 mL) ramekins. Cover. Chill for at least 8 hours or overnight until set. Carefully run knife around inside edge of each ramekin to loosen. Invert onto dessert plates. Serve immediately. Serves 8.

1 serving: 247 Calories; 15.1 g Total Fat (4.4 g Mono, 0.5 g Poly, 9.5 g Sat); 53 mg Cholesterol; 24 g Carbohydrate; trace Fibre; 6 g Protein; 68 mg Sodium

Pictured on page 111.

Note: To make strips of zest, use a vegetable peeler to remove thin strips of orange peel with no white pith.

Make Ahead: The panna cotta may be stored in the ramekins in the refrigerator for up to 3 days.

Cinnamon Panna Cotta, page 110, With Cranberry Pear Compote, below

Cranberry Pear Compote

The balance of sweet and tart flavours makes this an excellent dessert accompaniment for Cinnamon Panna Cotta, page 110. But you may also want to try it with roasted pork or turkey. Delicious served warm or cold.

Butter (or hard margarine)	2 tsp.	10 mL
Chopped peeled fresh pear	1 cup	250 mL
Brown sugar, packed	1/4 cup	60 mL
Orange liqueur	2 tbsp.	30 mL
Can of whole cranberry sauce	14 oz.	398 mL
Orange juice (see Tip)	1/4 cup	60 mL
Grated orange zest	1 tsp.	5 mL

Melt butter in large saucepan on medium. Add pear and brown sugar. Cook for 8 to 10 minutes, stirring occasionally, until pear is softened.

Add liqueur. Heat and stir for 1 minute.

Add cranberry sauce and orange juice. Cook for 5 minutes, stirring occasionally.

Add orange zest. Stir. Serves 8.

1 serving: 146 Calories; 1.1 g Total Fat (0.3 g Mono, trace Poly, 0.6 g Sat); 3 mg Cholesterol; 33 g Carbohydrate; 1 g Fibre; trace Protein; 30 mg Sodium

Pictured above.

Tip: When a recipe calls for both orange juice and zest, grate the orange first, and then juice it.

Make Ahead: The compote may be stored in a plastic airtight container in the refrigerator for up to 3 days, or in the freezer for up to 1 month. To serve it warm, reheat in a small saucepan on medium heat, stirring occasionally, until it is heated through.

Tartufi

That's Italian for truffles. Chocolate as an ingredient is to be expected, but balsamic vinegar adds a unique dimension. Use good-quality balsamic vinegar and dark chocolate for best flavour.

Dark chocolate bar, chopped	3 1/2 oz.	100 g
Whipping cream	1/3 cup	75 mL
Balsamic vinegar	2 tsp.	10 mL
Chocolate sprinkles	6 tbsp.	100 mL

Heat chocolate and whipping cream in small heavy saucepan on lowest heat, stirring often until almost melted. Do not overheat. Remove from heat. Stir until smooth.

Add vinegar. Stir. Chill, uncovered, for about 1 hour, stirring occasionally, until just firm enough to roll into balls. Roll into balls, using about 2 tsp. (10 mL) for each.

Roll each ball in chocolate sprinkles in small dish until coated. Place on waxed paper-lined baking sheet. Chill. Makes 16 truffles.

1 truffle: 62 Calories; 4.5 g Total Fat (1.4 g Mono, 0.1 g Poly, 2.7 g Sat); 7 mg Cholesterol; 6 g Carbohydrate; trace Fibre; 1 g Protein; 5 mg Sodium

Pictured at left.

Variation: Instead of balsamic vinegar, use 1 tbsp. (15 mL) orange liqueur.

Make Ahead: The truffles may be stored in an airtight container in the refrigerator for up to 1 week, or in the freezer for up to 1 month.

Christmas Celebrations – Sit-Down Meals

Special Touch

Candle Light, Candle Bright

Candles contribute beauty, mood, warmth, light and subtle scents to your party setting. Here are a few bright ideas for using candles:

✳ An unlit fireplace makes a beautiful frame or alcove for a collection of candles. Keep candles at a distance from lit fireplaces to avoid melting.

✳ Use a framed mirror or place a piece of pretty paper under the glass portion of a picture frame and lay it on the table to serve as a decorative base; set candles on heatproof coasters and group them on the frame.

✳ Set candles at different heights to illuminate every part of the table, from people's faces to their dinner plates.

✳ Tie a beautiful ribbon around a simple pillar candle. Add some Christmas balls and beads for a festive sparkle.

✳ On a heatproof plate, tie together a grouping of pillar candles of different heights.

Candle Care

Avoid setting candles in drafty areas: They will burn unevenly and drip.

Add a few drops of water to the bottom of a votive holder just before lighting. The candles and wax will release more easily later.

Rub nylon stockings along the outside of a candle to renew its sheen and aroma.

Keep candles away from harsh lighting or direct sunlight to avoid warping and fading.

Store candles in a dark, cool place.

Christmas Day Dinner

~

Christmas Day. At last! The long-awaited day unfolds, from an early morning spent diving into all those wonderful presents, to a casual, comfortable afternoon of playing games, visiting and maybe even catching a quick nap. But, always, the crowning moment is the celebratory dinner.

As befits the time-honoured tradition of the holiday dinner, we've created a menu that harkens back to old-world elegance. We've also included ways for you to add a stylish traditional touch through decor and table layout. After all, this is the highlight of the holiday season.

As for our festive dinner menu, we know that, for some families, it wouldn't be Christmas without a beautifully roasted turkey, but we also know some hosts like to include new dishes. So, every course offers mix-and-match choices for you to customize the dinner as you please, taking into account your schedule and your family's preferences.

Our menus and planning guide make it easy for you to enjoy this festive occasion without stress and fuss. And as the evening draws to a close, family and friends will remember with fondness the warm memories created around a Christmas dinner table that sparkled with love, life, laughter and good food.

1. Cinnamon Honey Carrots, page 126
2. Sweet And Smoky Brussels Sprouts, page 125
3. Creamy Parsnip Mashed Potatoes, page 120
4. Cranberry Marmalade, page 126
5. Holiday Turkey Roulade, page 122

Christmas Day Dinner

Special Family Feast for 12

The starter, sides, accompaniments and dessert dishes can be mixed and matched to suit your family's tastes. We suggest two main course meats—one served hot, the other cold—to save time and create an interesting, sophisticated Christmas dinner experience for your guests. To keep last-minute work to a minimum, prepare the potatoes or rice on the stovetop ahead of time, then transfer them to heatproof dishes for warming and serving. If Christmas isn't Christmas without your family's favourite turkey or roast beef, substitute either for one of the two meats and make the rest of the menu as suggested. With our plan, there's room in the oven and on top of the stove for the big bird and gravy.

Menu Choices

Starter
Silky Butternut Squash Soup, page 117, *or*
Festive Spinach Salad, page 119

Main Courses
Savoury Pork Roast, page 120, *and*
Holiday Turkey Roulade, page 122

Sides (Starch)
Creamy Parsnip Mashed Potatoes, page 120, *or*
Wild Rice Pilaf, page 124

Sides (Vegetable)
Sweet And Smoky
Brussels Sprouts, page 125, *or*
Zucchini In Walnut Butter, page 122, *and*
Cinnamon Honey Carrots, page 126, *or*
Roasted Dilled Beets, page 124

Accompaniments
Peach Chutney, page 126, *and/or*
Cranberry Marmalade, page 126

Dessert
Christmas Cranapple Pies, page 128, *or*
Snappy Pumpkin Pies, page 127

All of the menu items are included in this timeline so you can easily see what needs to be done and when, no matter which combination of recipes you choose to make.

Up to One Month in Advance
Make and freeze soup
Make and freeze pumpkin pies

Up to One Week in Advance
Make chutney and/or marmalade

Day Before
Bake cranapple pies
Thaw soup or make vinaigrette
Roast turkey roulade
Marinate pork roast
Prepare beets

Day Of
Up to 8 hours in advance:
Prepare Brussels sprouts or zucchini
Take pumpkin pies out to thaw

Up to 4 hours in advance:
Prepare salad or heat soup

2 1/2 hours in advance:
Cook pork roast

2 hours in advance:
Prepare potatoes or rice

30 minutes before serving:
Remove salad dressing from refrigerator
Slice roulade
Make Mushroom Sauce
Place potatoes or rice in oven to heat
Cook vegetable sides

15 minutes before serving:
Carve roast

At serving time:
Toss salad or serve soup
Warm cranapple pies in turned-off oven during dinner

Silky Butternut Squash Soup

'Tis in season, so there's no better time to serve butternut squash. It's perfectly partnered with leek and potatoes in this rich, velvety-textured soup. Serve with your favourite rolls or bread.

Cooking oil	1 tbsp.	15 mL
Thinly sliced leek (white part only)	1 1/2 cups	375 mL
Ground ginger	1 tbsp.	15 mL
Garlic cloves, minced (or 3/4 tsp., 4 mL, powder)	3	3
Chopped peeled butternut squash	10 cups	2.5 L
Chopped peeled potato	4 1/2 cups	1.1 L
Prepared chicken broth	8 cups	2 L
Pepper	1/2 tsp.	2 mL

Heat cooking oil in large pot or Dutch oven on medium. Add next 3 ingredients. Stir. Cook for about 5 minutes, stirring often, until leek is softened.

Add remaining 4 ingredients. Stir. Bring to a boil. Reduce heat to medium-low. Simmer, covered, for about 20 minutes, stirring occasionally, until squash and potato are softened. Remove from heat. Let stand for about 10 minutes until slightly cooled. Process squash mixture with hand blender (or in blender or food processor in small batches) until smooth. Heat and stir on medium for about 5 minutes until heated through. Makes about 16 cups (4 L). Serves 12.

1 serving: 151 Calories; 2.4 g Total Fat (1.1 g Mono, 0.6 g Poly, 0.4 g Sat); 0 mg Cholesterol; 28 g Carbohydrate; 3 g Fibre; 6 g Protein; 558 mg Sodium

Pictured below.

Make Ahead: The soup may be stored in an airtight container in the freezer for up to 1 month. Thaw overnight in the refrigerator. To reheat slowly, cook in a 4 to 5 quart (4 to 5 L) slow cooker on Low for 4 hours or on High for 2 hours. Or to reheat the soup more quickly, heat in a large pot or Dutch oven on medium heat for about 30 minutes, stirring occasionally, until heated through.

Christmas Day Dinner

Elegance and Grace at the Table

Achieving a beautiful, old-world look to your table presentation is as simple as spreading out a rich, heavy, white damask tablecloth: a blank canvas to handsomely set off china, crystal, silverware and the rich dark greenery of your centrepiece.

Here are a few suggestions for creating a beautiful table that will add to the charm and mood of your dinner party:

❋ **Table linens:** You don't want wrinkles and creases drawing attention away from your beautiful setting. Laundered and freshly pressed tablecloth and napkins set the stage.

❋ **China and crystal:** Set out your best plates, cups, saucers, water glasses and wine glasses, and your prettiest serving bowls and platters. Don't worry about all the pieces matching as long as they are coordinated. Bring out and show off that heirloom soup tureen or antique sugar and creamer set.

❋ **Cutlery:** Use your best silver or flatware, including large serving spoons, forks and lifters.

❋ **Accessories:** Add unique touches to the table with interesting items you've collected or inherited, such as tongs for sugar cubes, a knife rest at each place, porcelain place card holders, a covered butter dish or a silver serving tray for tea and coffee.

❋ **Inspired creations:** Maybe you've been impressed by little extras you've seen in a restaurant, magazine or old movie. Now's the time to add them to your own table: Instead of a glass pitcher for iced water, use a silver tea or coffee pot set on a napkin-covered plate to catch the beads of condensation; use an ice bucket for the wine and wrap a crisp white folded napkin around the neck of the bottle.

Christmas Greenery Centrepiece

Make this beautiful Christmas bough arrangement in almost any container in less than 30 minutes.

Place a block of soaked florist foam (use the one for fresh arrangements) in a shallow bowl and secure it with waterproof florist tape.

Start with four pieces of greenery. Insert one in the centre of each of the four outside edges of the foam. To make an oblong shape, insert longer pieces of greenery on the left and right sides, establishing the length, and shorter pieces in the front and back, establishing the width. Continue to insert greenery around the edge, slightly inward from the first four pieces, to fill in the oblong shape (see photo).

Insert a bow in the centre of the foam to establish the height of the centrepiece. Make sure the centrepiece is low enough for guests to see over when seated at the table. Insert more pieces of greenery in the foam to fill out the shape, making sure to leave enough room for your decorative elements.

Insert decorative picks, ribbons or bows, ornaments, fresh berries, flowers or fruits. Add a final touch of greenery around the decorative elements or to fill in any holes in the arrangement.

Festive Spinach Salad

A light, refreshing dressing brings out the flavours of this spectacular salad. If you prefer, serve the blue cheese on the side and allow your guests to add as much or as little as they like to their own salad serving.

Bag of fresh spinach, stems removed	10 oz.	284 g
Head of radicchio, chopped or torn	1	1
Raisins	1 cup	250 mL
Fennel bulb (white part only), thinly sliced	1	1
Crumbled blue cheese (optional)	3/4 cup	175 mL
Flaked hazelnuts (filberts), toasted (see Tip)	1/2 cup	125 mL

LEMON AND HONEY VINAIGRETTE

Olive (or cooking) oil	1/4 cup	60 mL
Lemon juice	3 tbsp.	50 mL
White wine vinegar	1 tbsp.	15 mL
Liquid honey	1 tbsp.	15 mL
Salt	1/4 tsp.	1 mL
Pepper	1/4 tsp.	1 mL

Put first 6 ingredients into large bowl. Toss.

Lemon And Honey Vinaigrette: Measure all 6 ingredients into jar with tight-fitting lid. Shake well. Makes about 1/2 cup (125 mL) vinaigrette. Drizzle over salad. Toss well. Serves 12.

1 serving: 136 Calories; 8.2 g Total Fat (6.0 g Mono, 0.8 g Poly, 0.9 g Sat); 0 mg Cholesterol; 16 g Carbohydrate; 1 g Fibre; 2 g Protein; 85 mg Sodium

Pictured above.

Tip: To toast the hazelnuts (filberts), place them in an ungreased frying pan. Heat on medium for 3 to 5 minutes, stirring often, until they are golden.

Make Ahead: The vinaigrette may be stored in an airtight container in the refrigerator for up to 1 week. Bring it to room temperature before tossing with the salad.

The salad may be stored in an airtight container in the refrigerator for up to 4 hours. Let it stand at room temperature for 30 minutes before tossing with the vinaigrette.

Savoury Pork Roast

This dressy dish is easy to serve and a perfect accompaniment or alternative to roast turkey. Serve with Peach Chutney, page 126, for another layer of flavour.

Olive (or cooking) oil	1/4 cup	60 mL
Finely chopped fresh parsley (or 1 tbsp., 15 mL, flakes)	1/4 cup	60 mL
Finely chopped onion	1/4 cup	60 mL
Garlic cloves, minced (or 3/4 tsp., 4 mL, powder)	3	3
Honey Dijon mustard	2 tbsp.	30 mL
Lemon pepper	2 tsp.	10 mL
Dried sage	1 tsp.	5 mL
Ground coriander	1/2 tsp.	2 mL
Boneless pork loin roast	3 – 4 lbs.	1.4 – 1.8 kg
MUSHROOM SAUCE		
Butter (or hard margarine)	2 tbsp.	30 mL
Olive (or cooking) oil	2 tbsp.	30 mL
Sliced brown (or white) mushrooms	6 cups	1.5 L
All-purpose flour	1/4 cup	60 mL
Dried sage	1/2 tsp.	2 mL
Salt	1/2 tsp.	2 mL
Pepper	1/4 tsp.	1 mL
Dry sherry	3/4 cup	175 mL
Prepared chicken broth	2 cups	500 mL

Sprigs of fresh parsley, for garnish
Lemon slices, for garnish

Combine first 8 ingredients in small bowl.

Score 1/4 inch (6 mm) deep diamond pattern in fat on top of roast. Rub parsley mixture evenly over entire surface of roast. Wrap with plastic wrap. Chill for at least 6 hours or overnight. Place roast on greased wire rack set in 9 x 13 inch (22 x 33 cm) pan. Cook, uncovered, in 400°F (205°C) oven for 30 minutes. Reduce heat to 325°F (160°C). Cover roast loosely with foil if browning too quickly. Cook for another 1 to 1 1/4 hours until meat thermometer inserted into thickest part of roast reads 160°F (71°C). Transfer roast to large plate. Cover loosely with foil. Let stand for at least 10 minutes. Pour juices from pan through sieve into small bowl. Set aside.

Mushroom Sauce: Heat butter and olive oil in large frying pan on medium-high until butter is melted. Add mushrooms. Cook for about 10 minutes, stirring occasionally, until mushrooms are browned and liquid is evaporated. Reduce heat to medium.

Add next 4 ingredients. Stir well.

Gradually add sherry, broth and pan juices, stirring constantly until smooth. Increase heat to medium-high. Heat and stir for about 5 minutes until boiling and thickened. Makes about 3 1/4 cups (800 mL) sauce.

Slice roast and arrange on large serving platter. Drizzle 1 cup (250 mL) sauce over roast slices. Garnish with parsley and lemon. Serve with remaining sauce. Makes 12 servings (3 oz., 85 g, each of pork).

1 serving of pork with sauce: 349 Calories; 23.9 g Total Fat (12.3 g Mono, 2.4 g Poly, 7.3 g Sat); 77 mg Cholesterol; 5 g Carbohydrate; 1 g Fibre; 25 g Protein; 449 mg Sodium

Pictured on page 121.

Creamy Parsnip Mashed Potatoes

Delicious mashed potatoes with a sweet parsnip flavour—so good it may become a favourite dish for all holiday gatherings.

Peeled baking potatoes, chopped	4 lbs.	1.8 kg
Parsnips, chopped	2 lbs.	900 g
Block of light cream cheese, softened	8 oz.	250 g
Sour cream	1 cup	250 mL
Grated Parmesan cheese	1/2 cup	125 mL
Chopped fresh chives	1/3 cup	75 mL
Butter (or hard margarine)	2 tbsp.	30 mL
Pepper	1/2 tsp.	2 mL

Cook potato and parsnip in boiling salted water in large pot or Dutch oven until tender. Drain. Mash.

Add remaining 6 ingredients. Mash well. Serves 12.

1 serving: 253 Calories; 10.5 g Total Fat (3.1 g Mono, 0.4 g Poly, 6.2 g Sat); 30 mg Cholesterol; 34 g Carbohydrate; 4 g Fibre; 8 g Protein; 269 mg Sodium

Pictured on pages 114 and 121.

Make Ahead: The mashed potato mixture may be prepared up to 2 hours ahead of time and put into a greased 3 quart (3 L) baking dish. Cover with a lid or with greased foil and let it stand at room temperature until ready to bake. Bake, covered, in a 375°F (190°C) oven for about 30 minutes or until heated through.

Clockwise from left:
Creamy Parsnip Mashed Potatoes, above
Roasted Dilled Beets, page 124
Savoury Pork Roast, this page

Holiday Turkey Roulade

For a spectacular presentation with no last-minute Christmas Day fuss, serve the turkey cold this year. You'll need to make this the day before, or use our make-ahead suggestions to prepare it even sooner. Pairs beautifully with Peach Chutney, page 126.

PISTACHIO APRICOT STUFFING

Cooking oil	1 tbsp.	15 mL
Finely chopped onion	3/4 cup	175 mL
Finely chopped celery	1/4 cup	60 mL
White bread slices, cut into 1/4 inch (6 mm) cubes (about 2 cups, 500 mL)	4	4
Coarsely chopped pistachios	3/4 cup	175 mL
Finely chopped dried apricot	1/2 cup	125 mL
Apricot jam	3 tbsp.	50 mL
Large egg, fork-beaten	1	1
Chopped fresh parsley (or 2 1/4 tsp., 11 mL, flakes)	3 tbsp.	50 mL
Salt	1/4 tsp.	1 mL
Pepper	1/4 tsp.	1 mL
Boneless, skinless turkey breast halves (about 2 1/4 lbs., 1 kg, each)	2	2
Bacon slices	8	8

Pistachio Apricot Stuffing: Heat cooking oil in large frying pan on medium. Add onion and celery. Stir. Cook for about 5 minutes, stirring often, until onion is softened. Transfer to large bowl.

Add next 8 ingredients. Stir well. Set aside. Makes about 4 cups (1 L) stuffing.

Cut 1 turkey breast half lengthwise, not quite through to other side (see photo 1). Press open to flatten, making sure that smooth side of turkey is face down and farthest away from you. Place between 2 sheets of plastic wrap. Pound with mallet or rolling pin to even 3/4 inch (2 cm) thickness. Discard plastic wrap. Spread 1/2 of stuffing on turkey, leaving 1/2 inch (12 mm) edge. Roll up from side closest to you to enclose stuffing (see photo 2). Tie with butcher's string.

Wrap 4 bacon slices around turkey. Place in large roasting pan. Repeat with remaining ingredients, placing second roulade in same roasting pan. Cook, uncovered, in 325°F (160°C) oven for 2 1/2 to 3 hours until meat thermometer inserted into thickest part of turkey (not stuffing) reads 170°F (77°C). Cool completely. Wrap each roulade with plastic wrap. Chill for at least 8 hours or overnight. Discard bacon and butcher's string. Cut into 1/2 inch (12 mm) slices. Makes 18 servings (3 oz., 85 g, each of turkey).

1 serving: 196 Calories; 4.4 g Total Fat (2.4 g Mono, 0.9 g Poly, 0.7 g Sat); 83 mg Cholesterol; 9 g Carbohydrate; 1 g Fibre; 30 g Protein; 119 mg Sodium

Pictured on pages 114 and 123.

Make Ahead: The cooked roulade may be stored in the refrigerator for up to 24 hours, or wrapped with an additional layer of foil and stored in the freezer for up to 1 month.

Zucchini In Walnut Butter

Christmas colours blend with the festive taste of walnuts. This dish comes together quickly on the stove while the Savoury Pork Roast, page 120, is resting.

Medium unpeeled zucchini	6	6
Butter (or hard margarine)	1/4 cup	60 mL
Walnut halves, coarsely chopped	2/3 cup	150 mL
Finely chopped red pepper	2 tbsp.	30 mL
Chopped fresh sage	1 tbsp.	15 mL
Salt	1/2 tsp.	2 mL

Quarter each zucchini lengthwise. Trim flesh containing seeds. Cut remaining zucchini into 1 inch (2.5 cm) pieces.

Melt butter in large pot or Dutch oven on medium-low. Add walnuts. Cook for about 5 minutes, stirring occasionally, until butter is bubbling and walnuts are heated through. Increase heat to medium-high. Add zucchini. Toss until coated. Cook for about 5 minutes, stirring occasionally, until zucchini is tender-crisp.

Add remaining 3 ingredients. Toss gently. Makes about 8 cups (2 L). Serves 12.

1 serving: 100 Calories; 8.4 g Total Fat (2.1 g Mono, 3.0 g Poly, 2.9 g Sat); 11 mg Cholesterol; 5 g Carbohydrate; 3 g Fibre; 3 g Protein; 145 mg Sodium

Pictured on page 123.

Make Ahead: Cut the zucchini and chop the red pepper and sage up to 8 hours ahead of time, then store them in separate airtight containers in the refrigerator. The walnuts may be chopped well ahead of time and stored in an airtight container. Cook as directed.

Clockwise from left:
Holiday Turkey Roulade, this page
Wild Rice Pilaf, page 124
Zucchini In Walnut Butter, above
Peach Chutney, page 126

Wild Rice Pilaf

The nutty flavour of wild rice goes well with almost any meat. Chopped vegetables add colour and crunch.

Wild rice	2 cups	500 mL
Prepared chicken broth	4 cups	1 L
Water	4 cups	1 L
Salt	1/2 tsp.	2 mL
Olive (or cooking) oil	2 tbsp.	30 mL
Sliced brown (or white) mushrooms	4 cups	1 L
Butter (or hard margarine)	2 tbsp.	30 mL
Chopped onion	1 1/2 cups	375 mL
Chopped celery	1 cup	250 mL
Chopped red pepper	1/3 cup	75 mL
Garlic cloves, minced (or 1/2 tsp., 2 mL, powder)	2	2
Can of sliced water chestnuts, drained and coarsely chopped	8 oz.	227 mL
Chopped fresh parsley (or 1 tbsp., 15 mL, flakes)	1/4 cup	60 mL
Dried thyme	1/2 tsp.	2 mL
Pepper	1/2 tsp.	2 mL

Put rice into fine sieve. Rinse with cold water. Drain.

Combine next 3 ingredients in large pot or Dutch oven. Bring to a boil on high. Add rice. Stir. Reduce heat to medium-low. Simmer, covered, for about 1 hour until rice is puffed and cracked. Drain. Cover to keep warm. Set aside.

Heat olive oil in large frying pan on medium-high. Add mushrooms. Cook for 5 to 10 minutes, stirring occasionally, until mushrooms are browned and liquid is evaporated. Reduce heat to medium.

Add butter. Heat and stir until butter is melted and bubbling.

Add next 4 ingredients. Stir. Cook for 5 to 10 minutes, stirring often, until onion is softened.

Add remaining 4 ingredients. Stir. Add to rice in pot. Stir well. Makes about 10 cups (2.5 L). Serves 12.

1 serving: 172 Calories; 5.0 g Total Fat (2.4 g Mono, 0.6 g Poly, 1.7 g Sat); 5 mg Cholesterol; 27 g Carbohydrate; 3 g Fibre; 6 g Protein; 221 mg Sodium

Pictured on page 123.

Make Ahead: The pilaf may be prepared up to 2 hours ahead of time and put into a greased 3 quart (3 L) ovenproof serving dish. Cover it with foil and let it stand at room temperature until ready to bake. Bake in a 375°F (190°C) oven for about 25 minutes or until heated through.

Entertaining Tip

Polished and Ready

Take time a week or so before Christmas to pull out and thoroughly clean and polish your table settings, from wine glasses and bread plates to sugar tongs and serving bowls. Involve the whole family—including children—in polishing the silver and they will appreciate even more the extra effort that goes into this special holiday meal.

Once done, lay tea towels over everything until you are ready to set the table. Everything will glisten beautifully!

Roasted Dilled Beets

Often under-appreciated, beets take on an entirely different personality when baked or roasted. Colour deepens and natural sweetness intensifies for a beautiful and flavourful addition to the holiday table.

Fresh medium beets (about 4 lbs., 1.8 kg), scrubbed clean and trimmed (see Tip)	10	10
Butter (or hard margarine)	3 tbsp.	50 mL
Chopped fresh dill	3 tbsp.	50 mL
Coarse ground pepper	1/2 tsp.	2 mL

Chopped fresh dill, for garnish

Wrap beets individually with foil. Bake directly on rack in 325°F (160°C) oven for about 2 1/2 hours until tender. Discard foil. Let stand for about 5 minutes until cool enough to handle. Peel beets. Cut into quarters.

Heat next 3 ingredients in large saucepan on medium. Add beets. Cook for 5 to 10 minutes, stirring occasionally, until heated through.

Garnish with second amount of dill. Serves 12.

1 serving: 70 Calories; 3.1 g Total Fat (1.9 g Mono, 0.2 g Poly, 1.8 g Sat); 8 mg Cholesterol; 10 g Carbohydrate; 2 g Fibre; 2 g Protein; 109 mg Sodium

Pictured on page 121.

Tip: Don't get caught red-handed—wear rubber gloves when handling the beets.

Make Ahead: Bake, peel and quarter the beets up to 24 hours ahead of time and store in an airtight container in the refrigerator. Continue as directed.

Sweet And Smoky Brussels Sprouts

A must-try side dish if Brussels sprouts are a traditional part of your Christmas dinner. The sweet peas, smoky bacon and earthy pine nuts are an intriguing and wonderful complement.

Bacon slices, diced	4	4
Finely chopped onion	1 cup	250 mL
Brussels sprouts (about 3 lbs., 1.4 kg), trimmed and halved lengthwise (see Tip)	12 cups	3 L
Prepared chicken broth	1 1/4 cups	300 mL
Frozen peas	2 cups	500 mL
Pine nuts, toasted (see Tip)	2/3 cup	150 mL
Grated Parmesan cheese	1/3 cup	75 mL
Butter (or hard margarine)	1 tbsp.	15 mL

Cook bacon in large pot or Dutch oven on medium until crisp. Transfer with slotted spoon to paper towels to drain. Set aside.

Heat 2 tsp. (10 mL) drippings in same pot on medium-high. Add onion. Cook for 5 to 10 minutes, stirring often, until softened.

Add Brussels sprouts and broth. Bring to a boil. Reduce heat to medium. Boil gently, covered, for about 10 minutes until Brussels sprouts are just tender-crisp.

Add bacon and peas. Stir. Cook, covered, for about 2 minutes until heated through and peas are tender.

Add remaining 3 ingredients. Heat and stir until butter is melted. Serves 12.

1 serving: 156 Calories; 8.2 g Total Fat (2.9 g Mono, 2.4 g Poly, 2.4 g Sat); 7 mg Cholesterol; 15 g Carbohydrate; 7 g Fibre; 10 g Protein; 238 mg Sodium

Pictured below and on page 114.

Tip: Select Brussels sprouts that are heavy for their size and bright green with tight leaves. Small heads, about 1 inch (2.5 cm) in diameter, are best. Before cooking, remove any brown leaves and trim the stem ends.

Tip: To toast the pine nuts, place them in an ungreased frying pan. Heat on medium for 3 to 5 minutes, stirring often, until they are golden.

Make Ahead: Chop the bacon and onion, trim the Brussels sprouts and grate the cheese up to 8 hours ahead of time, then store them in separate airtight containers in the refrigerator. Cook as directed.

The pine nuts may be toasted and stored in an airtight container well ahead of time to free up the stovetop.

Cinnamon Honey Carrots

Cinnamon is a favourite aromatic spice of the season. Often associated with beverages and baking, it also goes well with the natural—and honey-enhanced—sweetness of carrots.

Bags of baby carrots (2 lbs., 900 g, each)	2	2
Cinnamon honey (see Note)	1/2 cup	125 mL
Butter (or hard margarine)	1/2 cup	125 mL
Chopped fresh parsley (or 3 1/2 tsp., 17 mL, flakes)	1/3 cup	75 mL

Cook carrots in boiling salted water in large saucepan for about 8 minutes until tender-crisp. Drain. Transfer to medium bowl.

Put remaining 3 ingredients into same large saucepan. Cook on medium for about 5 minutes, stirring occasionally, until boiling and thickened. Add carrots. Heat and stir for about 3 minutes until carrots are hot and glazed. Serves 12.

1 serving: 158 Calories; 8.3 g Total Fat (2.4 g Mono, 0.4 g Poly, 5.1 g Sat); 22 mg Cholesterol; 22 g Carbohydrate; 2 g Fibre; 1 g Protein; 111 mg Sodium

Pictured on page 114.

Note: To make your own cinnamon honey, combine 1/2 cup (125 mL) liquid honey and 1/4 tsp. (1 mL) ground cinnamon in a small cup.

Cranberry Marmalade

Add another surprise to Christmas Day! This may look like regular cranberry sauce but the flavours of marmalade and orange liqueur make it a very special addition to your dinner.

Can of whole cranberry sauce	14 oz.	398 mL
Orange marmalade	1/4 cup	60 mL
Orange liqueur	1 tbsp.	15 mL

Combine all 3 ingredients in medium bowl. Makes 2 cups (500 mL).

1 tbsp. (15 mL): 28 Calories; trace Total Fat (0 g Mono, 0 g Poly, 0 g Sat); 0 mg Cholesterol; 7 g Carbohydrate; trace Fibre; trace Protein; 5 mg Sodium

Pictured on page 114.

Make Ahead: The marmalade may be stored in an airtight container in the refrigerator for up to 1 week.

Peach Chutney

Add some spice to your holiday season. The flavour of the chutney intensifies and improves with time. It's excellent with turkey or pork and is equally good served cold or at room temperature.

Cooking oil	1 tbsp.	15 mL
Finely chopped onion	2 cups	500 mL
Ground cumin	1/2 tsp.	2 mL
Chili paste (sambal oelek)	1/2 tsp.	2 mL
Cans of sliced peaches in light syrup (14 oz., 398 mL, each), drained and chopped	3	3
Brown sugar, packed	2/3 cup	150 mL
White wine vinegar	2/3 cup	150 mL

Heat cooking oil in large saucepan on medium-high. Add onion. Cook for 5 to 10 minutes, stirring often, until softened and starting to brown.

Add cumin and chili paste. Heat and stir for about 1 minute until fragrant.

Add remaining 3 ingredients. Stir. Cook for about 10 minutes, stirring often, until thickened. Makes about 3 2/3 cups (900 mL).

1 tbsp. (15 mL): 19 Calories; 0.3 g Total Fat (0.1 g Mono, 0.1 g Poly, trace Sat); 0 mg Cholesterol; 4 g Carbohydrate; trace Fibre; trace Protein; 2 mg Sodium

Pictured on page 123.

Make Ahead: The chutney may be stored in an airtight container in the refrigerator for up to 1 week, or in the freezer for up to 1 month.

Cooking Tip

Foil Pans

❋ Deep-dish foil pie plates are a great option for holiday pies. You can prepare pies in advance and store them in the freezer without worrying that your regular pie plates will be out of service. The foil plates also make it easier to get out that first slice and have it looking great!

❋ Place foil pie plates on a baking sheet for easy and safe transfer, and to capture any boil-over from the pies while they're cooking.

Snappy Pumpkin Pies

These family-favourite pumpkin pies are quick and easy to make. Traditional seasoning makes a classic filling for scrumptious pecan-gingersnap crusts. A food processor will make quick work of crushing the gingersnaps.

GINGERSNAP CRUST

Crushed gingersnaps (about 20 gingersnaps)	2 cups	500 mL
Ground pecans (or almonds)	1 cup	250 mL
Brown sugar, packed	1/4 cup	60 mL
Ground cinnamon	1 tsp.	5 mL
Butter (or hard margarine), melted	1/2 cup	125 mL
Boxes of instant butterscotch pudding powder (4 serving size, each)	2	2
Milk	1 1/2 cups	375 mL
Can of pure pumpkin (no spices)	14 oz.	398 mL
Ground cinnamon	1 tsp.	5 mL
Ground ginger	1/2 tsp.	2 mL
Ground nutmeg	1/2 tsp.	2 mL
Ground cloves	1/8 tsp.	0.5 mL
Frozen whipped topping, thawed	3 cups	750 mL
Chopped pecans (or almonds), toasted (see Tip)	1/3 cup	75 mL

Gingersnap Crust: Combine first 4 ingredients in medium bowl. Add butter. Mix well. Spoon into 2 ungreased 9 inch (22 cm) pie plates. Press firmly on bottom and up side of pie plates. Bake in 350°F (175°C) oven for about 12 minutes until firm. Let stand on wire racks until cooled completely.

Beat pudding powder and milk on low in large bowl for 1 minute.

Add next 5 ingredients. Beat on low for about 1 minute until well combined. Spread in pie shells.

Spread with whipped topping. Sprinkle with pecans. Chill for at least 4 hours until set. Each pie cuts into 6 wedges, for a total of 12 wedges.

1 wedge: 416 Calories; 25.1 g Total Fat (9.8 g Mono, 3.1 g Poly, 10.8 g Sat); 23 mg Cholesterol; 47 g Carbohydrate; 2 g Fibre; 4 g Protein; 478 mg Sodium

Pictured above.

Tip: To toast the pecans, place them in an ungreased frying pan. Heat on medium for 3 to 5 minutes, stirring often, until they are golden. To bake, spread them evenly in an ungreased shallow pan. Bake in a 350°F (175°C) oven for 5 to 10 minutes, stirring or shaking often, until golden.

Make Ahead: The pies may be stored in airtight containers in the freezer for up to 1 month. Thaw them in the refrigerator for at least 8 hours before serving.

Christmas Cranapple Pies

Keep your oven available on Christmas Day by making the pies the day before, then set them to warm while you're enjoying dinner. Delicious with eggnog or vanilla ice cream. And leftovers are just as good the next day!

Brown sugar, packed	1 1/2 cups	375 mL
All-purpose flour	1/4 cup	60 mL
Ground cinnamon	1/2 tsp.	2 mL
Ground allspice	1/2 tsp.	2 mL
Ground nutmeg	1/4 tsp.	1 mL
Peeled and sliced tart cooking apple (such as Granny Smith)	8 cups	2 L
Lemon juice	1 tbsp.	15 mL
Vanilla extract	1 tsp.	5 mL
Dried cranberries	2 cups	500 mL
Pastry for 2 double crust 9 inch (22 cm) pies, your own or a mix		
Water		
Large egg, fork-beaten	1	1
Granulated sugar	2 tsp.	10 mL

Combine first 5 ingredients in small bowl.

Put apple, lemon juice and extract into large bowl. Toss until apple is coated. Add brown sugar mixture and cranberries. Stir until fruit is coated.

Divide pastry into 4 equal portions. Shape each portion into slightly flattened disc. Roll out 2 portions, 1 at a time, on lightly floured surface to about 1/8 inch (3 mm) thickness. Line two 9 inch (22 cm) pie plates. Spoon fruit mixture into shells. Roll out remaining 2 pastry portions, 1 at a time, on lightly floured surface to about 1/8 inch (3 mm) thickness. Dampen edge of shells with water. Cover fruit mixture with pastry. Trim and crimp decorative edges to seal.

Brush tops of pies with egg. Sprinkle with granulated sugar. Cut 1 or 2 small vents in tops to allow steam to escape. Bake on bottom rack in 375°F (190°C) oven for about 1 hour until golden. Let stand on wire racks until cooled completely. Each pie cuts into 8 wedges, for a total of 16 wedges.

1 wedge: 222 Calories; 5.7 g Total Fat (2.6 g Mono, 0.7 g Poly, 1.8 g Sat); 13 mg Cholesterol; 43 g Carbohydrate; 3 g Fibre; 2 g Protein; 115 mg Sodium

Pictured on page 129.

Make Ahead: The pies may be baked up to 24 hours ahead of time and stored at room temperature until ready to serve.

Special Touch

Chair Bow

Cut a piece of pretty fabric ribbon. The length will vary depending on the height and width of your chair back, but it needs to be long enough to make a bow and tails. Centre the ribbon at the narrowest part of your chair back, near the top. Make a knot, then a bow (just like tying your shoelaces). Cut the ends of the ribbon tails on an angle and, using wire, adorn the bow with greenery, craft berries or a miniature musical instrument.

New Year's Day Reminiscing Supper

~

As the Christmas festivities wind down, it's time for one final celebration—a tribute to the end of one year and a toast to the start of another.

A casual, easygoing get-together that includes a relaxed, sit-down supper served family-style is a setting made for reminiscing…about the days just past and the best Christmas ever, highlights of the year gone by, trips taken, meals and laughs and conversations shared.

Two very different menus are suggested for this occasion—a traditional, warming meal takes the chill out of a cold winter's eve, and a lighter supper takes the first step toward a healthier outlook going into the new year. Set your table as simply or as formally as you like. Paper plates can even be used to make this final celebration of the season a breeze to clean up.

An easy way to bring the theme of your party into the decor and encourage reminiscing is to make place cards using photos of your guests. Or ask everyone to bring an item for a time capsule—it's sure to spark memories and lively discussion.

Left: Comfort Roast, page 133
Top: Mashed Dilled Potatoes, page 134
Right: Roasted Sesame Vegetables, page 134

New Year's Day Reminiscing Supper

Casual Dinner for 8

Menu 1 – Comfort Cooking

This menu offers a warm and comforting winter meal. Before preheating the oven, remember to adjust oven rack positions to accommodate all the pans. The only make-ahead we recommend is baking the bread pudding early in the day so your oven is available later on to cook the roast, which requires a higher temperature.

Comfort Roast, page 133
Creamy Horseradish Sauce, page 133
Mashed Dilled Potatoes, page 134
Roasted Sesame Vegetables, page 134

Marmalade Bread Pudding, page 135

Menu 2 – Light and Fresh

The charm and appeal of this fresh and lively menu is that it can be served hot or cold. Because the dishes are so quick and easy to put together, there is little need for much advance preparation.

Veggie Pesto Salad, page 136
Citrus Glazed Salmon, page 137
Mushroom Spinach Couscous, page 136

Caramel Latte, page 138

Timeline

Menu 1 – Comfort Cooking

Up to Two Days in Advance
Prepare horseradish sauce

Day Before
Prepare bread pudding
Rub beef with mustard mixture

Day Of
4 - 6 hours in advance:
Bake bread pudding
Peel potatoes, keep in water
Prepare vegetables, cover and chill

2 1/2 hours in advance:
Put roast in oven

2 hours in advance:
Put vegetables in oven

45 minutes before serving:
Cook potatoes

Just before dinner is served:
Warm bread pudding in turned-off oven during
    dinner (optional)
Carve roast
Set out horseradish sauce

Menu 2 – Light and Fresh

Day Of
Up to 4 hours in advance:
Prepare glaze for salmon
Make salad
Cut vegetables for couscous

30 minutes before serving:
Make couscous
Glaze and bake salmon

After dinner:
Make latte

Mashed Dilled Potatoes, page 134   Comfort Roast With Creamy Horseradish Sauce, below   Roasted Sesame Vegetables, page 134

Comfort Roast

This well-seasoned roast is tender and flavourful—and we've made sure there's enough for seconds! Delicious with Creamy Horseradish Sauce, this page.

Dijon mustard	3 tbsp.	50 mL
Prepared horseradish	1 tbsp.	15 mL
Garlic clove, minced	1	1
(or 1/4 tsp., 1 mL, powder)		
Montreal steak spice	1 tsp.	5 mL
Beef sirloin tip roast	3 lbs.	1.4 kg

Combine first 4 ingredients in small bowl.

Place roast on large plate. Rub mustard mixture over entire surface of roast. Chill, covered, overnight. Place roast on greased wire rack set in 9 x 9 inch (22 x 22 cm) pan (see Note). Bake, uncovered, on bottom rack in 475°F (240°C) oven for about 30 minutes until browned. Reduce heat to 300°F (150°C). Bake for another 2 to 2 1/2 hours until meat thermometer inserted into thickest part of roast reads 160°F (71°C) for medium or until desired doneness. Remove from oven. Cover with foil. Let stand for 10 minutes before serving. Makes 12 servings (3 oz., 85 g, each of beef).

1 serving: 258 Calories; 13.4 g Total Fat (5.5 g Mono, 0.8 g Poly, 5.0 g Sat); 70 mg Cholesterol; 1 g Carbohydrate; trace Fibre; 32 g Protein; 212 mg Sodium

Pictured above and on page 130.

Note: Using a 9 x 9 inch (22 x 22 cm) pan will ensure that the roast and vegetables will fit in the oven at the same time.

Creamy Horseradish Sauce

Classic and familiar—but still the perfect complement to a roast beef dinner. Delicious with potatoes and vegetables, too!

Sour cream	1 cup	250 mL
Prepared horseradish	1 tbsp.	15 mL
Dijon mustard	1 tbsp.	15 mL
Lemon juice	1 tsp.	5 mL
Salt	1/4 tsp.	1 mL
Pepper	1/8 tsp.	0.5 mL

Combine all 6 ingredients in small bowl. Makes about 1 cup (250 mL).

2 tbsp. (30 mL): 47 Calories; 4.2 g Total Fat (1.2 g Mono, 0.2 g Poly, 2.6 g Sat); 11 mg Cholesterol; 2 g Carbohydrate; trace Fibre; 1 g Protein; 111 mg Sodium

Pictured above.

Make Ahead: The sauce may be stored in an airtight container in the refrigerator for up to 2 days.

Mashed Dilled Potatoes

Creamy mashed potatoes speckled with dill and parsley are the perfect accompaniment for Comfort Roast, page 133, and Roasted Sesame Vegetables, this page.

Peeled potatoes, cut up	4 lbs.	1.8 kg
Butter (or hard margarine)	1/4 cup	60 mL
Garlic clove, minced (or 1/4 tsp., 1 mL, powder)	1	1
Milk	1/2 cup	125 mL
Sour cream	1/2 cup	125 mL
Chopped fresh dill (or 3/4 tsp., 4 mL, dill weed)	1 tbsp.	15 mL
Salt	1/2 tsp.	2 mL
Pepper	1/4 tsp.	1 mL
Chopped fresh parsley	1 tbsp.	15 mL

Cook potato in boiling salted water in large pot or Dutch oven until tender. Drain. Return to same pot. Place uncovered pot on hot burner. Turn off heat. Stir potato or shake pot until any excess liquid is evaporated. Mash. Cover to keep warm.

Melt butter in small frying pan on medium. Add garlic. Heat and stir for about 1 minute until fragrant. Add milk. Bring to a boil. Add to potato. Mash well.

Add next 4 ingredients. Mix well. Remove to large serving bowl.

Sprinkle with parsley. Serves 8.

1 serving: 219 Calories; 8.6 g Total Fat (2.4 g Mono, 0.4 g Poly, 5.3 g Sat); 23 mg Cholesterol; 32 g Carbohydrate; 3 g Fibre; 5 g Protein; 236 mg Sodium

Pictured on pages 130 and 133.

Roasted Sesame Vegetables

Herb-roasted veggies with a twist. For a supper that welcomes the start of a new year, we've hinted at the coming spring with a subtle hint of maple and lemon.

Parsnips, cut into 3/4 inch (2 cm) pieces	1 lb.	454 g
Medium carrots, cut into 1/2 inch (12 mm) slices	10	10
Large onion, cut into 12 wedges	1	1
Olive (or cooking) oil	2 tbsp.	30 mL
Dried thyme	1 tsp.	5 mL
Salt	1/4 tsp.	1 mL
Pepper	1/4 tsp.	1 mL
Maple (or maple-flavoured) syrup	2 tbsp.	30 mL
Frozen concentrated lemonade, thawed	1 tbsp.	15 mL
Sesame seeds, toasted (see Tip)	2 tsp.	10 mL

Put first 7 ingredients into large bowl. Toss until vegetables are coated. Spread evenly in greased 3 quart (3 L) shallow baking dish. Bake, covered, on bottom rack in 300°F (150°C) oven for 1 hour.

Combine maple syrup and concentrated lemonade in small bowl. Drizzle over vegetables. Stir until coated. Bake, uncovered, for another 1 to 1 1/4 hours until vegetables are tender-crisp.

Sprinkle with sesame seeds. Serves 8.

1 serving: 139 Calories; 4.2 g Total Fat (2.7 g Mono, 0.6 g Poly, 0.6 g Sat); 0 mg Cholesterol; 25 g Carbohydrate; 5 g Fibre; 2 g Protein; 116 mg Sodium

Pictured on pages 131 and 133.

Tip: To toast the sesame seeds, place them in an ungreased frying pan. Heat on medium for 3 to 5 minutes, stirring often, until they are golden.

Marmalade Bread Pudding

Served hot out of the oven, warm or even at room temperature, sweet bites of fruit and tangy marmalade make this raisin bread pudding delicious. An addition of cream or ice cream will make this an extra-special treat.

Homogenized milk	2 cups	500 mL
Eggnog	1 cup	250 mL
Large eggs	4	4
Brown sugar, packed	1/3 cup	75 mL
Vanilla extract	1 tsp.	5 mL
Ground cinnamon	1/2 tsp.	2 mL
Salt	1/8 tsp.	0.5 mL
Raisin bread slices	12	12
Orange marmalade	1 cup	250 mL
Orange liqueur	2 tbsp.	30 mL
Golden raisins	2 tbsp.	30 mL
Dried cranberries	2 tbsp.	30 mL
Chopped dried apricot	2 tbsp.	30 mL

Beat first 7 ingredients with whisk in large bowl.

Dip both sides of 6 bread slices into egg mixture. Arrange, slightly overlapping, in spiral pattern in greased 3 quart (3 L) round casserole.

Combine marmalade and liqueur in small bowl. Add remaining 3 ingredients. Stir. Spoon 1/2 of marmalade mixture evenly over bread slices in casserole. Dip both sides of remaining 6 bread slices into egg mixture. Arrange, slightly overlapping, spiralling in opposite direction on top of marmalade mixture. Spoon remaining marmalade mixture evenly over bread slices. Carefully pour remaining egg mixture over top. Chill, covered, for at least 8 hours or overnight. Bake, covered, in 325°F (160°C) oven for 1 hour. Remove cover and bake for another 15 minutes until top is golden and knife inserted in centre comes out clean. Serves 8.

1 serving: 394 Calories; 8.9 g Total Fat (3.2 g Mono, 0.8 g Poly, 4.0 g Sat); 136 mg Cholesterol; 70 g Carbohydrate; 2 g Fibre; 10 g Protein; 300 mg Sodium

Pictured below.

Veggie Pesto Salad

Transform raw veggies into a fresh, tangy salad guaranteed to lift winter spirits. Quick preparation with appetizing results.

Frozen peas, thawed	4 cups	1 L
Cauliflower florets, cut into 1/2 inch (12 mm) pieces	2 cups	500 mL
Diced red pepper	1 cup	250 mL
Coarsely grated carrot	1 cup	250 mL
PESTO VINAIGRETTE		
Cooking oil	6 tbsp.	100 mL
White wine vinegar	1/4 cup	60 mL
Sun-dried tomato pesto	1/4 cup	60 mL
Salt	1/2 tsp.	2 mL
Pepper	1/2 tsp.	2 mL

Put first 4 ingredients into medium bowl. Toss.

Pesto Vinaigrette: Combine all 5 ingredients in jar with tight-fitting lid. Shake well. Makes about 2/3 cup (150 mL) vinaigrette. Drizzle over vegetables. Toss well. Serves 8.

1 serving: 178 Calories; 11.3 g Total Fat (6.5 g Mono, 3.3 g Poly, 0.9 g Sat); 0 mg Cholesterol; 16 g Carbohydrate; 5 g Fibre; 5 g Protein; 257 mg Sodium

Pictured on page 137.

Make Ahead: The salad may be tossed with the vinaigrette up to 4 hours ahead of time and stored in an airtight container in the refrigerator. Toss again just before serving.

Special Touch

Photo Place Cards

Surprise guests with personalized place cards that say: Here's lookin' at you!

Choose photos of your guests that evoke memories of a specific event. It will get everyone talking, looking back and reminiscing about their lives and the experiences they've had over the past year.

Insert the photo in a simple silver picture frame. Glue a few embellishments on the frame, such as colourful rhinestones, if you'd like to add a bit of colourful sparkle. You can also crop photos and mount them on plain or patterned paper to match your table decor or colour scheme.

Mushroom Spinach Couscous

Looks as good as it tastes. Best of all, this dish comes together quickly so you can spend more time visiting and less time cooking.

Prepared chicken broth	3 cups	750 mL
Box of plain couscous	12 oz.	340 g
Salt	1/2 tsp.	2 mL
Butter (or hard margarine)	2 tbsp.	30 mL
Chopped onion	1/2 cup	125 mL
Garlic clove, minced (or 1/4 tsp., 1 mL, powder)	1	1
Sliced fresh white mushrooms	2 cups	500 mL
Boxes of frozen chopped spinach (10 oz., 300 g, each), thawed and squeezed dry	2	2
Prepared chicken broth	1/4 cup	60 mL
Dried tarragon leaves	1 tsp.	5 mL

Bring first amount of broth to a boil in medium saucepan. Add couscous and salt. Stir. Cover. Remove from heat. Let stand for about 5 minutes, without stirring, until broth is absorbed. Fluff with fork. Set aside.

Melt butter in large frying pan on medium. Add onion and garlic. Cook for 2 to 3 minutes, stirring often, until onion starts to soften.

Add mushrooms. Cook for 5 to 10 minutes, stirring occasionally, until mushrooms are softened.

Add couscous and remaining 3 ingredients. Heat and stir for 2 to 3 minutes until heated through. Serves 8.

1 serving: 227 Calories; 4.1 g Total Fat (1.1 g Mono, 0.5 g Poly, 2.1 g Sat); 8 mg Cholesterol; 38 g Carbohydrate; 4 g Fibre; 10 g Protein; 563 mg Sodium

Pictured on page 137.

Mushroom Spinach Couscous, page 136   Citrus Glazed Salmon, below   Veggie Pesto Salad, page 136

Citrus Glazed Salmon

Sweet and smoky with a hint of citrus, this beautifully glazed side of salmon is a light and fresh way to start the new year. Also great served cold.

Fresh (or frozen, thawed) salmon fillet, skin and any small bones removed	2 lbs.	900 g
Brown sugar, packed	1/3 cup	75 mL
Lime juice	3 tbsp.	50 mL
Frozen concentrated orange juice, thawed	2 tbsp.	30 mL
Hickory barbecue sauce	1 tbsp.	15 mL
Small garlic clove, minced (or 1/8 tsp., 0.5 mL, powder)	1	1
Salt	1/4 tsp.	1 mL
Pepper	1/4 tsp.	1 mL

Place salmon on greased foil-lined baking sheet with sides.

Combine remaining 7 ingredients in small bowl. Spread 1/2 of juice mixture on salmon. Bake in 400°F (205°C) oven for 10 minutes. Spread remaining juice mixture on salmon. Bake for another 4 to 5 minutes until fish flakes easily when tested with fork. Let stand for 5 minutes. Remove to large serving platter. Spoon glaze from baking sheet over top. Serves 8.

1 serving: 207 Calories; 7.2 g Total Fat (2.4 g Mono, 2.9 g Poly, 1.1 g Sat); 62 mg Cholesterol; 12 g Carbohydrate; trace Fibre; 23 g Protein; 144 mg Sodium

Pictured above.

New Year's Day Reminiscing Supper

Caramel Latte

Whipped cream drizzled with caramel topping converts this sweet caramel flavoured coffee from beverage to decadent dessert. Don't be surprised if your guests want to sit and reminisce through seconds!

Water	4 cups	1 L
Milk	4 cups	1 L
Caramel ice cream topping	1 cup	250 mL
Instant coffee granules	1/2 cup	125 mL
Vanilla	4 tsp.	20 mL
Whipped cream	1/2 cup	125 mL
Caramel ice cream topping	1/4 cup	60 mL

Combine first 5 ingredients in large pot or Dutch oven. Heat and stir on medium for 15 to 20 minutes until bubbles form around edge. Remove from heat. Ladle into 8 large mugs until about 3/4 full.

Top each with 1 tbsp. (15 mL) whipped cream. Drizzle with second amount of ice cream topping. Serves 8.

1 serving: 229 Calories; 4.0 g Total Fat (1.2 g Mono, 0.1 g Poly, 2.5 g Sat); 15 mg Cholesterol; 44 g Carbohydrate; 0 g Fibre; 6 g Protein; 256 mg Sodium

Pictured at left.

Special Project

Time Capsule

This supper is all about reminiscing, and what better way to do it than with a time capsule?

Invite each guest to bring along something special from the past year—photographs, newspaper clippings, a CD of their favourite music—or ask them to answer a few questions on paper about their favourite TV show, book, meal or celebrity. Or get your guests to write predictions about the coming year.

Put everything into a large coffee can or box that you've covered with paper. You might even want to seal the container with wax, just for fun. On the outside, write the year it was sealed, the year it's to be opened and list the guests at the party. Think of what fun it will be to crack open your time capsule at your next reminiscing supper!

Cocktail Parties

Cocktail Party Guide

Cocktail parties tend to be evening, adult-oriented gatherings. They can usually accommodate a larger guest list, especially for a come-and-go party spanning three or four hours.

A cocktail party is a good entertaining choice if your overall space is limited, or if you want guests to mingle rather than sit in one place. The ebb and flow of conversation and movement around the room makes a cocktail party, even at its most sophisticated, a relaxed and easygoing affair.

Circulation of guests—and food—lends a lively energy to this style of party, with the host in the middle of it all! Throughout the evening, visiting is interwoven with cooking (or at least reheating) and serving duties. This is one occasion when it's worth planning for some help, or accepting it when offered.

A tempting variety of finger foods—hot, cold or both—is an important element of the cocktail party. At first glance, it might seem an easier alternative to a full-fledged dinner party; however, bite-sized food is costly to buy, and making it yourself can be time-consuming. Taking into account time and dollars, a cocktail party is probably the most expensive style of entertaining—but find a balance that works, and you and your guests will have a great evening.

Cocktail Party Serving Style

Whether the party is casual or sophisticated, food is either brought around to guests or guests approach a table or tables and serve themselves. In either case, appetizers are set out and replenished on larger platters or trays. There is considerably less dinnerware and cutlery involved in a cocktail party, but significantly more glassware and napkins.

The food requires the host's attention for the duration of the cocktail party. That means short stints of kitchen duty throughout the evening, so it's good to figure out the demands while choosing the menu and make adjustments accordingly. Remember, too, each time you bring out food, you'll have an opportunity to circulate among your guests.

Planning Beverages

For a larger party, if you have the room, consider setting up more than one beverage bar. Ask a reliable friend or two to share bartending duty. If you're serving alcohol, talk with an expert at a liquor store about the type of party you're hosting and he or she can advise what amount and what type of different wines, beer or spirits to consider. Make sure to include a selection of alcohol-free cold and hot beverages.

Have some food set out when guests arrive and serve appetizers throughout the evening. It's best not to overdo the salty, sweet or greasy snack foods; they increase thirst. High-starch and protein foods are better choices.

For this type of gathering, you want to have plenty of extra glasses (to avoid doing wash-up during the party) and ice.

Planning a Menu

If variety is the spice of life, then cocktail parties are the spiciest and liveliest of gatherings. Appetizers can be hot, cold, sweet, savoury, meaty, veggie, dipped, skewered—the choices are truly endless! The best thing about a cocktail party is having a variety of tasty appetizers to nibble.

Theme, duration, number of guests and, especially, the time you have available are important considerations when planning a cocktail party menu. The appetizers should create an appealing and complementary variety of flavours, presentations and cooking styles. In planning for that, you can still make it easier on yourself, for example:

※ Make a double batch of one item instead of an additional recipe, or substitute convenience products for one or more homemade hors d'oeuvres.

※ Many cocktail food recipes lend themselves to make-ahead preparation, from single-serving morsels that can easily be frozen and reheated, to dips that actually taste better if made the day before.

A good starting point in planning your cocktail party menu is deciding whether you'll offer finger or fork hors d'oeuvres, or a combination. Then you can determine if you'll need cutlery and plates or just napkins. That will also define which recipes make your list of possibilities. Then decide if you want to serve only hot, only cold or both hot and cold appetizers. If you plan to include hot, you know you'll need to plan on some kitchen time during the party.

To make less adventurous guests feel more at ease, consider including a few familiar stand-bys that are easy to recognize.

Portion and Quantity

The variety and richness of the appetizers, as well as the timing and duration of the party, will have a bearing on the size and quantity of appetizers you serve. You'll have to plan differently if guests are coming for a couple of hours after work or dinner, stopping by during the dinner hour or spending the whole evening nibbling. Keep in mind that you might want to serve dips or spreads with accompaniments in addition to your hors d'oeuvres.

The following is a very general (and generous) guideline for a three- to four-hour-long cocktail party that's not over the dinner hour.

Number of guests	Varieties of hors d'oeuvres	Servings of each variety per guest
8 – 10	At least 4	3 or 4
12 – 16	5 or 6	2 or 3
18 – 30	7 or 8	1 or 2

Serving Tips

❋ Hors d'oeuvres should be easy to handle and, whenever possible, small enough to be eaten in one or two bites. This often eliminates the need for plates and is less messy for your guests.

❋ Food is most flavourful at room temperature but cold food should still be cool and hot food should be as hot as is comfortable to hold in your fingers.

❋ Keep an eye on replenishing as needed, making sure what's set out is eaten in a reasonable time and always looks appealing and presentable.

❋ To allow for regular and timely replenishing, use smaller serving dishes. Generously filled with food, they'll look abundant but guests will reach the bottom more quickly.

❋ Set out food in one or more locations, along with cocktail napkins and receptacles to hold used skewers, stir sticks, napkins and such.

❋ If you're passing around the appetizers, you can tell guests what they are. If guests are helping themselves, add a card beside each item with the name and a bit of description.

❋ Individual plates are an option, depending on the menu, but cocktail napkins are a must.

❋ Put coasters everywhere.

Tray Tips

❋ Gauge the amount of food you set out by the number of people at the party. There's no need to set out three dozen hors d'oeuvres on a passing tray if only half a dozen people have arrived.

❋ Trays should look plentiful but be small enough that they can be freshened up often.

❋ Large trays are difficult to maneuver through a crowded room. Use them primarily to set out food in a central location.

❋ Serve larger trays of cold appetizers and smaller trays of hot ones. Keep the remaining hot appetizers in the oven or ready to heat in the microwave. Use them to refill the first tray or have a second tray ready to fill when the first is finished.

Traffic Flow and Seating

There are usually more guests than chairs, so many will be standing or moving about as they visit, eat and drink. If necessary, move some of the furniture to allow more space for circulating or congregating. Be alert to any bottlenecks: You want guests to be able to easily access the food table and beverage bar. And think about removing any breakable or treasured objects that could be bumped because of crowding.

Food Safety

Two-hour rule To stay on the safe side, food should not sit at room temperature for more than two hours—the danger zone for bacterial growth is between 40°F (4°C) and 140°F (60°C).

Keep cold foods cold Put serving bowls or trays on crushed ice.

Keep hot foods hot Use chafing dishes or warming trays.

Set out small portions Serve dips and hors d'oeuvres in smaller portions and replenish them throughout the party.

Never add new to old If you have a little bit of dip left in the bottom of a dish, spread it on a few crackers and pass the plate around, then set out a fresh bowl of dip.

Wash before reusing Be sure to wash trays before adding new hors d'oeuvres.

Table Decor and Presentation

If you're setting out trays of food on a table or at several food stations, choose a festive table covering and coordinating napkins as a quick way to dress things up. If there's room, include a centrepiece and maybe some candles.

Cocktail picks, whether plain plastic or tasselled and beaded silver, are a fun, attractive and convenient way to present hors d'oeuvres. Be sure to use only plain wooden picks if the appetizers are being baked.

If napkins and small plates are being used, they won't take up much space. Set them out for easy access from different points around the table.

Be creative in your presentation of the food. Use skewers, fancy picks or individual cups. Fancy up your serving trays with pretty doilies or napkins. Choose some unusual vessels for serving, perhaps related to the theme of your party.

Holiday Cocktail Party

~

Santa makes a global trek every year, so why not host a trip of your own? A cocktail party is the perfect choice for a tasting tour that explores some of the world's most delectable cuisines. Fitting comfortably into those first days of the entertaining season, this party infuses the holidays with an international flavour.

Three casual menus are inspired by the cuisines of three different regions: Mexico, the Far East and India. The recipes include traditional ingredients, spices and cooking styles associated with these areas. The menus also feature ways to keep the dishes truly authentic, without placing extra demands on the cook, by offering suggestions on ways to include purchased items.

This party lends itself to a larger crowd. For easier circulation, we suggest three food stations throughout the party area and, ideally, a fourth table in a different area for extended beverage service. For a smaller gathering, you could serve one of the menus supplemented by purchased convenience products from that particular cuisine. We've also included suggestions for simple decor touches that will enhance the mood and experience for your guests.

What better way to enter the season of peace and goodwill than by creating a global village in your living room and inviting guests to explore traditions from other parts of this wonderful world we call home.

Top left: Coconut Shrimp With Thai Dipping Sauce below, page 146
Centre: Crunchy Asian Salad, page 146
Bottom: Sweet Ginger Cheese Spread, page 147

Holiday Cocktail Party

Casual Open House for 16

The ingredients and dishes in these three international menus offer your guests flavours that may already be familiar, as well as tastes of the new and exotic. To make sure it all comes together smoothly for you, we've organized the preparation timelines so you can move progressively through each menu until everything is ready. And to keep things nice and easy during the party, we've made sure that the oven temperature is the same for all the baking.

Menu 1 – The Far East
Sake-tini, page 145

Crunchy Asian Salad, page 146
Sweet Ginger Cheese Spread, page 147
Coconut Shrimp, page 146

∼

Menu 2 – Mexican
Pomegranate Margaritas, page 147

Tijuana Wedges, page 148
Cinnamon Chips With Fruit Salsa, page 148
Roasted Corn Crab Cakes, page 150

∼

Menu 3 – Indian
Spiced Apple Iced Tea, page 151

Seafood Curry Dip, page 151
Kofta, page 152
Curried Onion Paneer, page 152

Timeline

Menu 1 – The Far East

Day Before
Make cheese spread (except garnish)
Make sauce for shrimp
Make dressing for salad
Cut vegetables to accompany cheese spread

Day Of
Up to 8 hours in advance:
Prepare martini garnish

Up to 4 hours in advance:
Assemble and coat shrimp skewers
Make, toss and portion salad

1 hour before guests arrive:
Mix gin and sake for martinis
Remove cheese spread from refrigerator and sprinkle with sesame seeds and onion
Arrange vegetables and rice crackers for cheese spread

During the party:
Mix martinis
Bake shrimp in batches
Replenish vegetables, rice crackers, etc. as needed

Menu 2 – Mexican

Up to Three Days in Advance
Make Cinnamon Chips
Make Chipotle Mayonnaise for crab cakes

Up to Two Days in Advance
Assemble and shape crab cakes

Day Before
Assemble Tijuana Wedges

Day Of
Up to 4 hours in advance:
Combine ingredients (except ice) for margaritas
Garnish margarita glass rims
Prepare Fruit Salsa

During the party:
Bake crab cakes in batches
Brush Tijuana Wedges with cooking oil and bake
Finish making margaritas
Replenish dishes with any extra salsa, wedges, etc.

Christmas Celebrations – Cocktail Parties

Menu 3 – Indian

Up to One Month in Advance
Cook and freeze Kofta

Day Before
Steep iced tea
Make seafood dip
Make Mint Raita Sauce for Kofta
Cut vegetables to accompany dip

Day Of
Just before guests arrive:
Take seafood dip out of refrigerator
Set out vegetables or crackers for dip
Prepare pitchers of iced tea
Make curried paneer
Cut naan bread for paneer

During the party:
Reheat Kofta in batches

Sake-tini

This rice wine and gin martini trades the traditional olive for crunchy cucumber and sweet-and-spicy pickled ginger. Guests who enjoy pickled ginger as a sushi condiment will love it in this cocktail.

Thin unpeeled English cucumber slices	32	32
Pickled ginger slices, drained	16	16
Cocktail picks	16	16
Gin (or vodka)	2 1/2 cups	625 mL
Sake (rice wine)	1 1/2 cups	375 mL
Ice cubes	32	32

Stack 2 cucumber slices together. Place 1 ginger slice on top. Fold cucumber slices in half to enclose ginger. Secure with cocktail pick. Repeat with remaining cucumber and ginger slices.

Combine gin and sake in large pitcher. Measure 1 cup (250 mL) into cocktail shaker. Add 8 ice cubes. Replace lid. Hold firmly and shake vigorously until cold. Strain through sieve into 4 martini glasses. Repeat with remaining gin mixture and ice cubes. Garnish with cucumber picks. Serves 16.

1 serving: 106 Calories; trace Total Fat (0 g Mono, trace Poly, trace Sat); 0 mg Cholesterol; 2 g Carbohydrate; trace Fibre; trace Protein; 3 mg Sodium

Pictured above.

Make Ahead: The cucumber-ginger picks may be assembled up to 8 hours ahead of time. Place them on a large plate, cover with damp paper towels and plastic wrap, and store in the refrigerator until ready to serve.

Menu Additions

Whether you want to enhance your menu or be prepared for unexpected guests, here are some convenience items that fit nicely into each theme as additional dishes.

You can even order a couple of your favourite items, such as green onion cakes or pot stickers, from a local Chinese restaurant. If available, take advantage of home delivery.

Menu 1 – The Far East
Asian snack mix or wasabi peas
Heat-and-serve spring rolls or dumplings
from the grocery freezer section
Sushi from a local Japanese takeout or grocery store
Teriyaki chicken wings

Menu 2 – Mexican
Roasted pumpkin seeds
Salsa and tortilla chips
Heat-and-serve stuffed jalapeños
Layered taco dip from the deli

Menu 3 – Indian
Pistachios or curry roasted nuts
Heat-and-serve samosas or pakoras
Add a little curry paste to some hummus
and serve with pappadums

Crunchy Asian Salad

Ginger, orange and chili are a harmonizing thread of flavour among this dish and others in the menu. Be creative and serve this salad in individual mini takeout boxes.

Bag of broccoli slaw	12 oz.	340 g
Bag of coleslaw mix (16 oz., 500 g, size)	1/2	1/2
Cans of mandarin orange segments (10 oz., 284 mL, each), drained	2	2
Large red pepper, julienned (see Note)	1	1
Green onions, thinly sliced diagonally	4	4
ORANGE GINGER DRESSING		
Cooking oil	1/4 cup	60 mL
Rice vinegar	3 tbsp.	50 mL
Frozen concentrated orange juice, thawed	3 tbsp.	50 mL
Finely grated gingerroot (or 3/4 tsp., 4 mL, ground ginger)	1 tbsp.	15 mL
Sesame oil	1 tsp.	5 mL
Salt	3/4 tsp.	4 mL
Chili paste (sambal oelek)	1/4 tsp.	1 mL
Sesame seeds, toasted (see Tip)	2 tbsp.	30 mL

Combine first 5 ingredients in extra-large bowl.

Orange Ginger Dressing: Combine first 7 ingredients in jar with tight-fitting lid. Shake well. Drizzle over salad. Toss.

Sprinkle individual servings with sesame seeds. Makes about 10 cups (2.5 L). Serves 16.

1 serving: 70 Calories; 4.7 g Total Fat (2.5 g Mono, 1.5 g Poly, 0.4 g Sat); 0 mg Cholesterol; 7 g Carbohydrate; 1 g Fibre; 1 g Protein; 121 mg Sodium

Pictured on page 142.

Note: To julienne, cut into very thin strips that resemble matchsticks.

Tip: To toast the sesame seeds, place them in an ungreased frying pan. Heat on medium for 3 to 5 minutes, stirring often, until they are golden.

Make Ahead: The dressing may be stored in an airtight container in the refrigerator for up to 24 hours. The salad may be tossed with the dressing and portioned up to 4 hours ahead of time. Cover and chill until ready to serve. Sprinkle with the sesame seeds just before serving.

Coconut Shrimp

Sambal oelek, a popular South East Asian paste made from chilies, brown sugar and salt, spices up the shrimp batter and balances the coconut's sweetness. Bake these a dozen at a time so guests can enjoy hot hors d'oeuvres throughout the evening.

THAI DIPPING SAUCE		
Sweet chili sauce	3/4 cup	175 mL
Lime juice	3 tbsp.	50 mL
Chopped fresh cilantro or parsley	3 tbsp.	50 mL
Frozen uncooked medium shrimp (peeled and deveined), thawed	48	48
Bamboo skewers (4 inches, 10 cm, each), soaked in water for 10 minutes	48	48
All-purpose flour	1/3 cup	75 mL
Salt	1/8 tsp.	0.5 mL
Large eggs	2	2
Chili paste (sambal oelek)	2 tbsp.	30 mL
Shredded (long thread) coconut	2 cups	500 mL

Thai Dipping Sauce: Combine first 3 ingredients in small bowl. Makes about 1 cup (250 mL) sauce.

Thread 1 shrimp lengthwise onto each skewer. Set aside.

Combine flour and salt in small shallow dish.

Beat eggs and chili paste in separate small shallow dish.

Measure coconut into third small shallow dish. Holding 1 skewer, dredge shrimp in flour mixture until coated. Gently shake to remove any excess flour. Dip shrimp into egg mixture and press into coconut until coated. Place on greased parchment paper-lined baking sheet. Repeat with remaining shrimp skewers. Spray shrimp with cooking spray. Bake, uncovered, in 425°F (220°C) oven for about 8 minutes, turning once, until coconut is golden and shrimp are firm and fully cooked. Serve with sauce. Makes 48 skewers.

1 skewer with 1 tsp. (5 mL) sauce: 35 Calories; 1.4 g Total Fat (0.2 g Mono, 0.1 g Poly, 1.0 g Sat); 20 mg Cholesterol; 4 g Carbohydrate; trace Fibre; 2 g Protein; 89 mg Sodium

Pictured on page 142.

Make Ahead: The sauce may be made up to 24 hours ahead of time and stored in an airtight container in the refrigerator. Bring to room temperature before serving. Assemble the shrimp skewers up to 4 hours ahead of time and store in an airtight container in the refrigerator until ready to bake.

Pomegranate Margaritas

Although not native to Mexico, the pomegranate is a favourite ingredient in Mexican cuisine because of its intense colour and sweet flavour. Set one pitcher out when guests arrive and keep the other chilled for later in the evening.

Bottles of pomegranate juice (15 1/2 oz., 473 mL, each)	4	4
Tequila	2 cups	500 mL
Orange liqueur	1 cup	250 mL
Lime juice	1/2 cup	125 mL
Grenadine syrup	4 tsp.	20 mL
Ice cubes	32	32

Combine first 5 ingredients in 2 large pitchers. Chill.

Just before serving, add ice cubes. Stir well. Strain through sieve into margarita glasses (see Note). Makes about 12 cups (3 L). Serves 16.

1 serving: 187 Calories; 0.1 g Total Fat (0 g Mono, trace Poly, trace Sat); 0 mg Cholesterol; 21 g Carbohydrate; trace Fibre; 1 g Protein; 6 mg Sodium

Pictured on page 149.

Note: Your guests will be impressed if you've garnished the glasses prior to pouring the margaritas. To garnish, dampen the rims with a lime wedge or dip into lime juice in a small saucer. Press the rims into granulated sugar in a separate small saucer until coated.

Make Ahead: Rim the margarita glasses with sugar up to 4 hours ahead of time. The juice mixture may be stored in the refrigerator for up to 4 hours. Add ice cubes and stir just before serving.

Sweet Ginger Cheese Spread

Crystallized ginger, a popular treat on its own, melds seamlessly with other traditional Asian ingredients in this easy-to-make spread. Serve with rice crackers and vegetables cut at sharp angles (to mimic the clean lines in modern Japanese design).

Block of cream cheese, softened	8 oz.	250 g
Sweet chili sauce	2 tbsp.	30 mL
Minced crystallized ginger	1 1/2 tbsp.	25 mL
Finely chopped green onion	1 tbsp.	15 mL
Lime juice	2 tsp.	10 mL
Grated lime zest	1/2 tsp.	2 mL
Sesame seeds, toasted (see Tip)	1/2 tsp.	2 mL
Finely chopped green onion	1/2 tsp.	2 mL

Beat first 6 ingredients on low in medium bowl. Remove to small serving bowl. Chill, covered, for at least 6 hours or overnight to blend flavours.

Before serving, garnish with sesame seeds and second amount of onion. Makes about 1 1/3 cups (325 mL).

1 tbsp. (15 mL): 43 Calories; 4.0 g Total Fat (1.1 g Mono, 0.2 g Poly, 2.5 g Sat); 12 mg Cholesterol; 1 g Carbohydrate; trace Fibre; 1 g Protein; 55 mg Sodium

Pictured on page 143.

Tip: To toast the sesame seeds, place them in an ungreased frying pan. Heat on medium for 3 to 5 minutes, stirring often, until they are golden.

SWEET GINGER CHEESE BALL: Roll the chilled cream cheese mixture into a ball. Wrap with plastic wrap. Chill for another 3 hours until firm. Roll the ball in toasted black and white sesame seeds on a large plate until coated.

Special Touch

An Ethnic Setting

Create inexpensive but effective multi-ethnic settings from items you have on hand or can easily buy at a local dollar store or party shop. Because each table showcases a distinct region, reinforce each theme with elements that reflect that particular culture. Here are a few ideas:

The Far East Theme

Consider clean, straight lines, such as rectangular-shaped dishes, or the decorated takeout containers featured in our photos. As a colour accent, red is significantly used in many Far East celebrations and is symbolic of joy, happiness and prosperity.

Mexican Theme

Rustic, warm and bright colours will offer a festive welcome. Decorate your table with bright, patterned blankets and baskets. Mirror the colours of your patterned accents with a selection of solid-coloured plates.

Indian Theme

Indian designs can be characterized by exotic, rich patterns, highlighted by warm earth tones and jewel colours. A simple throw or length of sari fabric can be set out as a tablecloth or wall hanging. Candles set in containers of sand or beads can add to the atmosphere.

Tijuana Wedges

Packed full of refried beans, hot jalapeños, chili and a blend of mild cheeses, these wedges are a step above the regular quesadilla. A pizza cutter makes quick work of cutting the tortillas.

Canned refried beans	3/4 cup	175 mL
Chili powder	1 tsp.	5 mL
Dried oregano	1/2 tsp.	2 mL
Whole wheat flour tortillas (9 inch, 22 cm, diameter)	6	6
Deli chicken breast slices	6	6
Thinly sliced red pepper	1/2 cup	125 mL
Grated Mexican cheese blend	2 cups	500 mL
Can of sliced jalapeño peppers, drained and chopped (optional)	4 1/2 oz.	125 mL
Cooking oil	1 1/2 tbsp.	25 mL

Combine first 3 ingredients in small bowl.

Spread about 2 tbsp. (30 mL) bean mixture on each tortilla almost to edge.

Layer next 4 ingredients, in order given, on top of bean mixture on 1/2 of each tortilla. Fold each uncovered half over filling. Press down lightly.

Brush both sides of tortillas with cooking oil. Place on 2 greased baking sheets. Bake on separate racks in 425°F (220°C) oven for about 15 minutes, switching position of baking sheets at halftime, until cheese is melted and edges of tortillas start to brown. Let stand for 5 minutes. Cut each tortilla into 6 wedges, for a total of 36 wedges.

1 wedge: 82 Calories; 3.7 g Total Fat (1.3 g Mono, 0.6 g Poly, 1.6 g Sat); 14 mg Cholesterol; 7 g Carbohydrate; 1 g Fibre; 5 g Protein; 106 mg Sodium

Pictured on page 149.

Make Ahead: Assemble the tortillas up to 24 hours ahead of time. Wrap them tightly with plastic wrap and store in the refrigerator until ready to bake. Brush both sides with cooking oil and bake as directed.

Cooking Tip

Ingredient Focus

The culinary influences of the Far East, Mexico and India were chosen for these menus because, even though they have distinct differences in taste, they have many ingredients in common—cumin, cilantro, garlic, chilies and onions. Not only will similar and complementary flavours be woven throughout your menu, but you'll also be able to prepare ingredients for several dishes at once.

Cinnamon Chips With Fruit Salsa

This fresh and sweet dish is a splendid diversion from richer appetizers. Both the salsa and tortilla wedges offer subtle hints of sugar and the spices redolent of Mexico.

CINNAMON CHIPS

Granulated sugar	2 tsp.	10 mL
Ground cinnamon	1/2 tsp.	2 mL
Salt	1/8 tsp.	0.5 mL
Cayenne pepper, just a pinch (optional)		
Flour tortillas (6 inch, 15 cm, diameter)	6	6
Butter (or hard margarine), melted	2 tbsp.	30 mL

FRUIT SALSA

Chopped fresh strawberries	1 cup	250 mL
Tart medium cooking apple (such as Granny Smith), finely chopped	1	1
Kiwifruit, chopped	1	1
Orange juice	1 tbsp.	15 mL
Red jalapeño jelly	1 tbsp.	15 mL
Brown sugar, packed	1 tsp.	5 mL
Grated orange zest	1/2 tsp.	2 mL
Salt, just a pinch		

Cinnamon Chips: Combine first 4 ingredients in small bowl.

Brush 1 side of each tortilla with butter. Sprinkle sugar mixture over butter. Cut each tortilla into 8 wedges. Arrange on 2 greased baking sheets. Bake on separate racks in 375°F (190°C) oven for 8 to 10 minutes, switching position of baking sheets at halftime, until golden and crisp. Makes 48 chips.

Fruit Salsa: Combine all 8 ingredients in large bowl. Makes about 2 1/3 cups (575 mL) salsa. Serve with Cinnamon Chips.

3 chips with 2 tbsp. (30 mL) salsa: 65 Calories; 2.3 g Total Fat (0.7 g Mono, 0.4 g Poly, 1.0 g Sat); 4 mg Cholesterol; 10 g Carbohydrate; 1 g Fibre; 1 g Protein; 85 mg Sodium

Pictured on page 149.

Make Ahead: The chips may be baked ahead of time and stored in an airtight container at room temperature for up to 3 days. The salsa may be made up to 4 hours ahead of time and stored in an airtight container in the refrigerator.

Clockwise from top left:
Pomegranate Margaritas, page 147
Tijuana Wedges, this page
Roasted Corn Crab Cakes With Chipotle Mayonnaise, page 150
Cinnamon Chips With Fruit Salsa, above

Roasted Corn Crab Cakes

This dish will satisfy those who like it hot and those who do not! The mayonnaise sauce is for the guests who aren't afraid of a little heat in their food. For others who prefer less daring fare, the crab cakes are great on their own. These delectable cakes will disappear in a flash, so consider making a double batch.

CHIPOTLE MAYONNAISE

Mayonnaise	1 cup	250 mL
Frozen concentrated orange juice, thawed	3 tbsp.	50 mL
Chipotle chili peppers in adobo sauce (see Tip), finely chopped	2	2
Butter (or hard margarine)	1 tbsp.	15 mL
Chopped onion	1/3 cup	75 mL
Frozen kernel corn, thawed	2/3 cup	150 mL
Cans of crabmeat (4 1/4 oz., 120 g, each), drained, cartilage removed (or about 12 oz., 340 g, imitation), flaked	3	3
Mayonnaise	1/3 cup	75 mL
Yellow cornmeal	1/4 cup	60 mL
Roasted red peppers, drained, blotted dry, finely chopped	3 tbsp.	50 mL
Chopped fresh cilantro or parsley	3 tbsp.	50 mL
Dry mustard	1 tsp.	5 mL
Salt	1/4 tsp.	1 mL
Cayenne pepper	1/4 tsp.	1 mL
Cooking oil	2 tsp.	10 mL
Butter (or hard margarine), melted	2 tsp.	10 mL

Chipotle Mayonnaise: Combine mayonnaise, concentrated orange juice and chili pepper in small bowl. Chill, covered, until ready to serve. Makes about 1 1/3 cups (325 mL) mayonnaise.

Melt first amount of butter in small frying pan on medium. Add onion. Cook for 5 to 10 minutes, stirring often, until starting to soften. Increase heat to medium-high.

Add corn. Heat and stir for about 3 minutes until onion and corn start to brown. Cool.

Combine next 8 ingredients in large bowl. Add corn mixture. Stir. Let stand for about 15 minutes until cornmeal is softened. Shape into 1/2 inch (12 mm) thick patties, using about 1 tbsp. (15 mL) for each. Arrange on greased baking sheet.

Combine cooking oil and second amount of butter in small cup. Brush on patties. Bake in 425°F (220°C) oven for about 10 minutes per side until golden. Serve with Chipotle Mayonnaise. Makes about 32 crab cakes.

1 crab cake with 2 tsp. (10 mL) Chipotle Mayonnaise: 99 Calories; 8.9 g Total Fat (4.7 g Mono, 2.8 g Poly, 1.2 g Sat); 8 mg Cholesterol; 3 g Carbohydrate; trace Fibre; 2 g Protein; 149 mg Sodium

Pictured on page 149.

Tip: Chipotle chili peppers are smoked jalapeño peppers. Be sure to wash your hands after handling. To store leftover chipotle chili peppers, divide into recipe-friendly portions and freeze, with sauce, in airtight containers for up to 1 year.

Make Ahead: The Chipotle Mayonnaise may be stored in an airtight container in the refrigerator for up to 3 days.

Assemble and shape the crab cakes and store them in a single layer or between sheets of waxed paper in an airtight container in the refrigerator for up to 2 days. Brush with cooking oil mixture and bake as directed.

Entertaining Tips

A Festive Floor Plan

Expect an evening of activity with guests milling about, conversing with friends and making new acquaintances. Set out the food throughout the party area to encourage mingling and sampling. Choose three spots where tables can be arranged without disrupting foot traffic. These will become stations representing each country, colourfully decorated with accessories associated with the culture and people. In a fourth area, place a separate table for beverage service, again comfortably away from the elbows of passing guests who might accidentally jostle freshly poured drinks.

An Appetizing Introduction

The premise of this cocktail party is celebration with a multicultural flair—which means some of your guests may be unfamiliar with the culturally themed appetizers. Because people are most comfortable with the familiar, you can introduce each dish by telling your guests a little something about the ingredients. We've included snippets of information in the recipe introductions to help you ease your guests into more adventurous sampling. Or if you prefer, create cards with food descriptions and place them at each station.

Who to Invite

The animated conversation that often flows while socializing blends in well with the adventurous ingredients found in the menus created for this occasion. Remember, too, that shared experiences of new foods are a great ice-breaker. As you prepare your invitation list, keep these points in mind so that those you invite will be comfortable both with the idea of sampling new foods and of joining a lively conversation.

Spiced Apple Iced Tea

Due to the wide consumption and production of tea in India, it was declared the national beverage. For this cold version, black tea is steeped with exotic chai spices then mixed with apple juice and effervescent ginger ale. You can add a little apple brandy to turn this refreshing, family-friendly beverage into a cocktail for the grown-ups.

Water	12 cups	3 L
Granulated sugar	1/2 cup	125 mL
Orange pekoe tea bags	6	6
Whole green cardamom, bruised (see Tip)	6	6
Cinnamon sticks (4 inches, 10 cm, each)	3	3
Star anise	3	3
Whole cloves	3	3
Piece of gingerroot (1 inch, 2.5 cm, length), halved lengthwise	1	1
Apple juice	4 cups	1 L
Ginger ale	4 cups	1 L
Ice cubes		
Thin unpeeled red apple wedges, for garnish	16	16
Thin lemon wedges, for garnish	16	16

Bring water to a boil in large pot or Dutch oven. Remove from heat. Add sugar. Stir until dissolved. Add next 6 ingredients. Cool. Chill, covered, for at least 3 hours to blend flavours. Strain through sieve into 2 large pitchers. Discard solids.

Just before serving, measure 2 cups (500 mL) each of apple juice and ginger ale into each pitcher. Stir gently. Makes about 20 cups (5 L).

Pour over ice in large glasses. Garnish with apple and lemon wedges. Serves 16.

1 serving: 80 Calories; 0.1 g Total Fat (trace Mono, trace Poly, trace Sat); 0 mg Cholesterol; 20 g Carbohydrate; trace Fibre; trace Protein; 8 mg Sodium

Pictured on this page.

Tip: To bruise cardamom, hit the cardamom pods with a mallet or the flat side of a wide knife to "bruise" or crack them slightly open.

Spiced Apple Iced Tea, left

Seafood Curry Dip

This is a great introduction to Indian food. A hint of curry subtly enhances the mild flavours of shrimp and crabmeat in this not-too-spicy, Indian-inspired dip. Perfect with crackers or fresh vegetables.

Cream cheese, softened	1/4 cup	60 mL
Mayonnaise	1/4 cup	60 mL
Finely chopped green onion	2 tbsp.	30 mL
Curry powder	2 tsp.	10 mL
Lime juice	1 1/2 tsp.	7 mL
Coarsely chopped cooked salad shrimp	3/4 cup	175 mL
Can of crabmeat, drained, cartilage removed, flaked	5 oz.	142 g

Combine first 5 ingredients in large bowl.

Add shrimp and crabmeat. Stir well. Chill until ready to serve. Makes about 1 1/3 cups (325 mL).

1 tbsp. (15 mL): 39 Calories; 3.2 g Total Fat (1.5 g Mono, 0.8 g Poly, 0.8 g Sat); 15 mg Cholesterol; trace Carbohydrate; trace Fibre; 2 g Protein; 75 mg Sodium

Pictured on page 153.

Make Ahead: The dip may be stored in an airtight container in the refrigerator for up to 24 hours.

Kofta

A cocktail party favourite—meatballs—are infused with the flavours of India. If it suits your taste, try using ground lamb in place of beef or adding more chili paste for a hotter dish.

MINT RAITA SAUCE

Thick (Balkan-style) plain yogurt	1 cup	250 mL
Finely chopped green onion	2 tbsp.	30 mL
Finely chopped fresh mint leaves	2 tbsp.	30 mL
Lime juice	1 tbsp.	15 mL
Granulated sugar	1 tbsp.	15 mL
Finely grated gingerroot	1 tsp.	5 mL
Large eggs	2	2
Finely chopped fresh cilantro or parsley (or 1 1/2 tsp., 7 mL, dried)	2 tbsp.	30 mL
Finely grated gingerroot	1 tbsp.	15 mL
Garlic cloves, minced (or 1/2 tsp., 2 mL, powder)	2	2
Chili paste (sambal oelek)	1 tsp.	5 mL
Ground cumin	1 tsp.	5 mL
Salt	1/2 tsp.	2 mL
Lean ground beef	2 lbs.	900 g
Wooden cocktail picks	20	20

Mint Raita Sauce: Combine first 6 ingredients in small bowl. Chill, covered, until ready to serve. Makes about 1 1/4 cups (300 mL) sauce.

Combine next 7 ingredients in large bowl.

Add ground beef. Mix well. Roll into 1 inch (2.5 cm) balls. Arrange on greased baking sheet with sides. Bake in 375°F (190°C) oven for about 25 minutes until fully cooked, and internal temperature of beef reaches 160°F (71°C). Transfer to paper towels to drain. Makes about 60 meatballs.

Thread 3 meatballs onto each cocktail pick. Arrange skewers on serving platter. Serve with sauce. Makes 20 skewers.

1 skewer with 1 tbsp. (15 mL) sauce: 29 Calories; 1.5 g Total Fat (0.6 g Mono, 0.1 g Poly, 0.6 g Sat); 15 mg Cholesterol; 1 g Carbohydrate; trace Fibre; 3 g Protein; 31 mg Sodium

Pictured on page 153.

Make Ahead: The cooked meatballs may be assembled on the cocktail picks and stored in an airtight container in the freezer for up to 1 month. To reheat from frozen, arrange the skewers on a greased baking sheet. Bake, uncovered, in 425°F (220°C) oven for about 10 minutes until heated through.

The sauce may be stored in an airtight container in the refrigerator for up to 24 hours.

Curried Onion Paneer

Paneer, a fresh and delicate cheese similar in taste to cottage cheese, is used in Indian dishes such as dahl, as well as in salads and other vegetable dishes. Serve with naan or pita bread.

Butter (or hard margarine)	1 tbsp.	15 mL
Chopped onion	1 1/2 cups	375 mL
Dried crushed chilies (optional)	1/8 tsp.	0.5 mL
Brown sugar, packed	1 tbsp.	15 mL
Curry powder	1 tsp.	5 mL
Ground cumin	1/2 tsp.	2 mL
Salt	1/8 tsp.	0.5 mL
Can of diced tomatoes, drained	14 oz.	398 mL
Fresh spinach, stems removed, lightly packed, chopped or torn	1 cup	250 mL
Paneer cheese (see Note), cut into 1/4 inch (6 mm) cubes	1/2 lb.	225 g
Lime juice	2 tsp.	10 mL
Sprigs of fresh cilantro or parsley, for garnish		

Melt butter in large frying pan on medium. Add onion and chilies. Cook for 5 to 10 minutes, stirring often, until onion is softened. Reduce heat to medium-low.

Add next 4 ingredients. Stir. Cook for 5 to 10 minutes, stirring occasionally, until onion is caramelized. Increase heat to medium.

Add next 4 ingredients. Stir. Cook for about 10 minutes, stirring occasionally, until spinach is wilted and liquid is evaporated. Remove to small serving bowl.

Garnish with cilantro. Makes about 3 cups (750 mL).

3 tbsp. (50 mL): 59 Calories; 3.1 g Total Fat (0.9 g Mono, 0.1 g Poly, 1.9 g Sat); 9 mg Cholesterol; 4 g Carbohydrate; 1 g Fibre; 4 g Protein; 140 mg Sodium

Pictured on page 153.

Note: Paneer is available in specialty food stores or in the freezer section of some grocery stores.

Top: Curried Onion Paneer, above
Centre: Kofta With Mint Raita Sauce, this page
Bottom: Seafood Curry Dip, page 151

New Year's Eve Celebration

New Year's Eve. Three little words, but what a ripple of excitement and anticipation they create. This shining, shimmering evening celebrates the exhilarating promise of possibility.

Opportunities abound to party with a crowd on New Year's Eve—from formal, glam-and-glitter merrymaking in hotel ballrooms to casual community festivities in the great outdoors. But if you'd like to ring in the new year in your own home with a group of your nearest and dearest, our party guide helps you do it with dazzle and drama in an excitingly different way.

Because our cocktail party starts after supper and will likely wind up well after midnight, food is served all evening long. Nine courses of hot and cold hors d'oeuvres are presented one dish at a time, starting with lighter fare and progressing to more substantial dishes.

We've planned the preparation and clocked the warming and serving of every dish so you can smoothly and effortlessly host a smashing event.

As the final minutes tick down to midnight, pull out the noisemakers, hats and balloons, pass around celebratory drinks and invite everyone to raise their glass to a Happy New Year!

Clockwise from top left:
Bacon Feta Turnovers, page160
Raspberry Sparklers, page 166
Smoked Salmon Spears, page 160
Lemon Pepper Crisps, page 158
Chili Crab Dip, page 157

155

New Year's Eve Celebration

Cocktail Party for 12
This impressive collection of appetizers and finger food is listed in the order to be served. All include convenient make-ahead suggestions so there's little to do but warm and serve the food throughout the evening. Some appetizers are set out as guests arrive, and additional courses are served every 30 minutes or so. The alternating hot and cold courses progress from light to more substantial bite-sized fare. Fittingly, the dessert course is timed to welcome in the new year.

Timeline

Up to One Month in Advance
Make and freeze Lemon Pepper Crisps
Make and freeze pizzettes
Make and freeze turnovers
Make and freeze meatballs
Make and freeze Toast Cups
Make dipping sauce for lamb
Make, frost and freeze cupcakes

Up to Two Days in Advance
Prepare dip and spread
Make Butternut Blossoms and assemble meatball skewers

Day Before
Cut vegetables to accompany spread
Make filling for shrimp cocktails
Chill sparkling wine
Make mushroom filling and fill Toast Cups
Marinate lamb

Day Of
Up to 8 hours in advance:
Assemble shrimp cocktails
Sear lamb
Remove Lemon Pepper Crisps from freezer

Up to 4 hours in advance:
Wrap salmon spears

Up to 1 hour before guests arrive:
Place frozen cupcakes on serving tray
Arrange vegetables for spread

Step-by-Step Serving Plan

We suggest you start heating an appetizer about 30 minutes before serving it. This gives you enough time for the food to heat through, then cool slightly so your guests don't burn themselves on too hot hors d'oeuvres.

8:00 p.m.
Guests begin to arrive
Offer drinks
Set out dip and spread with Lemon Pepper Crisps, vegetables, rye bread, etc.
Bake pizzettes

8:30 p.m.
Serve pizzettes

9:00 p.m.
Serve shrimp cocktails
Reheat turnovers

9:30 p.m.
Serve turnovers

10:00 p.m.
Serve salmon spears
Reheat meatball skewers
Replenish dip, spread and accompaniments as needed

10:30 p.m.
Serve meatball skewers

11:00 p.m.
Serve mushroom cups
Bake lamb chops and heat dipping sauce

11:30 p.m.
Serve lamb chops
Brew coffee, steep tea
Clear away dip, spread, etc.
Mix Raspberry Sparklers

12:00 Midnight
Raise your glass in a toast to the new year
Serve cupcakes, coffee and tea

Chili Crab Dip

The zing of lemon and a little chili heat give this creamy appetizer a pleasant, peppery bite. Serve with small bread sticks and fresh vegetables for dipping.

Block of cream cheese, softened	8 oz.	250 g
Mayonnaise	1/3 cup	75 mL
Lemon juice	3 tbsp.	50 mL
Sweet chili sauce	2 tbsp.	30 mL
Chopped fresh dill	2 tbsp.	30 mL
Salt	1/4 tsp.	1 mL
Pepper	1/4 tsp.	1 mL
Cans of crabmeat (4 1/4 oz., 120 g, each), drained, cartilage removed, flaked	2	2
Chopped fresh chives	2 tbsp.	30 mL

Beat first 7 ingredients in medium bowl until smooth.

Add crabmeat and chives. Stir. Chill, covered, until ready to serve. Makes about 2 2/3 cups (650 mL).

2 tbsp. (30 mL): 137 Calories; 12.6 g Total Fat (4.9 g Mono, 2.0 g Poly, 5.1 g Sat); 27 mg Cholesterol; 2 g Carbohydrate; trace Fibre; 4 g Protein; 312 mg Sodium

Pictured on page 154.

Make Ahead: The dip may be stored in an airtight container in the refrigerator for up to 2 days.

Entertaining Tip

Change of Course

Our menu is a guide for a multi-course cocktail party but the number of courses and timing of service can be adjusted to suit your situation. We do suggest, however, that you try to maintain the progress of dishes from lighter to more filling throughout the evening.

If you want to include one of your signature appetizers or a convenience product, substitute it for something similar on our menu or add it where appropriate. For example, replace the Tourtière Meatball Skewers, page 162, with sautéed venison sausage, substitute a shrimp ring for the Thai Shrimp Cocktails, page 161, or offer your homemade truffles alongside the cupcakes.

And if you just don't have the time or the inclination to make the whole menu, start with the lighter fare and serve ready-to-bake pizzas at midnight!

Sun-Dried Tomato Spread

Sweet, tangy tomato and roasted garlic come together to create a tantalizing, smooth-textured spread. Serve with vegetables, cocktail rye bread or crackers.

Garlic bulb	1	1
Block of cream cheese, softened	8 oz.	250 g
Jar of sun-dried tomatoes in oil, drained, coarsely chopped	8 1/2 oz.	251 mL
Chopped fresh parsley	1/4 cup	60 mL
Sweet chili sauce	2 tbsp.	30 mL
Lemon juice	2 tbsp.	30 mL
Water	2 tbsp.	30 mL
Pepper	1/4 tsp.	1 mL

Trim 1/4 inch (6 mm) from garlic bulb to expose tops of cloves. Wrap loosely in foil. Bake in 375°F (190°C) oven for about 45 minutes until softened. Let stand until cool enough to handle. Squeeze garlic bulb to remove cloves from peel. Transfer cloves to blender or food processor.

Add remaining 7 ingredients. Process until smooth. Remove to small serving bowl. Cover. Chill. Before serving, let stand at room temperature for about 30 minutes to soften. Makes about 2 1/4 cups (550 mL).

2 tbsp. (30 mL): 63 Calories; 5.4 g Total Fat (1.7 g Mono, 0.3 g Poly, 3.0 g Sat); 15 mg Cholesterol; 3 g Carbohydrate; trace Fibre; 1 g Protein; 78 mg Sodium

Pictured on page 159.

Make Ahead: The spread may be stored in an airtight container in the refrigerator for up to 2 days, or in the freezer for up to 1 month. If frozen, let stand at room temperature for 1 1/2 hours to soften before serving.

Entertaining Tip

Be Prepared

The evening celebration promises to be a lot of fun. With a little advance preparation, it can be easy too. Here are a few strategies to help you manage the evening:

❋ Send your invitations early.

❋ Have some extra convenience foods on hand.

❋ Pre-set your television to a favourite countdown channel.

❋ Cue up a recording of *Auld Lang Syne*.

❋ Note the telephone number of a taxi service or volunteer driving club in a spot where everyone can see it as they arrive.

❋ Clear your driveway and front walk of ice and snow.

Lemon Pepper Crisps

A lemon tang is followed by a lingering peppery heat in these crunchy, piquant chips.

Cooking oil	1 tbsp.	15 mL
Corn tortillas (6 inch, 15 cm, diameter)	12	12
Lemon pepper	2 tsp.	10 mL
Pepper	1 tsp.	5 mL
Grated lemon zest	2 tsp.	10 mL

Brush cooking oil lightly on both sides of tortillas. Cut each into 8 wedges. Arrange wedges on ungreased baking sheets.

Combine lemon pepper and pepper in small cup. Sprinkle over wedges. Bake on separate racks in 350°F (175°C) oven for 8 minutes. Remove from oven.

Sprinkle with lemon zest. Switch position of baking sheets in oven. Bake for another 6 minutes until crisp and golden. Makes 96 crisps.

3 crisps: 25 Calories; 0.7 g Total Fat (0.3 g Mono, 0.2 g Poly, 0.1 g Sat); 0 mg Cholesterol; 4 g Carbohydrate; 1 g Fibre; 1 g Protein; 52 mg Sodium

Pictured on page 154.

Make Ahead: The baked crisps may be stored in an airtight container for up to 2 weeks, or in the freezer for up to 1 month.

Onion Pepper Pizzettes

*Simple ingredients, simply amazing appetizers!
Sweet, caramelized onion and mild goat cheese
will have your guests coming back for more.*

Olive (or cooking) oil	1 1/2 tsp.	7 mL
Diced onion	1 cup	250 mL
Roasted red peppers, drained, blotted dry, chopped	3/4 cup	175 mL
Red wine vinegar	1 tsp.	5 mL
Salt	1/8 tsp.	0.5 mL
Pepper	1/8 tsp.	0.5 mL
Basil pesto	1/4 cup	60 mL
Unbaked pizza crust (12 inch, 30 cm, diameter)	1	1
Goat (chèvre) cheese, cut up (see Tip)	2 1/2 oz.	70 g

Heat olive oil in large frying pan on medium. Add onion. Cook for about 15 minutes, stirring often, until caramelized.

Add next 4 ingredients. Stir. Remove from heat.

Spread pesto on pizza crust. Cut out circles with 2 inch (5 cm) round cookie cutter. Arrange on greased baking sheet. Spoon onion mixture onto rounds.

Sprinkle with cheese. Bake in 400°F (205°C) oven for about 12 minutes until cheese is melted and just golden. Makes about 30 pizzettes.

1 pizzette: 43 Calories; 1.9 g Total Fat (0.7 g Mono, 0.2 g Poly, 0.6 g Sat); 2 mg Cholesterol; 5 g Carbohydrate; trace Fibre; 1 g Protein; 68 mg Sodium

Pictured below.

Tip: To cut the goat cheese easily, place it in the freezer for 15 to 20 minutes until firm.

Make Ahead: Assemble the pizzettes, layer them between sheets of waxed paper in an airtight container and store them in the freezer for up to 1 month. Arrange the frozen pizzettes on a greased baking sheet and bake as directed.

Top: Sun-Dried Tomato Spread, page 158

Bottom: Onion Pepper Pizzettes, above

New Year's Eve Celebration

Smoked Salmon Spears

The varied textures of tender-crisp asparagus, velvety salmon and creamy herbed cheese combine in an appealing appetizer.

Fresh asparagus spears, trimmed of tough ends	24	24
Chive and onion spreadable cream cheese	3/4 cup	175 mL
Thin smoked salmon slices	24	24
Strips of lemon zest (see Note)	1 tbsp.	15 mL
Capers (optional)	1 tbsp.	15 mL
Coarse ground pepper, sprinkle		

Blanch asparagus in boiling water in large saucepan for about 5 minutes until bright green. Drain. Immediately plunge into ice water in large bowl. Let stand for 10 minutes until cold. Drain. Blot dry with paper towels.

Spread 1/2 tbsp. (7 mL) cream cheese on 1 slice of smoked salmon. Place 1 asparagus spear on top of cream cheese. Roll up, leaving tip and end of asparagus spear exposed. Repeat with remaining cream cheese, salmon and asparagus. Arrange on large serving plate.

Sprinkle with remaining 3 ingredients. Makes 24 spears.

1 spear: 40 Calories; 2.2 g Total Fat (0.8 g Mono, 0.2 g Poly, 1.0 g Sat); 9 mg Cholesterol; 1 g Carbohydrate; trace Fibre; 4 g Protein; 385 mg Sodium

Pictured on page 154.

Note: Use a vegetable peeler to cut a 1 inch (2.5 cm) slice of lemon peel (yellow part only), then cut the zest into 1/16 inch (1.5 mm) slices.

Make Ahead: Assemble the spears up to 4 hours ahead of time and store in an airtight container in the refrigerator until ready to serve. Arrange them on a serving plate then sprinkle with the lemon zest, capers and pepper.

SMOKED SALMON GRISSINI: Use long, thin Italian bread sticks (Grissini) instead of asparagus spears. Serve immediately.

Bacon Feta Turnovers

The savoury flavours of smoky bacon and feta cheese are a hit in these delicious and tempting turnovers. You may want to make extras because they freeze well and can be quickly reheated directly from the freezer.

Block of cream cheese, softened	8 oz.	250 g
Butter (or hard margarine), softened	1/2 cup	125 mL
All-purpose flour	1 1/2 cups	375 mL
Bacon slices, diced	5	5
Finely chopped onion	1 cup	250 mL
Crumbled feta cheese	1 cup	250 mL
Chopped fresh parsley (or 1 1/2 tsp., 7 mL, flakes)	2 tbsp.	30 mL
Dried oregano	1/2 tsp.	2 mL
Pepper	1/4 tsp.	1 mL
Large egg, fork-beaten	1	1

Beat cream cheese and butter in large bowl until smooth. Add flour. Mix well. Shape into slightly flattened disc. Wrap with plastic wrap. Chill for at least 1 hour.

Heat large frying pan on medium. Add bacon and onion. Cook for about 15 minutes, stirring occasionally, until bacon is crisp. Remove from heat. Drain.

Add next 4 ingredients. Stir well. Transfer to small bowl. Cool to room temperature.

Roll out pastry on lightly floured surface to 1/8 inch (3 mm) thickness. Cut out circles with 2 1/2 inch (6.4 cm) round cookie cutter. Spoon 1 tsp. (5 mL) bacon mixture onto centre of each circle.

Brush 1/2 the edge of each circle with egg. Fold pastry over filling. Press edges together with fork to seal. Arrange on 2 greased baking sheets. Brush tops with egg. Cut small vents in tops of turnovers to allow steam to escape. Bake in 450°F (230°C) oven for about 10 minutes until golden. Makes about 42 turnovers.

1 turnover: 77 Calories; 5.8 g Total Fat (1.7 g Mono, 0.3 g Poly, 3.5 g Sat); 22 mg Cholesterol; 4 g Carbohydrate; trace Fibre; 2 g Protein; 99 mg Sodium

Pictured on page 154.

Make Ahead: The baked turnovers may be stored in an airtight container in the freezer for up to 1 month. Arrange the frozen turnovers on a greased baking sheet and bake in a 400°F (205°C) oven for about 10 minutes or until heated through.

Thai Shrimp Cocktails

The exotic Thai flavours of curry, sweet chili and lime liven up a cocktail party classic.

Cooking oil	1 tbsp.	15 mL
Garlic cloves, minced (or 1/2 tsp., 2 mL, powder)	2	2
Finely grated gingerroot	1 tsp.	5 mL
Red curry paste	1 tsp.	5 mL
Bags of frozen uncooked shrimp (12 oz., 340 g, each), peeled and deveined, thawed, coarsely chopped	2	2
Sweet chili sauce	2 tbsp.	30 mL
Lime juice	2 tbsp.	30 mL
Fish sauce (or low-sodium soy sauce)	1 tbsp.	15 mL
Fresh bean sprouts	1 cup	250 mL
Coarsely chopped unsalted peanuts	1/2 cup	125 mL
Coarsely chopped fresh cilantro or parsley	1/4 cup	60 mL
Small butter lettuce leaves	24	24

Heat cooking oil in large frying pan on medium. Add next 3 ingredients. Heat and stir for 1 to 2 minutes until fragrant.

Add next 4 ingredients. Heat and stir for about 3 minutes until shrimp turns pink. Remove from heat.

Add next 3 ingredients. Stir. Transfer to medium bowl. Chill for about 1 hour until cold.

Press lettuce leaves into 12 small wine glasses (see Note). Spoon shrimp mixture on top of lettuce. Makes 12 shrimp cocktails.

1 shrimp cocktail: 121 Calories; 5.6 g Total Fat (2.5 g Mono, 1.8 g Poly, 0.7 g Sat); 86 mg Cholesterol; 4 g Carbohydrate; 1 g Fibre; 14 g Protein; 166 mg Sodium

Pictured above.

Note: For easy cleanup, use small disposable stemware.

Make Ahead: Prepare the shrimp mixture and store it in an airtight container in the refrigerator for up to 24 hours. The shrimp cocktails may be assembled up to 8 hours before serving, covered and chilled.

Special Touches

Charming Champagne Flutes

The climax to this special night of shimmer and sparkle is the toast to the new year, so why not add some pizzazz to your champagne flutes? Cut lengths of glitter wire in half. Twist a piece once or twice around the stem of each glass, wrapping each end around a pencil to make a spring-like coil. Attach a little bauble or miniature decoration, or maybe a tag if you'd like to personalize each glass or write a wish for the new year.

Dazzling Ideas

Dress up each course you serve by adding a festive touch to the serving trays (just make sure nothing touches the food). It can be as simple as tying a ribbon on the handle or attaching a small ornament to the corner. Foil doilies quickly transform any serving platter with a bright flash of metallic colour.

Sprinkle metal confetti to reflect candlelight or arrange curled paper and foil streamers to add colour on tables or mantels.

As the crowning touch, make sure bright, shiny hats, horns and noisemakers find their way into everyone's hands as the magical midnight hour approaches, so everyone can ring in the new year with all the noise and fanfare it deserves!

Tourtière Meatball Skewers

These tasty meatballs have all the traditional flavours of the French-Canadian tourtière. Use a food processor to achieve a fine texture. Winter squash adds a pretty touch, but the meatballs are also great served on their own.

White bread slices	3	3
Coarsely chopped onion	1 cup	250 mL
Milk	2 tbsp.	30 mL
Salt	3/4 tsp.	4 mL
Pepper	1/4 tsp.	1 mL
Ground allspice	1/4 tsp.	1 mL
Ground cloves	1/8 tsp.	0.5 mL
Lean ground pork	1 lb.	454 g
BUTTERNUT BLOSSOMS		
Large butternut squash (about 2 1/2 lbs., 1.1 kg), peeled	1	1
Maple (or maple-flavoured) syrup	1 tbsp.	15 mL
Wooden cocktail picks	36	36

Process bread slices into crumbs in food processor. Add next 6 ingredients. Process for about 20 seconds until onion is finely chopped.

Add ground pork. Process for about 20 seconds until smooth. Roll into 36, 1 inch (2.5 cm) balls. Arrange on greased baking sheet with sides. Bake in 400°F (205°C) oven for about 15 minutes until fully cooked, and internal temperature of pork reaches 160°F (71°C). Transfer to paper towels to drain.

Butternut Blossoms: Cut squash crosswise into 1/2 inch (12 mm) slices. Cut out 36 flowers from squash slices with 1 1/4 inch (3 cm) flower-shaped metal cookie cutter. Keep remaining squash for another use. Arrange squash flowers on greased baking sheet. Brush tops with maple syrup. Bake in 400°F (205°C) oven for about 15 minutes until tender and golden. Makes 36 blossoms.

Thread 1 blossom and 1 meatball onto each cocktail pick. Makes 36 skewers.

1 skewer: 47 Calories; 1.9 g Total Fat (0.8 g Mono, 0.2 g Poly, 0.7 g Sat); 8 mg Cholesterol; 5 g Carbohydrate; 1 g Fibre; 3 g Protein; 69 mg Sodium

Pictured on page 163.

Make Ahead: The cooked meatballs may be stored in an airtight container in the freezer for up to 1 month. The blossoms may be baked and the skewers assembled up to 2 days ahead of time and stored in an airtight container in the refrigerator. To reheat the skewers, arrange them on a greased baking sheet and bake in a 400°F (205°C) oven for about 8 minutes or until heated through.

Stilton Mushroom Cups

Intense, earthy flavours in a satisfying appetizer that's delicious either hot or cold. Use a food processor to make quick work of chopping the onions and mushrooms.

TOAST CUPS

White bread slices, crusts removed	36	36
Butter (or hard margarine), melted	1/3 cup	75 mL
Butter (or hard margarine)	1 tbsp.	15 mL
Finely chopped fresh white mushrooms	2 cups	500 mL
Finely chopped onion	1 1/2 cups	375 mL
Garlic cloves, minced (or 1/2 tsp., 2 mL, powder)	2	2
Salt, just a pinch		
All-purpose flour	2 tbsp.	30 mL
Dry white wine (or prepared chicken broth)	1/4 cup	60 mL
Prepared chicken broth	1/2 cup	125 mL
Crumbled Stilton cheese	1 3/4 oz.	49 g
Chopped fresh chives	2 tbsp.	30 mL
Finely chopped walnuts	2 tbsp.	30 mL
Chopped fresh chives	1 tbsp.	15 mL

Toast Cups: Roll out bread slices to 1/8 inch (3 mm) thickness. Cut out circle from each slice with 3 inch (7.5 cm) round cookie cutter. Brush 1 side of bread rounds with first amount of butter. Press, buttered-side down, in bottom and up side of 36 mini muffin cups. Bake in 375°F (190°C) oven for about 15 minutes until crisp and golden. Makes 36 Toast Cups.

Melt second amount of butter in large frying pan on medium. Add next 4 ingredients. Cook for about 15 minutes, stirring occasionally, until onion is softened and liquid is evaporated.

Add flour. Heat and stir for 1 minute. Slowly add wine, stirring constantly. Heat and stir for about 2 minutes until thickened. Slowly add broth, stirring constantly. Heat and stir for 2 to 3 minutes until boiling and thickened. Remove from heat.

Add cheese and first amount of chives. Stir. Spoon into Toast Cups.

Sprinkle with walnuts and second amount of chives. Makes 36 mushroom cups.

1 mushroom cup: 94 Calories; 3.6 g Total Fat (1.1 g Mono, 0.4 g Poly, 1.8 g Sat); 7 mg Cholesterol; 12 g Carbohydrate; 1 g Fibre; 3 g Protein; 173 mg Sodium

Pictured below.

Make Ahead: The Toast Cups may be stored in an airtight container in the freezer for up to 1 month. The mushroom cups may be assembled up to 24 hours ahead of time and stored in an airtight container in the refrigerator. Just before serving, sprinkle with the walnuts and second amount of chives.

To serve them warm, arrange the mushroom cups on a greased baking sheet with sides and bake in a 400°F (205°C) oven for about 10 minutes or until the filling is heated through. Sprinkle with the walnuts and second amount of chives.

Lemon Herb Lamb Chops

A zesty marinade lends fabulous flavour to these succulent chops. Varying the size of the chops will result in a range of doneness to suit your guests' preferences. Thinner ones will be medium-well while the thickest ones will be medium-rare.

LEMON HERB MARINADE

Lemon juice	1/3 cup	75 mL
Chopped fresh oregano leaves (or 2 1/4 tsp., 11 mL, dried)	3 tbsp.	50 mL
Chopped fresh mint leaves (or 2 1/4 tsp., 11 mL, dried)	3 tbsp.	50 mL
Olive (or cooking) oil	3 tbsp.	50 mL
Liquid honey	2 tbsp.	30 mL
Grated lemon zest	2 tbsp.	30 mL
Garlic cloves, minced (or 1 tsp., 5 mL, powder)	4	4
Coarse ground pepper	2 tsp.	10 mL
Chili paste (sambal oelek)	1 tsp.	5 mL
Salt	1/2 tsp.	2 mL
Racks of lamb with 8 ribs each, cut between ribs into 24 chops	3	3
Cooking oil, approximately	1 tbsp.	15 mL

MUSTARD APRICOT DIPPING SAUCE

Apricot jam, fruit finely chopped	2/3 cup	150 mL
Dijon mustard	1/4 cup	60 mL
Soy sauce	4 tsp.	20 mL

Lemon Herb Marinade: Combine first 10 ingredients in large resealable freezer bag. Makes about 3/4 cup (175 mL) marinade.

Add lamb chops. Seal bag. Turn until coated. Marinate in refrigerator for at least 6 hours or overnight, turning occasionally. Discard marinade.

Heat cooking oil in large frying pan on high. Cook chops, in small batches, for about 1 minute per side until browned, adding more cooking oil if necessary to prevent sticking. Arrange on parchment paper-lined baking sheet with sides. Bake in 400°F (205°C) oven for about 8 minutes until desired doneness.

Mustard Apricot Dipping Sauce: Combine all 3 ingredients in small saucepan. Heat and stir on medium for 5 to 7 minutes until jam is melted. Makes about 3/4 cup (175 mL) sauce. Serve with lamb chops. Serves 12.

1 serving: 371 Calories; 26.5 g Total Fat (12.1 g Mono, 2.6 g Poly, 9.8 g Sat); 72 mg Cholesterol; 17 g Carbohydrate; trace Fibre; 17 g Protein; 350 mg Sodium

Pictured above.

Make Ahead: The dipping sauce may be stored in an airtight container in the refrigerator for up to 1 month. Reheat before serving. The cooled, browned chops may be stored, covered, on the baking sheet in the refrigerator for up to 8 hours. Bake them in a 400°F (205°C) oven for about 10 minutes or until desired doneness.

Raspberry-Kissed Cupcakes

Dainty lemon cupcakes with a raspberry swirl. These mini cupcakes accommodate those who like just a touch of sweet, while those who live for dessert can help themselves to two or three!

Sour cream	2/3 cup	150 mL
Lemon juice	1 tbsp.	15 mL
Grated lemon zest	1 1/2 tsp.	7 mL
All-purpose flour	1 1/2 cups	375 mL
Baking powder	2 tsp.	10 mL
Salt	1/4 tsp.	1 mL
Butter (or hard margarine), softened	1/2 cup	125 mL
Granulated sugar	3/4 cup	175 mL
Large eggs	2	2
RASPBERRY FROSTING		
Icing (confectioner's) sugar	3 cups	750 mL
Butter (or hard margarine), softened	3/4 cup	175 mL
Frozen concentrated raspberry cocktail, thawed	1/4 cup	60 mL

Combine first 3 ingredients in small bowl. Set aside.

Measure next 3 ingredients into separate small bowl. Stir.

Cream butter and sugar in medium bowl. Add eggs 1 at a time, beating well after each addition. Add flour mixture in 2 parts alternately with sour cream mixture, stirring after each addition until just combined. Line 36 mini muffin cups with paper liners (see Note). Spoon batter into liners until full. Bake in 350°F (175°C) oven for about 18 minutes until just golden and wooden pick inserted in centre of cupcake comes out clean. Let stand in pans for 10 minutes before removing to wire racks to cool completely.

Raspberry Frosting: Beat all 3 ingredients on low in medium bowl until smooth. Beat on high for another 1 to 2 minutes until light and fluffy. Makes about 2 1/2 cups (625 mL) frosting. Spoon into piping bag fitted with large star tip. Pipe frosting onto cupcakes. Makes 36 mini cupcakes.

1 mini cupcake: 153 Calories; 7.7 g Total Fat (2.3 g Mono, 0.3 g Poly, 4.7 g Sat); 32 mg Cholesterol; 21 g Carbohydrate; trace Fibre; 1 g Protein; 112 mg Sodium

Pictured on page 167.

Note: If you don't have enough pans to bake 36 mini cupcakes at once, this batter stands up well in the bowl so you can bake in smaller batches. Be sure to cool the pan in between batches.

Make Ahead: The frosted cupcakes may be stored in an airtight container in the freezer for up to 1 month. Arrange them on the serving tray right from the freezer, when they're very easy to handle. Thaw them at room temperature for at least 1 hour before serving.

Raspberry Sparklers

Serve these dazzling cocktails just before midnight, and bring in the new year with style. Cheers!

Raspberry syrup (such as Torani's)	3/4 cup	175 mL
Frozen whole raspberries	12	12
Bottles of sparkling white wine (or champagne), 26 oz. (750 mL), each	2	2

Divide syrup among 12 champagne flutes. Add 1 raspberry to each. Slowly pour wine into flutes until full. Serves 12.

1 serving: 153 Calories; trace Total Fat (0 g Mono, trace Poly, 0 g Sat); 0 mg Cholesterol; 19 g Carbohydrate; trace Fibre; trace Protein; 21 mg Sodium

Pictured on page 155.

Variation: Use ginger ale or sparkling pear juice instead of sparkling white wine.

Special Touch

Ribbons and Tiers

Raspberry-Kissed Cupcakes, on this page, are even more tempting when festively wrapped and presented. All it takes is a multi-tiered tray with a handle and some decorative ribbon. Choose wireless, sheer ribbon for best effect, either in a single solid colour or several coordinating colours. Cut three lengths so that each piece, once tied to the handle, drapes down the side of the tray and onto the table. Add a bow on top and, finally, fill the stand with frozen cupcakes (so the frosting doesn't smear the ribbon) and your dish is ready to serve.

Measurement Tables

Throughout this book measurements are given in Conventional and Metric measure. To compensate for differences between the two measurements due to rounding, a full metric measure is not always used. The cup used is the standard eight fluid ounce. Temperature is given in degrees Fahrenheit and Celsius. Baking pan measurements are in inches and centimetres as well as quarts and litres. An exact metric conversion is given on this page as well as the working equivalent (Standard Measure).

Oven Temperatures

Fahrenheit (°F)	Celsius (°C)	Fahrenheit (°F)	Celsius (°C)
175°	80°	350°	175°
200°	95°	375°	190°
225°	110°	400°	205°
250°	120°	425°	220°
275°	140°	450°	230°
300°	150°	475°	240°
325°	160°	500°	260°

Spoons

Conventional Measure	Metric Exact Conversion Millilitre (mL)	Metric Standard Measure Millilitre (mL)
1/8 teaspoon (tsp.)	0.6 mL	0.5 mL
1/4 teaspoon (tsp.)	1.2 mL	1 mL
1/2 teaspoon (tsp.)	2.4 mL	2 mL
1 teaspoon (tsp.)	4.7 mL	5 mL
2 teaspoons (tsp.)	9.4 mL	10 mL
1 tablespoon (tbsp.)	14.2 mL	15 mL

Cups

1/4 cup (4 tbsp.)	56.8 mL	60 mL
1/3 cup (5 1/3 tbsp.)	75.6 mL	75 mL
1/2 cup (8 tbsp.)	113.7 mL	125 mL
2/3 cup (10 2/3 tbsp.)	151.2 mL	150 mL
3/4 cup (12 tbsp.)	170.5 mL	175 mL
1 cup (16 tbsp.)	227.3 mL	250 mL
4 1/2 cups	1022.9 mL	1000 mL (1 L)

Pans

Conventional Inches	Metric Centimetres
8 × 8 inch	20 × 20 cm
9 × 9 inch	22 × 22 cm
9 × 13 inch	22 × 33 cm
10 × 15 inch	25 × 38 cm
11 × 17 inch	28 × 43 cm
8 × 2 inch round	20 × 5 cm
9 × 2 inch round	22 × 5 cm
10 × 4 1/2 inch tube	25 × 11 cm
8 × 4 × 3 inch loaf	20 × 10 × 7.5 cm
9 × 5 × 3 inch loaf	22 × 12.5 × 7.5 cm

Dry Measurements

Conventional Measure Ounces (oz.)	Metric Exact Conversion Grams (g)	Metric Standard Measure Grams (g)
1 oz.	28.3 g	28 g
2 oz.	56.7 g	57 g
3 oz.	85.0 g	85 g
4 oz.	113.4 g	113 g
5 oz.	141.7 g	140 g
6 oz.	170.1 g	170 g
7 oz.	198.4 g	200 g
8 oz.	226.8 g	225 g
16 oz.	453.6 g	454 g
32 oz.	907.2 g	1000 g (1 kg)

Casseroles

Canada & Britain		United States	
Standard Size Casserole	Exact Metric Measure	Standard Size Casserole	Exact Metric Measure
1 qt. (5 cups)	1.13 L	1 qt. (4 cups)	900 mL
1 1/2 qts. (7 1/2 cups)	1.69 L	1 1/2 qts. (6 cups)	1.35 L
2 qts. (10 cups)	2.25 L	2 qts. (8 cups)	1.8 L
2 1/2 qts. (12 1/2 cups)	2.81 L	2 1/2 qts. (10 cups)	2.25 L
3 qts. (15 cups)	3.38 L	3 qts. (12 cups)	2.7 L
4 qts. (20 cups)	4.5 L	4 qts. (16 cups)	3.6 L
5 qts. (25 cups)	5.63 L	5 qts. (20 cups)	4.5 L

Index

Christmas Celebrations

N - O

Index